D0088780

HOW TO BE A
WORKING
ACTOR

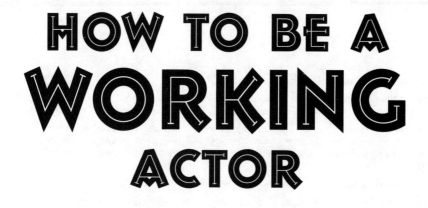

HOW TO BE A WORKING ACTOR

REVISED AND ENLARGED THIRD EDITION

THE INSIDER'S GUIDE TO FINDING JOBS IN THEATER, FILM, AND TELEVISION

MARI LYN HENRY AND LYNNE ROGERS

BACK STAGE BOOKS
AN IMPRINT OF WATSON-GUPTILL PUBLICATIONS
New York

Copyright © 1994 by Mari Lyn Henry and Lynne Rogers

This third, revised edition was first published in 1994 in the United States by Watson-Guptill Publications, a division of BPI Communications, Inc., 1515 Broadway, New York, NY 10036

All rights reserved. No part of this publication may be reproduced or used in any form or by any means—graphic, electronic, or mechanical, including photocopying, recording, taping, or information storage and retrieval systems—without written permission of the publisher.

Cataloging-in-Publication Data for this book is available from the Library of Congress.

All photographs are used with the kind permission of the actors and photographers.

Chapter 19:
"Emotional Recall" is excerpted from *Impassioned Embraces* by John Pielmeier, copyright © 1988, by Courage Productions as an unpublished dramatic composition; copyright © 1989, by Courage Productions.
        CAUTION: The reprinting of *Impassioned Embraces* in this volume is reprinted by permission of the author and Dramatists Play Service, Inc. The stock and amateur performance rights in this play are controlled exclusively by Dramatists Play Service, Inc., 440 Park Avenue South, New York, N.Y. 10016. No stock or amateur production of the play may be given without obtaining, in advance, the written permission of the Dramatists Play Service, Inc., and paying the requisite fee. Inquiries regarding all other rights should be addressed to Jeanine Edmunds, c/o Curtis Brown, Ltd., 606 Larchmont Blvd., Suite 300, Los Angeles, CA 90004.
"Hut, Hut," by Charles Sexton; "Happy Birthday," by Caroline White; "Angie's Song," by Ruth Jacobson; "He Told Me . . . #1," by Jessica Jory; and "He Told Me . . . #2," by Meghan Love, are reprinted with the kind permission of Nancy Niles Sexton, Walden Theatre, 233 West Broadway, Louisville, KY 40202, and the publisher, The Dramatic Publishing Company. All inquiries regarding purchasing of playbooks and stock and amateur performance rights should be addressed to The Dramatic Publishing Company, 311 Washington St., Box 129, Woodstock, IL 60098.
Excerpts from *Bless Me, Father* and *A Crooked Flower* copyright © by William Hathaway. All Rights Reserved.
Any inquiries about the plays *Bless Me, Father* and *A Crooked Flower* should be addressed to the author: William Hathaway, 402 Park Avenue, Rutherford, NJ 07070.

Chapter 20:
Excerpts of scripts from *General Hospital* and *All My Children* reprinted with the permission of American Broadcasting Companies, Inc., copyright © 1994.

Chapter 21: Excerpts from audition scripts for *The Wonder Years* reprinted with the kind permission of Carol Black and Neal Marlens.

Chapter 22:
Excerpts from *The Stranger Within* by John Pielmeier reprinted by permission of the author.

Chapter 23:
Page 304: Wind Drift® After-Shave and Cologne: Copy reprinted with the permission of Mem Company, Inc., Northvale NJ 07647.
Page 305: Easy-Off® is the registered trademark of American Home Products Corporation.
Page 306: Jergens Direct-Aid®: Copy reprinted with the permission of the Andrew Jergens Company, Cincinnati, Ohio.
Page 307: White Cloud® Tissue: Copy reprinted with the permission of the Procter and Gamble Company, Cincinnati, Ohio.

Manufactured in the United States of America
 2 3 4 5 / 98 97 96 95

This book is dedicated to the men in our lives.

This book could not have been written without the assistance and support we received from our many, many friends and industry professionals:

the actors,

agents,

casting directors,

designers,

directors,

managers,

producers,

writers,

union representatives,

and the members of professional organizations on both coasts and throughout the country who were happy to be interviewed, who took the time to answer our questionnaires (and kindly sent copies to colleagues), who made room for us in their studios, provided insight, and generously volunteered to share their expertise.

We are very grateful to William Hathaway and John Pielmeier for allowing us to use their work. We also deeply appreciate Carol Black and Neal Marlens, co-creators and producers of *The Wonder Years*, granting us permission to reprint two audition scenes.

CONTENTS

PART TWO
THE BREAKS

INTRODUCTION

*Acting is half shame, half glory; shame at exhibiting
yourself, glory when you can forget yourself.*

—SIR JOHN GIELGUD

You are about to enter a strange and wondrous land.

You are approaching that singular community of theater–TV–film which lies somewhere between the Twilight Zone and the Land of Oz and is known as The Business. It is a world of bright lights and frenzy, where the inhabitants love what they do with a passion that sustains them, often for years, and that enables them to exist under primitive conditions, working frequently for no compensation other than the thrill of participating in the endeavor and the shimmering prospect of future greatness.

Within the past decade we have witnessed what must be described as a seismic change in The Business. Digital communications technologies have propelled us to the brink of what pundits refer to as the Information Superhighway. Our universe of 500 television channels, interactive programming, CD-Rom, E-Mail, Pay-per-View, video games, and the heretofore undreamt-of possibilities of programming on demand is making "science fiction" an obsolete term. The future — particularly as drawn by Ray Bradbury in *Fahrenheit 451* — seems to have arrived.

Nevertheless, The Business remains a very accepting community. There is always room, at least on the outskirts, for a newcomer — someone who responds to the brightness and the energy and the lure of personal satisfaction. The primary requisite is dedication. It is the devoted ones who, eventually, make their way toward the centers of recognition, money, and power. It is this journey that concerns us now.

We are going to chart the territory for you, provide you with a map, show you how to proceed from where you are now to where you want to be — enjoying a career as a working performer who is part of the delicious excitement that characterizes life in the two magical cities, New York and Los Angeles. Along the way we may open your eyes to opportunities in new production centers blossoming across the country — in places like Dallas, Miami, and Chicago.

13

We've been living in this community for a long time; we know the way. And we have asked our friends — performers whose names or faces you know well and casting directors and talent agents whose names you will *want* to know — to share with us the benefit of their experiences in The Business. Their wisdom is here too.

Some sobering facts before we begin: as we write this guidebook, there are some 150,000 professional performers, by which we mean members of AEA (Actors Equity Association), SAG (Screen Actors Guild), and AFTRA (American Federation of Television and Radio Artists), in New York and Los Angeles. You should know that only 20 percent of those people earn more than $5,000 per year. Performers who earn more than $25,000 per year constitute about 8 percent of the membership. The number of actors who earn more than $100,000 per year is approximately 2,000 people. They are the ones you recognize working in commercials and in major roles on soap operas; they're "bankable" names in feature films and starring on Broadway.

Do these numbers mean that you should abandon the idea of trying to make your journey? Only if you are not serious about your commitment. If there are other things that you can see yourself doing, that will bring you just as much happiness, offer a higher ratio of success, and demand less application, then by all means involve yourself in those activities.

The gifted actor Jim Dale, speaking to a seminar of young AFTRA and SAG members, put it this way:

> If you are looking for security, go into some other business. I don't want that. We create magic. That's what I want to do. It's what I've wanted ever since I was nine years old and my father first took me to see a live performance.

If that is how you feel, if acting is what you know you absolutely must do, welcome to our world. (Incidentally, the play Jim's father took him to see was a musical, *Me and My Girl*. Decades later, when the London revival played in New York, the star of the show was Jim Dale!)

We believe that, despite the numbers, there is always room for talent. Every day another new face "makes it." Consider these recent Tony Award winners, all of them new on Broadway: Stephen Spinella, *Angels in America*, Brent Carver, *Kiss of the Spider Woman*, and Daisy Egan, *The Secret Garden*. New to TV audiences are Brett Butler of *Grace Under Fire*, David Caruso, the red-headed cop on *N.Y.P.D. Blue*, and Fred Savage, who starred on *The Wonder Years*. And plenty of new faces have been seen in films: Chris O'Donnell in *Scent of a Woman*, Leonardo DiCaprio in *This Boy's Life*, Angela Bassett in *Malcolm X*. Each season — on Broadway, on television, and in films — brings new shows with new people, and some of them are marvelous and they will last.

One of the most important things to keep in mind is that the casting director (or the producer or the network) and the actor share aspects of the same problem: one is constantly hoping to find new, interesting, arresting talent, and the other is talent hoping to be found. Whenever these two forces get together, the result is always jobs. And careers and recognition and, sometimes, fame and fortune.

Fame and fortune, however, are accidental, and they are not the immediate goal of this journey. Too often they are the result of being in the right show in the right season, on the right day of the week, on the right channel, in the right time slot, or in the right commercials — or some other outrageous, unpredictable bit of luck. Many people believe that appearing in a deodorant commercial was the spark that ignited Diane Keaton's illustrious career. Her sweetly daffy portrayal of an exhausted but fastidious jogger was viewed coast to coast, several times a day, for many months.

Before you can have a chance at fame and fortune you need to have a job. And to do that you must be a talented, determined performer who knows how to get seen by the people who can give you a job. That is what we call knowledgeable job-seeking, and that is what this book — this journey — is all about: getting to the centers of activity, knowing exactly how to function even in the wildest circumstances.

Jobs, careers, and recognition are what we hope you are after. Then you can try for fame and fortune.

Are you ready?

PART ONE

NUTS AND BOLTS

CHAPTER 1

WHAT YOU WILL NEED TO GET STARTED

Success is a journey, not a destination.
—ANONYMOUS

The best thing to have is wealthy or powerful or famous parents who are willing to support you in your chosen career.

No joke intended. We are simply trying to be realistic — and inject a little humor into the reality.

If you were planning a career in dentistry, archaeology, or accounting instead of performing, you would not be at all surprised to learn that establishing yourself requires the mastery of specific skills as well as the investment of serious amounts of time and dollars. Yet The Business (as we like to call it), more than any other field of endeavor, is so loaded with legends of success achieved by accident, and with tales of plucky but enthusiastic amateurs winning out over seasoned professionals, that it is frequently perceived as a fantasy playground even by those who would make their living in it.

Every dramatic genre has glorified the waif who gets off the bus in Los Angeles or New York with little more than a knapsack, a pair of tap shoes, and a load of moxie. She then collides with a powerful producer, celebrity, or agent who, struck by her art-less quality, declares, "You're what this tired old town needs," makes a few phone calls, and, in minutes, transforms her into a superstar. Doesn't that sound like the plot of a movie you've seen several times? It's a wonderful story. Let's hope you can audition for the lead when they cast the next remake. In the meantime, let's not confuse myth with reality. The recipe for success in The Business, as in any other, calls for a mixture of talent and study, plus hefty amounts of discipline and determination.

This book is all about how to be a *working* actor. We do not aim to tell you how to enjoy being a struggling, unemployed actor. While we may acknowledge the magic and passion and immeasurable satisfaction of performing, we have been careful to point out that there are thousands of dedicated professionals who earn very little money.

Auditioning for and winning an acting job is an accomplishment. Doing the job once you get it demands total concentration. Having to contend with the pressures of rehearsal, production, and performance while at the same time worrying about whether you'll have enough money to pay the rent or the telephone bill is, to our way of thinking, worse than foolish. It's suicidal and should not be attempted.

An actress we know tells us that she never could have succeeded without the help and understanding she received from her parents. She was able to study with the best teachers and not worry about the time it took her to develop as an artist. Jacklyn Zeman, who plays Bobbi Spencer on *General Hospital*, says:

> Don't put a time limit on yourself. Don't give yourself the added pressure of a time limit.

Veteran Helen Wagner, who arrived in New York a generation before Jacklyn, says almost the same thing:

> There were many other girls — friends of mine — who came here at the same time I did, and who knows if I was more or less gifted than they? But I saw their careers get postponed or sidetracked because of the need to do other things to earn money. I am so glad that I was able to hang in there until the work started to come.

Among the jobs to come her way was a role in what today would be called the pilot of a show. In 1956, it was a daring project — a thirty-minute live soap opera. (At that time, TV soaps, like the radio serials they sprang from, were fifteen-minute programs, performed live each weekday.) That show was *As the World Turns*, and Helen appeared as Nancy Hughes. In the thirty-plus years that have elapsed since its premiere, *As the World Turns* has expanded into a sixty-minute videotaped program — and Helen Wagner still appears as Nancy Hughes. Who says there's no security in this business?

Imagine for a moment that you are not a talented performer but a computer programmer looking for a job. Would you pack your duffel bag, head for Silicon Valley, and simply hope for the best? Of course not. You'd make certain you had sufficient resources to enable you to lead a relatively normal life until you found the position you were seeking. Aware that you'd be interviewed by a slew of personnel directors, you'd want nothing to interfere with your ability to impress them as the ideal candidate for their needs.

The aspiring performer requires and deserves no less.

Think, now, of the times you've gone on vacation — alone or with friends or family. Remember the hours of planning — figuring out whether to fly or drive, which clothes to pack? And, most important, how much this trip was going to cost? Could you afford it? That's the sort of preplanning you need to do now.

Before you go anywhere, make a list of what it costs you to live where you are now. Every day, write down how much you spend on food, clothes, rent, transportation, utilities, magazines, movies and video rentals, cable TV — on all the things that comprise your current life-style. If you're living at home, in a dorm, or in an apartment you share, find out how much it would cost to live the same way on your own.

This will give you some idea of your current expenses and prepare you for the job you must master — that of being your own financial planner.

YOUR MONEY

In the pages that follow, we are going to explain both the start-up costs and the continuing costs of living sensibly, not lavishly, in New York or Los Angeles for six months with *no squeeze*. By that we mean that you should not need, or expect, to earn one cent during the starting-out period. We've offered current figures to help you plan, but remember that there is always going to be some inflation; everything will surely be a bit more expensive in the future.

INITIAL COSTS

The first item to consider is what it costs to travel to Los Angeles or New York City. This trip can be planned far enough in advance to allow you to take advantage of whatever bargain fares may be offered by the buses, trains, or airlines.

Ideally, you should plan a preliminary scouting trip with your family and/or your potential roommate. High school seniors will visit several campuses to acquaint themselves with various college communities and evaluate their similarities and differences before deciding where to apply for admission; and corporate personnel, when engaged or transferred, are escorted on a tour of their soon-to-be-new location. If you've never been to the city before, it makes particularly good sense to do an exploratory trip.

New York and Los Angeles, while totally different in appearance and atmosphere, are awesome places. Even the most sophisticated traveler needs time to absorb their impact. Yes, you will be dumbfounded by New York's tall buildings and the crowds hurrying along the streets night and day. Yes, in Los Angeles there is smog you can see and flotillas of cars perpetually zooming ninety miles an hour along the endless freeway!

> I'm from Pittsburgh, and when I got to New York, it was a little bit more than I expected. I didn't realize it really was as difficult as everybody said. You hear it's difficult, but you think, yeah, that's what everybody else says, it'll be different for me. And it's not. New York is very expensive, so you have to have a job, and having a job means you aren't free to do the things you really want to do during the day, like meeting people and networking.
> —NOELLE NEAL, *actress*

Devote ten days or two weeks to discovering the places that are, or will be, significant in your life as a performer. See as much as you can of the city in the daytime, beginning with a sight-seeing tour. Listen to the spiel of the tour guides and ask questions, then venture out on your own. Scout for your location — just as a film production company would do when shooting outside the studio. You are seeking the best background for you — and trying to effect a workable compromise between comfort and affordability.

It should not be necessary to squander thousands of dollars on this visit. This is not the time to indulge in the splendors of the Four Seasons or Beverly Wilshire hotels (though you may wish to saunter through their lobbies). There are plenty of small hotels near New York's theater district or near the Hollywood power base that offer cleanliness and convenience at a modest price. You can find out about them, and get information on cultural attractions as well as maps of subway and bus routes, by writing to the Convention and Visitors Bureau in New York (2 Columbus Circle, New York, NY 10019) or in Los Angeles (505 South Flower Street, Los Angeles, CA 90071).

From the network of bed-and-breakfast establishments you may learn about attractive accommodations at fairly reasonable rates, often in the residential areas where you may want to look for an apartment. The number of bed-and-breakfast places increases steadily. For information, write to the Bed & Breakfast League, Ltd., 2855 29th Street, N.W., Washington, D.C. 20008.

RENT
Here, of course, is where the major chunk of your capital will go. It should come as no surprise that apartments in New York and Los Angeles cost more than in other cities.

In Atlanta, five minutes from the heart of town, one can select a two-bedroom, two-bath apartment with on-site swimming pool and garage for something like $750 a month. For that amount of money you *may* be able to find a studio apartment in Los Angeles, possibly large enough for two to share.

Try not to be shocked to learn that the same size studio can cost $1,200 a month in Manhattan. Or more, or less, depending upon the neighborhood. Neighborhoods affect the price of everything — even tomatoes. The neighborhoods we are talking about are decent, safe. Generally, the apartment buildings either employ a twenty-four-hour doorman or have a good security system. It is essential that you be able to come and go at all hours: rehearsals and theater will keep you out late; calls for TV and film jobs are usually early.

Most actors share apartments. If you have friends or relatives already living in the city, they may have, or know of, a place for you. Someone from your school, town, or club may be moving to New York or Los Angeles to pursue a career. Consider sharing your apartment with a novice lawyer and/or broker. If you are unable to find a roommate through these sources, you may wish to take advantage of notices posted on all the bulletin boards where you take classes, and at the unions (if you are a member). Tack your own "Roommate Wanted" notice up at your health club, your dance studio, the supermarkets where you shop. Besides getting more space for less money, you will gain the valuable sense of support that comes from being with people who know and care about you.

The frantic scramble for space in New York has, in large part, to do with the gradual phasing out of rent control. Whenever long-term tenants, paying rents that controls have kept affordable, vacate their premises, landlords are permitted to raise rents to the fair market level. These apartments then become rent-stabilized, and rent increases (according to numerical formulas that change annually) are permitted with each new lease. While the recent downturn in the economy may have depressed the prices of housing that is for sale, the cost of rental space has not dropped at nearly the same rate. Rent-controlled or rent-stabilized apartments that become vacated are considered lost to the Stratospheric Rent Monster, and performers are not the only ones who will resort to every conceivable strategy — be it sublet or share — to keep that from happening.

> I called everybody I knew and ended up with a place in SoHo that I learned about in a restaurant. It was a sublet, for $1000, which was just about manageable for two people. But in a sublet you have no rights or protection. Then I called a friend who was being killed off on a soap, and asked if his place was available, or if he knew of anything. He happened to have a girlfriend who wanted to share her two-bedroom with someone who would just live by himself. It was $650, and I grabbed it. But for a while there, I was talking to every superintendent in every building. There is a lot of rent-stabilized housing if you can just tap into it. You can get a place for $750, if you really ask. No one will know what you want unless you ask.
>
> —BRYAN LEDER, *actor*

To add to the complexity of this situation, apartments in newer buildings may be totally unregulated. For these, landlords are free to charge whatever they can get. The rent specified on the lease becomes the amount due each month, for the duration of that contract.

Though an ideal apartment in Manhattan would be within walking distance of the studios, theaters, and offices, it is certainly not a necessity. There are subways and buses to other boroughs. Plenty of performers enjoy living in Astoria, Jackson Heights, and Long Island City — which are convenient residential neighborhoods in Queens — and others rave about bargain spaces they've found twenty-five minutes from Times Square in Park Slope, Carroll Gardens, or Cobble Hill — in Brooklyn.

Actors are even venturing across the Hudson River to New Jersey, finding in nearby Weehawken and Hoboken housing that is grander and far less costly than anything Manhattan has to offer — and even boasts a view of Manhattan's magical skyline. However, there may be a drawback to living according to a train or bus schedule, for you can miss out on opportunities to spend time networking over coffee with other actors.

> I called everyone I knew from college — U. of Tennessee — asking if they needed or knew of anyone who needed a roommate. I found a schoolmate who lives in Astoria, with two bedrooms and a balcony, and it's safe, and she has a car. It's $950 a month. It takes about as long to get to midtown from the Upper West Side as from there. It was either that or sharing a one-bedroom on 14th Street for $940, and that was crowded.
>
> —MELISSA RITZ, *actress*

New York seemed so vast. How the money flowed out of my pocket! I wasn't ready for the cost of things. A few people from my college — Niagara University — were living in Weehawken. I sublet from a girl going on tour with *Starlight Express*, and because she knew me I didn't have to pay the security! It's $800, split two ways — two bedrooms — and we have a washer and dryer, which saves a fortune! My view of Manhattan is incredible.

—THOMAS RYAN, *actor*

In L.A. we had an apartment for $400 each in Studio City, but it was so boring, I'd lie on the grass and watch cars go by. Then I moved to Marina Del Rey, and that cost $900 for the two of us. But the pollution and the traffic were so bad. Yes, there was a pool, and it's very outdoorsy, and people are superficially friendly. But you feel you can't talk to them. And you can't do anything out there. In New York there's always something you can do, there's a great sense of community.

—BRITT SADY, *actress*

When you rent an apartment, you (and your roommate) will be expected to sign a lease for one or two years. You'll also be required to plunk down one or two months' rent as security.

The situation in Los Angeles differs to the extent that the entertainment industry plays such an enormous part in the local economy that real estate people are accustomed to serving a transient population — the performers, technicians, and production people who come and go according to TV and movie industry shooting schedules. Furnished apartments can be had on a monthly basis. Studio apartments will begin at $600 and go up. Again, prices will depend upon neighborhood, and in a city seventy miles wide, there are plenty of neighborhoods. It is truly impossible to be near everything, which is why your rent may include the cost of garage space for the car you will definitely need.

It's customary in Los Angeles to pay the first and last month's rent in advance, plus a security deposit, and even a cleaning fee. As we've said, you will not necessarily be required to sign a long-term lease, but you will have to commit for a definite period of time.

Sublets and Shares There are such things as leases for sub-tenants, but you and the person who has the lease for the apartment may simply make a private arrangement on a month-to-month basis, allowing you to move as soon as you find a place of your own. Before you do business on the basis of a handshake, though, it's a good idea to specify your privileges and responsibilities on a written document of which both of you will keep a copy.

Rent.......$800 to $1,500 per month, with two additional months as part of initial cost

In an Emergency If you find that you are totally without a place to stay or even park your belongings for a few days, consider the YMCA — in Hollywood at 1553 Hudson Avenue; in New York at 5 West 63rd Street. Both are centrally located. Their minimal accommodations are probably the least expensive you can find and will provide a brief respite until you can make arrangements to share or rent space.

Another low-cost option is Hosteling International, New York's facility at 103rd Street and Amsterdam Avenue. The cost of their dormitory rooms is $20 per night for members, $23 for nonmembers. For further information, write Hosteling International, 891 Amsterdam Avenue, New York, NY 10025.

UTILITIES

Heat and water are included in the rent for apartments in New York and Los Angeles. Energy for cooking (either by gas or electricity), and electricity for lights, air conditioning, and other appliances is additional; you are billed for gas and electric each month by the utility company. Of course, the more you use these appliances, the higher your bill.

Electricity/Gas..*about $75 and up per month*

TRANSPORTATION

Los Angeles Los Angeles has been described as a sprawl of suburbs in search of a city. You can travel for hours along crowded highways, from one small community to another, and never reach anything that looks like the center of town. Headquartered in sleekly modern office towers or homey bungalows, production houses, networks, studios, and casting people are scattered in all directions.

Los Angeles does have a bus system, the RTD. Check the local directory for the current number to call for instructions on getting to your destination. You can request route maps from the L.A. Convention and Visitors Bureau. You could memorize one or two of Hamlet's soliloquies while waiting for the right bus to come along. Great for seeing the town, they are not efficient for actors engaged in serious job hunting.

Los Angeles also has a recently-opened segment of its long-awaited mass-transit railway system. The 1993 earthquake joggled residents into using it, and reports are that they're finding it a surprisingly pleasant and safe way to travel. When a larger area is accessible, this may turn out to be the most efficient way to get places.

There are plenty of taxis, and you can hail them as they cruise by. The meter seems to drop twenty cents every few seconds, so paying thirty dollars for a taxi ride is not uncommon. It's foolish to consider this mode of travel, except in emergencies.

Driving becomes the only sensible way to get from one appointment to the next. The low-cost car-rental company Rent-A-Wreck was born in Los Angeles. Their vehicles are far from decrepit, just a few seasons away from being new. In 1994, their monthly rental cost for a subcompact car was $495 per month, including liability insurance. Their low-cost competitor is Ugly Duckling, whose rates begin at $119 per week (they have monthly specials), plus insurance. Drivers who prefer current models will find them at the nationally advertised rental outlets; lowest monthly rates hover around $650, plus insurance.

Lately, the practice of leasing cars directly from local auto dealers has become popular. Some people say that the cost is lower and cars and services are better.

If you intend to stay in Los Angeles for at least a year, it might be smart to buy a car where you currently live, from a local dealer you or your family know, and then drive (with all your possessions in a rented trailer) to California.

Car owners, of course, will have to budget for maintenance and insurance on a yearly basis. Depending upon the make and condition of the vehicle, estimates for maintenance are $300 and up per year; insurance costs $1200 and up. The common wisdom regarding insurance is that one should opt for the maximum coverage. In view of the cost of gasoline and the great distances to be covered, most performers prefer small, economical cars.

Car Rental..*from $119 per week*
$495 to $650 per month

Car Insurance ....*$100 and up per month*

Other Protection...................................... *(Wheel-locking attachment, car alarm, etc.)*
$60 and up

To the cost of renting (or leasing), operating, and insuring your vehicle, you must add the daily expense of parking at or near each office you visit. Actors learn to carry a supply of coins of all denominations to feed the parking meters. When you are on a business call, you may often park free if you have your parking-lot or garage ticket validated by a company receptionist. Rates vary — here, too, it all depends upon the neighborhood.

Parking...*$10 and up per week*

One of the stops on your exploratory trip to California should be at the office of the Motor Vehicle Bureau, to acquire a copy of the California Drivers' Handbook and the Registration Handbook. If you own your car, find out about the state's regulations concerning private vehicles. There are requirements for smog certification, registration, service and vehicle license fees, and a use tax. Also check the bookstores for *Thomas' Book of Maps*; it's invaluable.

New York New York, on the other hand, is a walking city, further enriched by an elaborate subway system and dozens of bus lines. For the most part, theater, film, and television offices are clustered in the heart of Manhattan, which is about a mile wide at 42nd Street. The farthest outposts — the Kaufman Astoria (Queens) Film Studios and the NBC Brooklyn TV Studio — are near bus and subway lines.

It's not unlikely that you would have a commercial audition at an advertising agency at 54th Street and Third Avenue, which is on the East side, followed by an interview for a play reading 'way west at 42nd Street and Tenth Avenue, at Theater Row, and then have to rush to an acting class downtown on Bank Street in Greenwich Village. You can take buses and subways to all these appointments, for $1.25 a ride (and bus transfers, or Add-A-Rides, are free).

Taxi rides, which really should be saved for emergencies, start at $1.50 and drop 25 cents every one-ninth of a mile. The average trip may cost five dollars or more, plus a tip for the driver.

New York Mass Transit ....*$50 or more per week*

TELEPHONE — AND THE LIKE

The phone is your lifeline to jobs, appointments, news about what's happening in The Business and at home, and just plain gossip. Apartment sharers should have separate telephones. Unless you have a poor record of payment with the phone company, there is, at this writing, no up-front security charge.

Telephone Connection ....*from $75 up for installation*

For your connection to the service, you should allow several days' lead time.

If your habit is to use the phone as a permanent attachment to your arm, your bills will be comparatively high.

Telephone Bill..*about $60 and up per month*

Optional services, such as Call Waiting (which tells you when someone else is trying to reach you while you are on the line) and Call Forwarding (which allows you to transfer incoming calls to another telephone number), may be worth investing in. These, of course, will add to your monthly bill:

Optional Telephone Services ....*about $10 per month*

And, of course, you should investigate the low-cost long-distance services offered by MCI, Sprint, and AT&T. Their special plans may lower the cost of calls home.

Answering Services and Machines The twenty-four-hour-a-day, seven-day-a-week answering service devoted to the special needs of actors blossomed during the wonderful days of radio drama. The major services maintained direct-line telephones outside the door of every radio studio and in the CBS and NBC restaurants so that their busy clients could check in for messages during rehearsal breaks, while waiting to grab a sandwich and coffee, or before dashing from a broadcast of *Our Gal Sunday* at CBS on East 52nd Street all the way across Fifth Avenue to Rockefeller Center for the first read-through of *Life Can Be Beautiful* in Studio G on the third floor at NBC.

Most important, the services could be relied upon to deliver calls for auditions, rehearsals, and jobs. A call confirmed through a performer's answering service was recognized throughout the business as a commitment. It was equivalent to a signed contract.

In addition to locating you quickly and relaying messages from agents, casting people, or friends, the service can be instructed to deliver crucial wake-up calls and function as a kind of appointments secretary. A charge — about fifty cents — is added to the basic monthly fee for each call made on your behalf. Reliable answering services advertise in all the trade papers. It might be sensible to use the same service that most of your friends do — when you're out together, one call will let you all know whether there are any messages.

Answering Service ....*$20 to $40 per month*

The actor selecting a telephone answering machine opts for the one-time purchase price over the continuing monthly service charge. Agents do not hesitate to say that they feel a certain frustration when they dial a client's home number and, instead of reaching the person, hear a recorded message — especially one in which the actor tries to be clever, offers heavy breathing, the soundtrack from *Jurassic Park*, or one-liners delivered in various dialects. On a heavy business day, that can work against you. Many casting people and agents prefer to leave messages with a real person — the service operator, whom they may already know — rather than with a machine. There is never a concern that the service will be out of commission, whereas machines have been known to break down.

If you decide that you prefer an answering machine, be sure you get one that is highly rated, with a call-in beeper that works. Above all, make it a habit to call in to your machine frequently. Your answering machine can also be had with a fax—which can be a lifesaver.

Telephone Answering Machine...*$40 to $200*
With Fax...*from $350*

Voice Mail, Message Banks, Beepers, and Pagers It becomes ever more necessary, especially in Los Angeles, to answer messages almost as soon as the calls are placed, so you may want to consider these relatively new, personalized services which allow you to be in touch with everyone connected to your business at all times. Some services assign you a local voice-mail phone number that you can keep even if you change your address. Add a beeper, and you know instantly when there is a call for you. You pay a few cents per minute of air time when you retrieve messages. It is also possible to have a personal 800 number, a small investment which makes it easy for people in other areas to contact you.

Voice Mail, Message Banks, Beepers, and Pagers.....................*$15 and up, per month*

Outside Calls Remember that you will need to make phone calls while you are out. Lacking a cellular phone, for this you will probably have to use a pay phone. Agents, secretaries, or receptionists do not take kindly to anyone who visits their office tying up and, essentially, doing private business on the company phone. (When you become a big money-producer for an agent, his or her office's attitude may change.) Local calls to any of the five boroughs in New York currently cost twenty-five cents; charges are the same at AT&T phones in Los Angeles.

Pay Phones...*$60 a month*

FOOD

New York and Los Angeles boast fantastic restaurants at all price levels, but this is one pleasure you should treat yourself to only occasionally. Let's face it, eating in restaurants is never cheap. So, if you have not yet mastered the technique of boiling an egg, think of this as a marvelous opportunity to learn. In both Los Angeles and New York there are plenty of markets offering fine, fresh produce, in addition to all the canned and packaged stuff you grew to love at home.

What cannot be overemphasized is the need to nourish yourself adequately. One cannot bear up under the rigors of a twelve-hour camera day on a diet of junk food, soft drinks, and candy bars. Sharing meals with friends, roommates, or scene partners is a way to reinforce relationships while making certain that you take the time to eat well.

You would be amazed at the number of high-profile performers who brown-bag it to rehearsals and to film shoots. This is not because they are penny pinching, but because they know they have to be in control of what they eat and, especially on location, when they eat.

> I cook for myself every day. I happen to enjoy it, and I am a good cook,
> but I also couldn't afford to live any other way.
>
> —NOELLE NEAL, *actress*

Start with the excellent basic, *The James Beard Cook Book*, treat yourself to a copy of esteemed actress Uta Hagen's *Love for Cooking*, or succumb to Rombauer and Becker's classic, the encyclopedic *Joy of Cooking*.

Costs can be contained. Watch the ads and clip the coupons in the food sections of the newspapers each Wednesday; shop for specials and stock up on staples. Some stores offer better prices on essentials than others; take note, and make lists when you go marketing.

Food...*$80 and up per week (for two people)*

Add to the costs of your food whatever you're accustomed to drinking — beer, wine, or liquor are additional. Then give yourself a separate food-budget category called "Incidentals" for lunches, snacks, and after-theater and after-work meetings with colleagues and casting people.

Incidentals..*$150 per month*

ENTERTAINMENT

Movies, theater, ballet, and concerts represent more than diversion for you: they are opportunities to learn more about your profession. You should see as much as you can. Of course, with first-run films costing eight dollars in many Manhattan cinemas, and Broadway theater seats edging up beyond sixty-five dollars, this can be a costly assignment. Fortunately, you can get half-price tickets to theater, concerts, and dance programs. The well-known TKTS booths in both cities sell discount tickets for same-day performances. In New York, there is also a discount-ticket booth for music and dance events located in Bryant Park, at the corner of 42nd Street and Sixth Avenue. You will need to bring cash to these services, and prepare to stand in line awhile.

Reduced-price tickets to long-running Broadway shows, commonly called twofers, are available through local merchants or through the mail if you apply to the Hit Show Club, at 630 Ninth Avenue, 8th floor, New York, NY 10036. Many shows, if they are selling out, make standing room available at very low cost about an hour before curtain time.

The Theater Development Fund, or TDF, makes mail-order sales of selected theater, cabaret, and dance tickets at cut-rate prices to members (membership costs $10 per year). TDF also sells sets of vouchers that can be used for showcase and off-

off-Broadway productions. These can help introduce you to a whole world of theater that you will want to become a part of. Write to TDF, 1501 Broadway, New York, NY 10036.

Actors Equity Association frequently has free passes to plays on and off Broadway.

Audience Extras, Inc., is a unique organization operating in New York and Los Angeles, through which people interested in the theater have a chance to see plays at reduced cost. For details, write to them at 109 West 26 Street, NY 10001.

New Yorkers can also take advantage of myriad opportunities to see exciting performances at absolutely no cost, at the open-air Delacorte Theater in Central Park (during the summer, that is), at the Bruno Walter Auditorium of the Library of Performing Arts in Lincoln Center, and in many of the library branches throughout the city. Symphony Space, in a former movie palace on the Upper West Side, offers a wide variety of cultural programs. Check the Arts and Leisure sections of the Sunday papers for programs in these places and elsewhere.

> If you can't even afford TKTS, you can "second-act" some shows. At institutional theaters, like Manhattan Theater Club, Playwrights Horizons, Circle Rep, and Second Stage, you can volunteer to usher for free. Aside from seeing the work, you meet other ushers doing the same thing. You involve yourself in a community.
>
> — MEG SIMON, *casting director*

Screen Actors Guild (SAG) members can join the union's Film Society ($65 per year) and attend screenings of more than twenty films each year. Members of the Television Academy (NATAS in New York, ATAS in Los Angeles) who purchase membership in their Cinema Club — the latest cost is $95 per year — see more than twenty-five new films annually at biweekly screenings.

Entertainment...up to $75 per week

CREATING YOUR NEST

Maintenance of your living space, which we assume you intend to clean yourself, will require more time than money. Expect that whoever lived in an apartment before you will have left a mess that you will need to scour away. To do this you will have to purchase basic supplies, such as a mop, broom, and household products.

Cleaning Supplies..$75

Invest also in a steam/dry iron, an ironing board, and handy items such as spot cleaners for the necessary daily touch-ups on your clothing. Laundry (there's usually one in the building or nearby), dry cleaning, and shoe repair are costs that come to about the same.

Iron, Ironing Board, Spot Cleaner...$75

Laundry, Dry Cleaning, and Shoe Repair...$75

Marin Mazzie, actress, recalls her first day in New York, several years ago:

> The one thing I didn't expect was that I'd have to exterminate the apartment! We must've spent a fortune on roach bombs. I was terrified that if I went to sleep I'd get a cockroach in my ear. We also spent money on locks for the front door and gates on the windows. The apartment was on the first floor on West 47th Street. It was great to be in the theater district — and rent-controlled, which was lucky. The apartment cost $800 a month. I figure my first day in New York I dropped $1,750 without batting an eyelash — that's including transportation, my share of the apartment deposit, the roach bombs, and the gates.

The amounts you spend for your bed, linens, utensils, appliances, and furniture will depend upon your bargain-hunting skills, your sense of style, and whether the apartment you find is already furnished or is a pristine, empty space waiting to be transformed into your personal environment. Some furnished apartments may be stocked with knives, china and glass, flatware, and an array of kitchen utensils, in addition to the expected sofa, tables, and chairs. Others may provide only the barest essentials to qualify as "furnished."

Whatever the case, make certain that the bed you'll be sleeping on provides proper support. There are few things more aging to your face or detrimental to your body attitude and general health than inadequate sleep and bad sleeping posture. Even if space is tight in your apartment, there are sofa beds and sleep sofas nowadays with firm mattress and spring combinations. Get the best you can afford.

Sleep Sofa or Sofa Bed..*$500 and up*

A traditional mattress and box spring may cost about $400. You may wish to purchase a platform-style bed and allow a bit more than half of that for the mattress alone.

Mattress and Box Spring...*$400*

Smart shoppers know that by taking advantage of white sales — usually held in January, May, and August — and patronizing the discount outlets on both coasts, they'll be able to save money on linens, towels, and so on. If you buy two sets of linens, you'll be able to use one while the other is being laundered.

Bed Linens..*$100 and up*

Towels, Bath Mat, Shower Curtain..*$100 and up*

Other immediate necessities are a clock radio and a can opener — the foolproof, hand-held kind.

Clock Radio..*$20 to $80*

Can Opener..*about $5*

Items you may not need to purchase but should have with you are grooming aids such as an electric razor, styling/blow dryer, and hot rollers.

Some people will not travel without their beloved rocking chair, their stereo and record collection, their electric frying pan. One of the leading ladies on *All My Children* confessed that she was permanently attached to her microwave oven. Obviously, these are personal choices. This is the time to make yourself aware of what you already have and what you need.

If furnishing your apartment is going to be one of your projects, there are less expensive ways to accomplish this than by heading for the nearest department store with your list. Bulletin boards — at the unions, in your neighborhood, and wherever you take classes — almost always carry notices of objects for sale by owners who may be relocating just as you are. Nowadays there are very good discount outlets for just about everything, and mail-order catalogs can offer terrific bargains. Furniture finds are plentiful at Salvation Army thrift shops, secondhand furniture stores, auctions, and warehouse or outlet clearance sales. Housing Works, a charity operated by volunteers at 136 West 18th Street in Manhattan, is a good source of used furniture and accessories, and all proceeds go to help persons with AIDS.

Flea markets are great places to find things, especially china, glass, and silverware, often with a prestigious design history. Frequenting these outlets can be great fun, save you money, and serve as a great opportunity to become better acquainted with your new hometown. The amounts you spend for these items will depend upon your taste and what you can afford.

Protection Devices Nowadays it takes more than a lock on your door to keep your premises burglar-proof. On the other hand, scenes (such as in Neil Simon's uproarious *The Sunshine Boys*) in which characters studiously close six or more complicated bolts, and then, just as laboriously, have to open them each time someone comes to call, are best left for comedy. Sensible protection lies somewhere between these two extremes: a foolproof lock, such as a Medeco, a police lock, and sturdy bars or gates on accessible windows, patio doors, and fire escapes. The cost of these devices will depend on what your surroundings call for, what has been previously installed in your living quarters, your personal choices, and your neighborhood locksmiths' prices (shop around!).

Or, you may opt for an alarm system which alerts an outside security company in case of emergency. The community liaison at your local police precinct will be able to advise you. Remember, while you want to keep intruders out, you also want people to be able to get in, in case you need assistance.

Alarm System *$1,000*

Installation ....*$350 annual maintenance*

PROFESSIONAL ORGANIZATIONS

We devote Chapter 7 to the performing unions. Their dues appear in Table 2 (page 35). Membership in these unions is not a prerequisite for joining the National Academy of Television Arts and Sciences (NATAS) in New York or the Academy of Television Arts and Sciences (ATAS) in Los Angeles. These organizations join to bestow the annual Emmy and Daytime Emmy awards; local awards ceremonies are conducted by academy chapters throughout the country. Membership activities can be informative and may offer chances to network with people active in The Business.

NATAS/ATAS Annual Membership ....*$134 first year, $99 thereafter*

Other professional organizations you may not necessarily join — their criteria are strict — but which offer tremendous opportunity for networking, are the following:

- Women in Film & TV (WIFTV), based in New York, is open to performers as well as writers, directors, agents, casting directors, producers, programming executives, and technical people. They have screenplay readings every season, and they do cast from their files. Actors and actresses interested in being part of the series should send their photo and résumé to WIFTV, 274 Madison Avenue, 12th floor, New York, NY 10016.

- Women in Theater, based in Los Angeles, is a full-service organization where one can take classes, work on scenes, attend seminars, prepare staged readings, meet agents, casting directors, and photographers, and network with colleagues. Contact Women in Theater, Box 3718, Hollywood, CA 90078.

- The Players, at 16 Gramercy Park, in Manhattan, is the oldest theatrical club in this country. Founded in 1889 by Edwin Booth, it was the great American actor's personal residence. Its Hampden-Booth Library can be a valuable resource for theatrical research.

- The Lambs, no longer in its splendid building on West 44th Street, is a venerable theatrical club now headquartered at 3 West 51st Street, right near Rockefeller Center. They frequently have performance nights — a good opportunity to see theater stalwarts and possibly join them in a production.

- And we must not forget HOLA, the Hispanic Organization of Latin Actors, 250 West 65th Street, New York, NY 10023.

All these organizations have membership fees. The amounts vary.

YOUR CLOTHES

As a performer, you really have two wardrobes: the clothing you wear to interviews and auditions (see Chapter 5), and the outfits you wear in what we refer to as "real life."

With casual clothing the order of the day everywhere — and nowhere more so than in Los Angeles — we doubt that you will need to plan on purchasing "real life" clothing during the first six months of your stay in either city. Of course, New York winters can be brutally cold, so if you don't already own a heavy coat and all-weather boots, you will surely need to buy them before the first snowfall. A good raincoat with a warm zip-out lining can be useful all year round; the classic trench coat, with its "I've just dashed in from the airport" look, is always in style.

Winter Coat..*$200 and up, depending on where you shop*

All-Weather Boots ....*$80 and up*

TABLE 1. **WHERE THE MONEY GOES**

ITEM	NY COSTS	LA COSTS
Rent	$800–$1,200	$600–$800
Add'l two mos. security (one time)	$1,600–$2,400	$1,200–$1,600
Gas & electric	$80 & up	$70 & up
Transportation:		
Car rental	$650 approx.	$650 approx.
Insurance	$100 & up	$100 & up
Maintenance (yearly)	$300 & up	$300 & up
Gasoline	$1.10 or so/gallon, depending on locale	
Public transportation	$200 & up	avoid at all costs!
Telephone:	$60 & up	$60 & up
Hook-up (one time)	$75	$75
Outside calls	$60	$60
Optional services	$10 & up	$10 & up
Cellular/car phones	determined by area & use	
Fax costs	$10–$25	$50
Answering service	$20–$40	$20–$40
Answering machine (one time)	$60–$200	$60–$200
Answering machine w. fax (one time)	$350 & up	$350 & up
Beeper/voice mail	$15 & up	$15 & up
Food:		
Essential groceries	$80 & up	$60 & up
Incidentals	$150 & up	$150 & up
Entertainment:		
Theater, movies, restaurants	$300	$300
Furnishings (one time):		
Linens	$100 & up	$100 & up
Sofa/sofa bed/mattresses	$300 & up	$300 & up
Clock radio	$20	$20
Kitchen gear (beyond can opener)	$200 & up	$200 & up
Supplies	$135 & up	$135 & up
Personal expenses:		
Haircut & style	$40–$60/session	$40–$60/session
Hair color & highlights	$100–$200/session	$100–$200/session
Cosmetics (yearly)	$150	$150
Exercise classes	$15 & up/session	$15 & up/session
Laundry/shoe repair	$80	$80

TABLE 2.   **PROFESSIONAL EXPENSES**

The following expenses concern the choices that will affect your career. (The reasons for most of these expenses are given in Chapter 2 and Chapter 7). Here, for the purpose of arriving at a realistic financial plan, we show you approximately how much they will cost.

ITEM	COSTS	
Photograph:		
Photo session	$125–$650	
Duplicating	$85 & up per hundred	
Résumes:		
Layout	$10–$40	
Copying	$5–$25 per hundred	
Photo-postcards	$48 per hundred	
Mailing expenses:		
Manila envelopes	$25 per hundred	
Cardboards	$10 per hundred	
Postage per 8 x 10" photo	Postal Service price	
Postage per card	Postal Service price	
Stationery	$25 & up	
Mailing labels	$5 per set	
Trade publications (monthly)	$25 or more	
Classes:		
Acting workshop	$20 & up per class	
Acting coach	$50 & up per session	
Commercial technique course	$350 & up	
Dance class	$10 & up per class	
Voice lessons	$30–$70 per hour	
Vocal coaching	$45–$75 per hour	
Speech lessons	$50 & up per hour	
Tape recorder	$60 & up	
Cable TV hook-up and monthly cost	$30 & up	
Dues for performing unions:		
AEA	$800 Initiation fee	$39 semi-annual dues
AFTRA	$800 Initiation fee	$35 semi-annual dues
SAG	$1,008 Initiation fee	$42.50 semi-annual dues
Talent directory listing:		
Players' Guide	$80 year; $40 renewals	
Academy Players Directory	$60 per year	
Public library card	FREE!	

Your Fabulous Face

The way you look is, obviously, of vital importance (as President Bill Clinton demonstrated when a runway was closed at a busy airport while a superstar stylist boarded Air Force One to trim his hair). For both men and women, professional hair care is a necessity.

Bargain-hunting colleagues may suggest that you take advantage of free haircuts and coloring services available at beauty schools, salons, or cosmetic companies. We consider this a foolish economy. You have little or no control over what your hair will look or feel like. Spend the money so that you will always be sure you look the way you must — your best. Search around: many stylists and colorists will gladly consult with you at no charge. Explain that you are a performer and that you may frequently need an emergency touch-up, trim, or comb-out.

Hair Styling (women)...*$60 and up per visit*

Hair Styling (men)..*$30 and up, per cut*

Highlights..*$100 to $200 every three months*

Remember that all actors need makeup onstage and off. For people with skin discoloration, there are special products sold under the Dermablend label. There are also nonreflective cosmetics designed particularly for use on-camera.

Remember, also, that everything you put on your face can take its toll on the skin and make you look older than you are. Skin care is a necessity for both men and women: cleansing, moisturizing, toning and conditioning — ridding the surface of dead skin (that's what is meant by exfoliating).

Makeup and Skin Care Products..*about $150 and up per year*

Makeup Application...*$45 and up*

Makeup Application Lesson..*$90*

Health

Young people accustomed to consistently good health may think that allowances for doctors' and dentists' bills and health insurance are optional expenses. That would be a mistake. Accidents happen, emergencies arise. And they inevitably occur when you least expect them and cannot afford them. Not every emergency is life-threatening, but even tripping on uneven pavement can lead to serious and painful injury that can keep you out of work for weeks.

Until you have worked under union jurisdiction and have become eligible for no-cost medical coverage (see Chapter 7), you must provide your own health insurance. If you do not now have some health coverage, arrange for such insurance as quickly as you can, where you are now living. Once you have moved, you can inform the insuring organization of your new address.

You should also have a complete medical checkup before you embark upon this journey.

Medical Insurance and Medical Care...*Varies enormously!*

Tell your regular physicians that you're moving — they may be able to recommend colleagues practicing in New York or Los Angeles. Friends, too, may know internists, dentists, gynecologists, chiropractors, or podiatrists whom they admire. Anyone with special problems, such as allergies or blood, back, skin, or eye ailments, should ask for copies of all past medical records. The same holds true for prescriptions for lenses and/or medication.

ARRANGING FOR CREDIT

Now you have an idea of the *costs*. To deal with them, any person moving to a new location needs to establish *credit*. You want to be able to buy things without always paying for them with cash or in advance. You will have to arrange for services that are delivered after a period of time but require credit.

Because they do not usually have permanent employment — looking for work is the "steady job" in The Business — actors more than most people have historically found it a problem to establish credit. You can circumvent much of this difficulty by making your arrangements ahead of time — ideally during your preliminary visit. You can do this by opening a savings account, preferably at a bank located near your apartment. The simplest way to handle this is to have a certified check (or a cashier's check) drawn on your current account by your hometown bank for the amount you wish to deposit in your new bank. These checks are considered immediate cash; regular checks drawn on out-of-town banks may take as long as three weeks to clear.

In some locales, depositors need to show some proof of residence. If you are a sub-tenant, you may not have a lease, so your current passport and voter registration card may be suitable identification.

Most savings banks, which pay interest at slightly higher rates than commercial banks, offer checking accounts as well. You will definitely need a checking account and should pay by check whenever you can. The reasons for doing this should be evident: it's never smart to carry large amounts of cash because money can be lost or stolen. A canceled check serves as your record of payment, useful for tax purposes and in case of any problem with your purchase.

Banks automatically print the depositor's name and address on checks. We think it's sensible to omit your address. You may change your address before you've used all the checks, which would be confusing to the people you're paying. And, nowadays, one never knows who will gain access to the information.

A major credit card is another method of payment that gives you a record of the purchase. Promptly paid bills add to your credit rating. If you don't already have one, apply for a credit card while you are still at home. Several credit card companies permit family members to have separate cards issued in their own name; the bill will then be sent to the original card holder (you can repay your family at the end of the month).

Union members have the opportunity to join the Actors Federal Credit Union, which offers such banking services as savings and checking accounts as well as a low-interest credit card. You'll learn more about this in Chapter 7.

Proper Identification Two forms of identification are usually necessary when paying by check, when cashing a check, or when purchasing an unusually expensive item. A valid driver's license will be fine, as is a major credit card or a charge card from a department store. Your Social Security card is not acceptable identification.

Frequent travelers are accustomed to carrying their passport. Because this is a valuable article that's easily lost and takes time and money to replace, we suggest xeroxing the necessary passport information, then obtaining the other forms of ID as quickly as you can.

Becoming Your Own Accountant   Canceled checks, as we've already noted, are records of purchases made. You will need to keep these records, as well as all receipts for every penny you spend on the tools of your trade. Keep a daily diary of pay phone calls, trade papers, entertainment costs, transportation to and from auditions and jobs, and all other expenses related to your business. You will need these records at income tax time.

FRILLS

We have limited our lists above to items we consider necessary. The allotted amounts are sensible and not sparse. Now we append a wish list of sorts, to show how you might augment your possessions or embellish your life-style — in the event that you enjoy a marvelous streak of good luck!

First, invest in a videocassette recorder (VCR), not only to "time-shift" your viewing (that is, tape broadcasts to view at other times), but to record your performances (and those of other good actors). It is also a resource for taping and replaying commercials that you think are right for you.

VCR, Cable-ready with Remote Control..*about $300 and up*

For West Coast people, who spend so much time driving that they almost seem to live in their cars, a car phone can seem more a necessity than a frill. What with the density of the traffic and the great distances to be covered in the course of a normally busy day, working actors need to be able to pick up messages quickly and talk to their agents, all the while heading to suddenly arranged auditions, interviews, or callbacks. Having a car phone is also an increasingly important safety measure: you may need to call for help on the highway.

A cellular phone is costly: the price of the instrument may range from $75 to close to $200. In addition, there is a hefty activation charge of several hundred dollars, and a monthly service charge, plus the cost of air time whenever you make a call (the clock keeps ticking when you are on hold, waiting to talk to your party). In a city the size of Los Angeles, when you drive from one vicinity to the next, you may even incur long distance charges. These costs vary, according to the neighborhood, or the phone company.

Cellular Phone ....*$75 to $200 for the phone,*
plus activation and monthly service, plus variable
local company charges per month for calls

Rehearsing an audition monologue can be much more valuable if you are able to record your own performance with a video camera, or camcorder.

Camcorder..*$700 and up*

Talent agent Carole Ingber says: "Today, everybody's faxing for dollars!" If you need a script in a hurry, it can be faxed to you; if someone wants your bio, that can be faxed. This has become a business about time and money. Fortunately, faxing costs are deductible business expenses.

Plain Paper Fax ....*$550 and up*

Once you've had a chance to get semi-settled in your new home, a session with an image consultant who can determine your best colors, silhouettes, and styles would be an excellent investment. This is as true for men as it is for women.

> Having my colors done by a professional image consultant changed my life. I booked three industrials in a row because I knew I was wearing the right outfits. And the confidence that gave me meant I could concentrate on the audition without having to worry about my appearance.
> —KITTY LUNN, *actress*

> Going to a professional consultant was just the kick in the ass I needed!
> —MICHAEL RYAN, *actor*

Image Consultant..*$75 and up per session*

Keeping yourself in good shape is, obviously, essential to looking and feeling your best. Membership in a health club, complete with swimming pool and lots of exercise classes, is a worthwhile investment. Yoga is another practice that adds to one's vitality.

Health Club ....*$600 and up per year*

Yoga Classes..*$10 and up per class*

While we're at it, massages, manicures, and pedicures help you look good — and feel good, too.

Massage..*$50 and up*

Manicures and Pedicures ....*$10 to $30 each*

And, to be able to keep your head in place with all this excitement, you might want to visit an understanding therapist from time to time, or locate a clinic for much less. Fees can vary a lot.

Therapist ....*$40 to $100 or more per session*

THAT PERSON IN THE MIRROR

Starting to think of yourself as a business, with categories of expenses and professional needs, is undeniably exciting. At this time many young people begin to scrutinize themselves in mirrors that seem to magnify every slight deviation from perfection. They suddenly decide that what they really need is a new face — or at least a better nose or chin. The brown-eyed girl shakes her head sadly, because blue eyes are what she knows she should have. Most of this self-dismay is merely a manifestation of fear of the unknown, an outburst of insecurity — and a feeling that will subside. (Chapter 5 is devoted to helping you package yourself successfully.)

However, if your dissatisfactions are real and long-standing, do have them attended to before you set out. There are several good reasons for doing so. The most practical consideration, if you are contemplating surgical, medical, or dental work, is the cost, which will surely be more expensive in New York or Los Angeles than almost anywhere else. The physician you are now seeing knows you, your needs, and your temperament. You will also save yourself time and anxiety by starting your career already looking your best.

To venture out on interviews when you are unhappy about your teeth, your nose, your hair, or your weight is to give yourself an unnecessary handicap. It means your concentration is centered upon what's wrong with you and whether or not the interviewer will notice. Yes, the interviewer will notice, and will either note your deficiency on the back of your photo (bad teeth, needs to lose weight) or tell you to come back when you have lost twenty pounds.

Why give yourself that pressure? Lose the weight! Get your hairline improved, or your eyebrows tweezed, or that unsightly mole removed. Feel confident that you look terrific when you go out on the first meeting!

THE GRAND TOTAL

As we indicated at the start of this chapter, the performer, like any other professional, needs to plan ahead for a successful career. The best way to proceed is to be able to devote yourself totally to the task of getting interviews and jobs without worrying about supporting yourself, at least for the first six months.

Once you've arrived and had a chance to unpack, you can pay attention to the real task, which is getting a job!

CHAPTER 2

THE TOOLS OF THE TRADE

Learn to listen. Opportunity sometimes knocks very softly.
—CHINESE PROVERB

You've found a place to live. You've unpacked your bags. The phone is hooked up and you're eager to get started. As the sole proprietor of your one-person business, what you need now is customers and a way to attract them.

THE PICTURE AND YOU

If you were working in any other business, you'd hand out little calling cards with your company logo, your name, your title, and direct telephone number. In The Business, your calling card is an 8 x 10" black-and-white photo. Actors introduce themselves with a photo; they refresh contacts' memories with a photo. That picture is you to all the people you've met and hope to meet.

The picture must look like *you*. Not what you want to look like, your fantasy image; not what the photographer thinks you should look like, with elaborate make-up and lighting tricks and fans blowing your hair. You. The you that is going to walk into the casting office or the agent's office. An extended handshake.

> I like a natural shot, a picture that looks like you.
> —FERN CHAMPION, *independent casting director*

> We receive 350 photos a week and, when we are doing a search for a principal role, 800 to 900 photos of actresses twenty-one to twenty-six. I look at every piece of mail that comes in.
> —MARK TESCHNER, *casting director,* General Hospital

Among all the pictures that casting people receive, certain people are going to stand out — the ones who are using a good picture.

WHAT MAKES A PICTURE GOOD

Naturalness is important. Casting directors and talent agents are looking for real people. Isn't that what you see every day on television, at the movies, or in commercials?

41

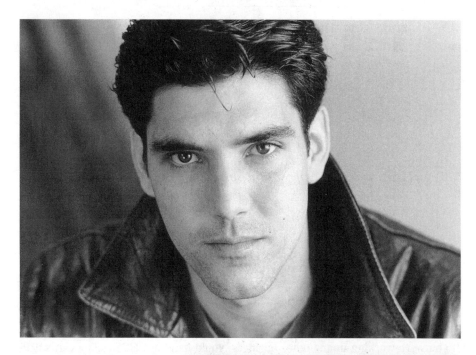

The actor Paul Stevenson
has chosen the closeup
"letter-box" format (top)
and the standard 8 x 10"
(right). Photos by
Hoebermann Studio.

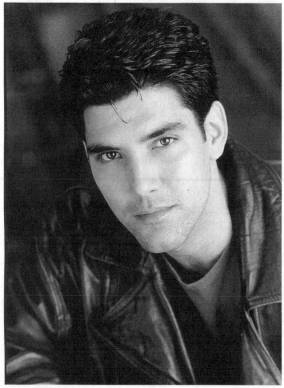

Even onstage, where distance allows us to be less specific, we're not transforming ourselves into outrageous apparitions; we are doing plays about people who are somewhat like ourselves.

Naturalness is reflected in your attitude — it should be open, friendly. Your shoulders should be relaxed. Your hands should rest in your lap, not cradle your cheek or your chin. Your smile should be easy, not a clenched-teeth pose you held until the photographer released you.

Most important, warmth should radiate from your eyes — they are "the windows of the soul." They reflect you, your quality, the quality that gets you into the agent/producer/casting director's office. A veteran casting director told us:

> The first thing that I look for is the eyes. I believe all film acting is in
> the eyes.

Study yourself in the mirror and, if you haven't already, practice expressions. It may sound childish or phony, but how else can you discover that when you smile, you squint or your gums show, you wrinkle your nose and your forehead. Be on the lookout for double chins or hunched shoulders. If there's a noticeable gap between your front teeth (and comedy is not your forte), get the temporary filler that so many performers and models use.

Actor Bernard Ferstenberg works as a comedian and clown. We think the photo exhibits an impish, warm, accessible quality. Photo by David Morgan Photography.

There's nothing distracting in Vince Viverito's shot. Your attention goes right to the face, the eyes looking at you. Photo by Glenn Jussen.

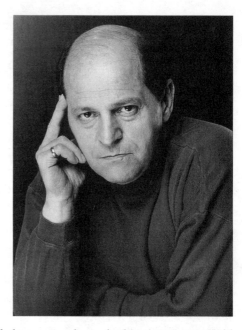

The Simple Picture Test If you already have your photo, do this picture test: Hold your 8 × 10" photo right next to your face and look in the mirror. Do you and that black-and-white image look like the same person? Does one of you look older, younger, tense, relaxed? Do you have freckles, laugh lines, or little puffs of skin under your eyes when you smile? The photographer who, aiming for the perfection of a 1940s movie still, airbrushes those out of the picture does you no service. The lines, freckles, and beauty marks, the bumps on your nose — those will all be there when you walk into the office.

If you are really concerned about puffy eyelids, dark circles, lines, bumps, crooked teeth, or other shortcomings, have them attended to by a plastic surgeon or orthodontist before you have your photo session.

The lighting should frame your face and not hide it with shadows, harden your features, or make you look as if you have a halo. The background must never upstage you. Nor should we be distracted by any metallic accessories, dangling earrings, or bold prints, plaids, or stripes. Avoid sharp contrasts between hair and complexion tones, or between fabric and hair or skin tones.

Color Photos Redheads are the only people we can think of who would benefit from using color photos. These pictures are more expensive, but they do show that wonderful hair color and peaches-and-cream complexion.

THE RIGHT PHOTOGRAPHER

Almost inevitably, the picture you have taken in Peoria, Battle Creek, or Billings will have to be discarded when you are trying to make it in the major talent centers. It's not that local photographers are untalented; they simply do not have the frame of reference necessary to provide you with a photo that will do the job you need. They don't do such work often enough. Photographers in New York, Los Angeles, and Chicago understand what The Business is looking for because they are part of it. They're dealing with thousands of people; they know what's happening *now!*

Choosing your photographer is an important decision. Select the photographer as carefully as you would a surgeon. It is essential that you trust and feel comfortable with your doctor, and so it is with your photographer. Your professional life is in his or her hands, after all.

> When it comes to my professional life I am not going to be cheap. Best classes, best coach, best photographer. I always interview before I decide on an acting school or a photographer, and I always look for the right clothing.
>
> —LAURA BONARRIGO, One Life to Live

Interview at least eight photographers before you make a choice. Examine their portfolios carefully. Do you like the work? Is the style so forceful that you feel the actor takes second place? Sense where the photographer is coming from. Do you feel comfortable with this person? How does he or she see you? Avoid anyone giving you a hard sell or trying to intimidate you by bragging about the "big name" performers in the portfolio, rather than focusing on you.

Find out, in advance, how long the photographer allows for each sitting. You want to be sure that you have all the time *you* need. Find out, in advance, how many shots are taken. Find out, in advance, how many prints are included in the cost of the sitting. If the photographer makes a number of the shots available to you, how much will they cost?

Also ask whether the photographer uses a makeup artist and/or hair stylist, or whether you should consider employing your own. Discuss the clothes you intend to bring to the session.

Photo session fees range from $125 to $650. Professional photographers advertise in the trade papers: *Back Stage* in New York, *Perform-Ink*, the Chicago paper, and *Drama-Logue, Back Stage—West*, and *The Working Actor's Guide to Los Angeles* in California. We've included the names of some photographers whose pictures consistently get attention.

New York

Arthur Cohen	Glen Jussen	
Jinsey Dauk	James Kriegsman	
John Dean	Bob Newey	
Nick Granito	Ron Rinaldi	
John Hart	David Rodgers	
Joe Henson	Tess Steincolk	
Kristin Hoebermann	Marsha Taylor	
Eric Stephen Jacobs	Denise Winters	

Los Angeles

Laura Burk
Janice Heiden
Bader Howar
Robert Kim
Minda
Alison Reynolds
Buddy Rosenberg
Darryl Schiff
Ron Sorenson
Toris von Wolfe

Shooting Outdoors

A number of photographers prefer to work in natural light. This is particularly true in California, where climate and landscape are so conducive to outdoor photography. If you are more comfortable outside a studio, look for someone whose pictures share that same feeling. But realize that the weather has to be totally in your favor — not so sunny that you automatically squint, not so breezy as to play havoc with your clothing or hair style. If your hair frizzes when there's a bit of humidity, stick to the studio shot.

More than Headshots

Only a few seasons ago the totally "in your face" headshot was the standard. Now, thanks to the interesting results achieved by some innovative photographers, the format has become looser. More of the performer's body is being seen; we get a better idea of the performer's physique. A relaxed pose can give a hint of the actor's personality. Again, it all depends upon the message you want to communicate. What are you selling? Do you want to be cast in *Beverly Hills 90210?* Are you the gal or guy next door? Cat-suit seductive? Rumpled intellectual? Certainly, the better physical shape you're in, the more you'll be inclined to show how you look. Dancers, of course, love the chance to reveal how well they carry themselves and how graceful they can be.

We liked the attitude of Joe Rivera's straight-on shot. There's strength in the upper body, but we respond to his "huggability." Photo by Hoebermann Studio.

Going in the opposite direction, Kristin Hoebermann has had an enthusiastic response to her ultra-tight shots; she uses the page sideways, like a still from a wide-screen movie. As shown in the example on page 42, there's an intensity, a sense of urgency and activity in this close-up, which has been called the "letter-box" shot.

> I was looking to do something more interesting than the standard head-shot. It's more challenging to me as a photographer. The letter-box is more "up close and personal" than the general portrait.
> —KRISTIN HOEBERMANN, *photographer*

BODY PARTS

Yes, there is a definite need for lovely hands and beautiful, slender feet. Yours can be the photogenic hands that open the mayonnaise jar, scrub out the grungy pan, or model elegant diamond rings. Think of the countless shoes, socks, stockings, and slacks you've seen featured in commercials. If you want to be considered for those jobs, use a photo-postcard of your hands or feet in an attractive, graceful position, with your name and answering-service number printed below the picture. Be sure to tell agents and casting directors that you are looking for such assignments. Again, this is a specialty, and the industry has definite standards.

THE PHOTO SESSION

Now that you understand how important the right picture is to your job-seeking, and you realize what an investment of dollars and time getting the right picture represents, the thought of actually having your picture taken may seem about as delightful as a visit to the dentist. However, if you think constructively, and prepare, you can transform the dreaded ordeal into a swell party.

What to Wear Before the session, before you even schedule the appointment, take the time to figure out how you are selling yourself. In other words, what kinds of parts do you think you can play? Are you the up-scale country-club and fine restaurant patron? Then choose the wardrobe, makeup and hairstyle for that person. Do you belong to the truck-driver, push-the-shopping-cart-around-the-supermarket set? Are you a young on-the-go executive or a suburban stay-at-home? Dedicated athlete or couch potato? How do you see yourself when you see yourself performing? Dress for those roles.

Veteran photographer John Hart believes there are four kinds of shots. In the *commercial* shot, what you want to project to the camera is your wholesome, outdoorsy, sincere self. The clothing reflects the outdoor feeling, the casual sunlight-in-the-hair quality. The *legit* look is quieter, yet more intense. While "laid back", it is still direct, but with a hidden agenda; it's the "soap" picture. The third type is for the industrial or *corporate* look: the news anchorman or successful professional male, with more tailored, traditional clothing, and the female executive, showing that she is in charge, has authority, is efficient, calm, cool, and collected. The fourth type, the *glamour* shot, is not for everyone. It is pure "Hollywood": the glitzy MTV performer who has made it, the Whitney Houston or *Dynasty* types.

In choosing your wardrobe, remember: bright whites and dull blacks are taboo; large buttons, particularly mother-of-pearl, are eye-catchers that take attention away from you. Again, busy prints, bold plaids, or stripes tend to leap out of the picture and overwhelm you. Look for varieties in texture rather than blocks of color. Medium tones of silk knit, coarse linen, ribbed cotton, and blue denim are comfortable to wear, present no lighting problems, and direct attention where it belongs — to you.

If you're uncertain about which necklines, collars, fabrics, and colors will be most flattering to you, consider seeking the advice of an image consultant. The objective, professional eye can survey your closet, create and coordinate outfits, determine what you need to buy or borrow. After you (and the image consultant) have chosen your wardrobe, try each outfit on, and check your appearance in a full-length mirror. Notice how the different fabrics feel, observe how you move in each.

Ask the consultant, or a friend, to take Polaroids of you in each outfit. Carry them with you. Become accustomed to seeing, and liking, yourself in the clothes. This will help you feel secure when you finally dress for the camera.

Press or steam your clothes in advance. When you pack them, try to use a garment bag rather than a suitcase. There'll be fewer wrinkles. Remember to include a clothes brush, as well as a supply of pins, clips, clothes pins, scissors, needle and thread. Buttons do drop off, and seams split, always at the worst time. And if the photographer doesn't have an iron — ask about this when you make the appointment for the session — tote your own along.

Your Makeup and Hair If you're really, really good at it, do your own makeup. If you'd feel more confident in the hands of a professional, by all means get made up before you go to the session, or have a makeup artist with you at the studio.

Your hair will probably need a professional's touch. For example, very dark hair, while it may have a healthy shine and be a breeze to manage, can contrast too greatly with pale skin. Even though you look sensational in real life, that sharp contrast will present problems for the TV and the movie camera.

> Dark hair can seem one-dimensional. The trick is to have a colorist give you some well-placed highlights, so your hair can have a feeling of movement and dimension.
>
> —TOM FRASCA, *colorist, Gerard Bollei Salon, New York*

A good hair stylist, particularly one who serves a theatrical clientele, will be able to advise men as well as women about length and shaping. Tell the stylist what kinds of roles you are promoting yourself for. The good ones will know how to help you look outstanding.

> Actresses feel that they can perform a fuller range of roles if they keep their hair long. I think longer than the collarbone is pushing it. The eighteen-year-old college freshman look isn't attractive after eighteen. Sure, you want some versatility. Too short is going to keep you too commercial. Keep it to shoulder length. Once you are famous you can do anything you want.
>
> —ALAN ADLER, *hair stylist, Gerard Bollei Salon, New York*

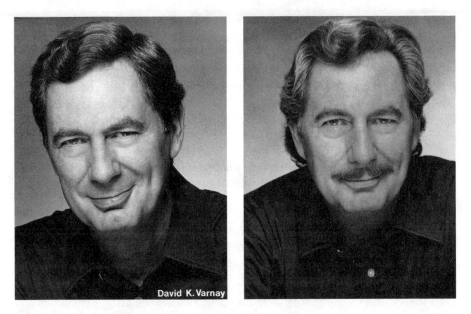

Longer hair and a mustache have given David K. Varnay
a more romantic look. Photo by Nick Granito.

Some people like to have their hair done right before the shoot. The hair will relax, or fall, in the three hours that a session usually lasts, so you should plan to do glamour or seductive shots (if any) first, and then relax into the commercial, energetic shots. Then, if your hairdo starts to relax, combing it casually into place will be fine. Similarly, your makeup will soften, becoming less dramatic as the time goes by.

How to Enjoy Your Photo Shoot   Plan to bring your music with you! Find out if the photographer has a tape or CD player, or bring one along. You want to be able to listen to sounds that relax you, give you energy, put you in a great mood, be it ocean waves, new age music, Sinatra, Streisand, or Pavarotti. And why not carry along your favorite fragrance too? If a scented candle or a spritz of something lovely enhances your mood or inspires you, use it.

Seriously consider having your spouse, your best friend, your significant other, or your image consultant accompany you. That other person who knows you well can not only provide support, but will also be able to help you with your outfits. You need another's watchful eye to spot wrinkles, loose buttons, wild threads. Don't depend upon the photographer to pay attention to those details. The photographer's job is to know how to focus the lights and the camera on you and take a great picture.

If you intend to show a variety of looks or a range of moods, begin with the most dramatic or glamorous look. Then, as you "bond" with the photographer and the inevitable early tension evaporates, you can loosen up into the freer, more casual images. Treat your photo session as a part of your acting career, as a visual monologue. The photo session is your chance to show all that you can do. You can decide how you're going to look, and you can rehearse until you learn how to make all those moments happen.

You don't have to skip blindly into the studio, spending your money and time and trusting that a photographer will make everything come out O.K. Remember, the photographer should be working for you. Take the responsibility of managing this moment in your career. Empower yourself. You may be amazed at how good it feels.

SELECTING AND PRINTING YOUR PHOTO

A few days after your photo session, the photographer will give you a set of *contact sheets* — pages filled with small prints of all the shots taken. With a magnifying glass (preferably one with a light) you can see the contact prints clearly.

If there are so many good pictures that you cannot decide, try to get the advice of a casting director or agent. It is very difficult to see ourselves objectively, as we must for these choices. (Examine the sample headshots in the illustrations; there we provide a few guidelines for choosing.) One terrific photo is all you really need.

Composites   Single shots are used for theater, films, television, and commercials in New York. But the composite — an 8 x 10" that shows you in different outfits and with various props — is favored by commercials agents in Los Angeles. The photos you select and the costumes you wear should be discussed with your commercials agent. Do not attempt to put a composite together without direction.

Duplication   Once you have chosen the shot (or shots) you want, you will need to take the photographer's finished print (and negative, if it was included) to a duplicating service and have your copies printed. Shop around. These businesses advertise in the trade papers. The photographer may wish to recommend a service whose work is consistently good.

Photos can be printed on a variety of papers. The semi-matte finish is popular now. It has an attractive, friendly tone. Glossies tend to reflect light and show smudges. The matte finish is too light-absorbing.

For a slight additional charge you may have your name and telephone service number printed on the front of the photo. This is a good idea: pictures and the résumés frequently get separated.

Order 300 pictures as a start. Your photos should be ready within ten days to two weeks. The original and the negative should be returned to you to keep. Additional reprints, when you need them, will be less costly than this first batch.

You should also order 200 *photo-postcards*. These are photos printed on card stock. The size of a postcard, they can be mailed at postcard rates, although you may prefer to send the card in an envelope to make certain that the Post Office doesn't imprint a postmark on your face or your message. Have your name and contact number printed beneath your picture.

The *photo business card* is a new and popular marketing tool. This is the size of a regular business card, with a postage-stamp-size photo of you on it with your name and contact number. It's great for parties, where you might meet, say, Steven Spielberg's right-hand person. Handing out your 8 x 10" seems tacky — where is the

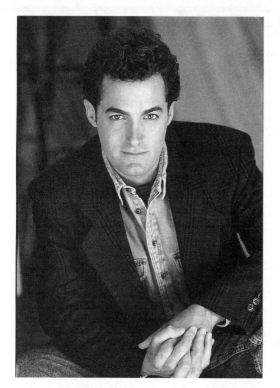

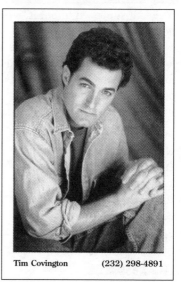

Tim Covington   (232) 298-4891

Actor Tim Covington came up with two good "sporty" looks and put one on a photo-postcard. In both pictures he looks relaxed; there's warmth in his eyes. Photo by Hoebermann Studio.

Photo business cards of Lee Kopp and Eileen Finn. Photos by Mike Humphrey.

recipient supposed to put it?—but exchanging business cards is the way the world networks nowadays.

If your photo session yields two or three absolutely marvelous shots that you love, use one for the 8 x 10" and the second for the postcard, with the third possibly for the business card. Or use your second and third for the postcard (a mini-composite) if they show really different aspects of you. Then you can get feedback about both pictures.

Here are some photo duplicators whose work we know and recommend:

New York

Dan Demetriad

Reproductions

Ken Taranto

Exact Photo

Shakespeare Mailing Service

Los Angeles

Ray the Retoucher

Paper Chase Printing Inc.

THE RÉSUMÉ

Your résumé should accompany your headshot at all times. To the back of your photo you staple the résumé, print side out, and trim the 8½ x 11" paper to match the 8 x 10" photo. We know a casting director who automatically discards photos if the résumé has not been cut to the same size and thus will not fit into file drawers without tearing.

It is your responsibility to attach it to the back of the photo. This may sound elementary, but performers have been known to hand them to casting directors separately — "This is my photo. And here's my résumé" — and then sit back as if it were part of the casting person's job to hunt for the stapler that will marry the two.

You don't have to write "Résumé" or "C.V." (Curriculum Vitae) at the top of your paper. We know what it is. The tips you may have gotten about writing a business résumé do not apply in the entertainment business. Your résumé should not list job experience chronologically or state your career goals and salary expectations. It should tell us all about the work you have done and with whom you have studied. The information should fit neatly on one side of one page and should be arranged with a certain artfulness. You don't have to hire an art director, but at the very least, the page should be neatly typed and easy to read. Tiny print causes eye strain, which will work against you. If you have access to a word processor, you should be able to compose a very acceptable page. Two examples are shown on pages 53 and 54.

Your name must be at the top — center stage or up left. Underneath, give your union affiliations, if any, and the telephone number where you can be reached. If you have a professional answering service, write *(service)* next to the number. If you are using an answering device, write *(machine)* next to the telephone number. If you have a pager, designate that number also. *Never include your home address or your home telephone number on your résumé.* Pictures are passed around to many hands and unfortunately may end up with some people whose interest in your career is questionable.

Vital statistics — your height and your hair and eye color — should be grouped

RECOMMENDED RÉSUMÉ FORM (NEW YORK)

YOUR NAME
UNION AFFILIATIONS

SERVICE #   HEIGHT:
AGENT: WEIGHT:
AGENT'S PHONE #   HAIR:
                                                    EYES:

THEATER

Hello, Dolly!	Minnie	National Tour
House of Blue Leaves	Bananas	Theatre Four
Summer and Smoke	Alma	Circle in the Square
Ethan Frome	Mattie	Cherry Lane Theatre
Mame	Miss Gooch	Allenberry Playhouse
Leading lady, four seasons		Falmouth Playhouse
Twelfth Night	Viola	
Lysistrata	Casseiopia	
Shadow and Substance	Thomasina	
A Streetcar Named Desire	Stella	
Bell, Book, and Candle	Gillian	

TELEVISION

Guiding Light	Marie Wallace (2 years)	CBS
As the World Turns	Julie Lester	CBS
Another World	Nurse Adams (recurring)	NBC
All My Children	Harriet Stark	ABC
The Edge of Night	Prison guard	ABC

FILM

Marigolds	Connie Dix	Pare Lorentz, dir.
The Wrong Man	Neighbor	Laurence Heath, dir.

INDUSTRIALS

Management training films	On-camera host	AT&T
Weigh of Life	Lead	Heart Association

COMMERCIALS
On camera and voice-overs — list and tape upon request

EDUCATION
Yale Drama School, MFA

TRAINING
Uta Hagen / Robert "Bobby" Lewis / Andy Thomas (vocal)

SPECIAL SKILLS
Fluent French, Spanish, piano (classical), dialectician

SPORTS
Champion bowler (New Haven, 1989), all racket sports, rollerblading

RECOMMENDED RÉSUMÉ FORM (LOS ANGELES)

YOUR NAME
UNION AFFILIATIONS

SERVICE #	HEIGHT:
AGENT:	WEIGHT:
AGENT'S PHONE #	HAIR:
	EYES:

FILM

Marigolds	Connie Dix	Pare Lorentz, dir.
The Wrong Man	Neighbor	Laurence Heath, dir.
The Stranger Within (M O W)	Gal next door	Lee Grant, dir.

TELEVISION

Guiding Light	Marie Wallace (2 years)	CBS
As the World Turns	Julie Lester	CBS
Another World	Nurse Adams (recurring)	NBC
All My Children	Harriet Stark	ABC

THEATER

Hello, Dolly!	Minnie	National Tour
House of Blue Leaves	Bananas	Theatre Four
Summer and Smoke	Alma	Circle in the Square
Mame	Miss Gooch	Allenberry Playhouse
Leading lady, four seasons		Falmouth Playhouse
Twelfth Night	Viola	
Lysistrata	Casseiopia	
Shadow and Substance	Thomasina	
A Streetcar Named Desire	Stella	
Bell, Book, and Candle	Gillian	

INDUSTRIALS

Management training films	On-camera host	AT&T
Weigh of Life	Lead	Heart Association

COMMERCIALS

On camera and voice-overs — list and tape upon request

EDUCATION

Yale Drama School, MFA

TRAINING

Uta Hagen / Robert "Bobby" Lewis / Milton Katselas / Andy Thomas (vocal)

SPECIAL SKILLS

Fluent French, Spanish, piano (classical), dialectician

SPORTS

Champion bowler (New Haven, 1989), all racket sports, rollerblading together. Your weight is optional, but height is essential. Don't waste your time (and the company's) by appearing at an audition when the lead is 5'5" and you, who hope to play opposite, are 6' tall.

If you sing or dance, state your voice type and the kind of dancing you do. It's not necessary to indicate your age range. That's an old stage habit. If they want an actor to look forty-five years old, they'll hire an actor who is forty-five years old. If you are in a wheelchair (see Chapter 9), use the universal symbol for disability, as Kitty Lunn has done (see illustration, page 156).

Now list your credits. In New York, the résumé lists *theater* credits first. Give the name of the play, your role, and the theater that produced it. If you've played a great many parts at one or two theaters, use a heading such as "Leading Lady, Forest Glen Theater, 4 seasons, Representative Roles" and select the most important plays. Next list your *film* credits. Your *television* credits are third. Roles in well-known films should head the list, as sample résumés illustrate.

In Los Angeles, the preferred order is film first, then television and theater.

> Film is a director's medium. In terms of your résumé, you can leave the producer's name off, the distributor's name off, you can even leave the name of the movie off, but put the director's name on. If your agent sends your résumé and you've worked for the director whose picture I'm casting, I'd be a fool not to go to the director with it.
>
> —MIKE FENTON, *casting director*

If you do commercials, state only whether you have been an on-camera and/or voice-over performer and whether you have a commercial reel or tape. *Do not list the products*. Your local spot for Dazzle Toothpaste may be canceled three days after you meet the person who casts for Stunning Toothpaste. That person may want to consider you for the upcoming Stunning commercial, but if your résumé says you already have a toothpaste commercial, you will not be called to audition for the competing product. You will lose the chance at a job you are right for.

Your training should be the next category. List where you studied, with whom, and for how long. Then tell us about your education. For performers who have not done a great deal of work, this section is particularly important: experienced casting people know the teachers and the schools. A casting director who hasn't had the chance to see your work can at least have an opinion about the people you have studied with.

Here's what some leading casting people have to say about training:

> I'm a great résumé reader, and an actor may have worked with somebody or studied with somebody I know.
>
> —JANE ALDERMAN, *independent casting director, Chicago:*

> The first thing I look at on young actors' résumés is their training . . . who have they studied with, who are they studying with now? Even if they don't have many credits, I want to know how committed they are to learning their craft.
>
> —MARK TESCHNER, *casting director,* General Hospital

What impresses me on a résumé is training, the people you are working
with.

—BETTY REA, *casting director,* Guiding Light

Your special skills are listed next. By this we mean whatever language you speak or
dialects you do *well*; whether you're a concert pianist (or play any instrument rea-
sonably well); whether you're an expert at anything — sculpture, even twirling a
baton. . . .

> It's important to include special abilities, languages, any specialties. I
> once had to find a man who could do bird calls. Be it ever so strange, put
> it on, because you never know!
>
> —BETTY REA

Sports, such as martial arts, diving, racquet sports, acrobatics, horseback riding, aerobics, or swimming, as well as any awards you might have won, get a separate listing. But list only the ones you do expertly at present; in commercials, particularly,
you'll be asked to perform a feat such as diving off a high board again and again for
repeated takes from a number of camera positions. Or you may have to skate on an
ice rink for several hours, jog all day, or serve a tennis ball in the noonday sun. When
you list sports you must be in superb physical condition and be able to perform these
feats well. Lying could be hazardous to your health.

PADDING YOUR CREDITS
There is a temptation to embellish your résumé, especially if you feel that your list
of credits could be more impressive. Wrong-headed advisers will suggest you add a
credit to "look more experienced." Our advice is *don't*. This is a very small business.
You will surely regret it, lose credibility, and be embarrassed.

> People lie on résumés, and I've always caught them. If people put down
> that they were in the national company of *Evita*, I have to say, "I don't
> think you were, because I cast it, and I'd remember you."
>
> —JANE ALDERMAN

> I padded my résumé a bit by adding parts in plays that I had never even
> seen. . . . I wrote down as part of my experience that I had played George
> in *George and Margaret*, a very popular repertory play. I was summoned
> to an audition, and when I walked into the theater the first thing the pro-
> ducer said to me was, "What have we here, then, apart from a bloody
> liar!" . . . The plot of that play centers on the fact that the entire cast
> spends the whole duration of the play waiting for George and Margaret
> to turn up, and they never do.
>
> —MICHAEL CAINE, *in his autobiography,* What's It All About?

A long time ago, Mervyn Nelson, actor, casting director, teacher, and great man of
the theater, said it so well: "You can't tell me this little girl in front of me with pigtails
and a pigeon-toed walk has played Medea!"

THE PHOTO RÉSUMÉ

With the addition of the same postage-stamp-size picture you use on your photo business card, the résumé becomes a far better marketing tool. It can be computer-generated, as Michael Latshaw has done (below), or applied by means of a process called Veloxing. Place the picture wherever there's enough white space for it to stand out. Then, if your photo and résumé happen to get separated, the casting director still knows who you are and what you look like.

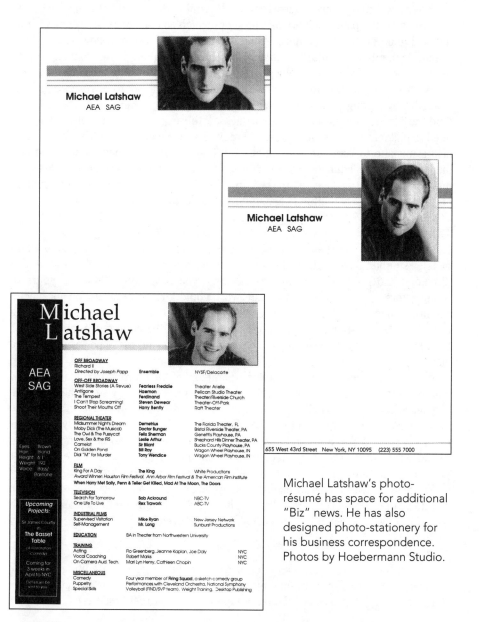

Michael Latshaw's photo-résumé has space for additional "Biz" news. He has also designed photo-stationery for his business correspondence. Photos by Hoebermann Studio.

MAKING COPIES

Copies of your résumé can be made cheaply at any copying center. The Staples office-products stores will copy in quantity for only a few cents per copy. PIP and Kinko's are nationwide franchises that do reliable work quickly, and have a variety of papers to choose from. New York's Shakespeare Mailing Service does copying at a reasonable price, offers pre-addressed mailing labels to all casting contacts, and will even send your photos and résumés out for you.

Select a weight that prints clearly and will stand up to a lot of handling. You don't have to use white paper — ivory or a pastel tint such as blue, rose, or green is attractive and generally costs no more. Avoid bright orange, purple, yellow, red, or lime green. Remember, one must be able to read the information. Order as many copies of your résumé as you do of your photo.

Avoid the temptation to save yourself the work of stapling the résumé to your headshot by having your résumé printed on the back of the photo. The lettering tends to bleed through and mar your face on the front. Revisions, which you will need to make as you get more jobs, will require a new batch of headshot prints. It is also a mistake to laminate your photo and résumé. Besides being expensive and inappropriate, the laminated photo will end up being oversized and unsuitable for filing, and the shiny surface will make it impossible for anyone to write an evaluation on your résumé — something casting directors do all the time.

THE VIDEOTAPE

Nowadays actors find that an effective videotape is as instrumental in getting a film or television job as a photo and résumé can be in opening a door. Agents, casting directors, and producers are always asking if you have some "film" on yourself. Many actors who have done important work could kick themselves for not having acquired copies of their performances over the years. They may have played leading roles in top-rated shows, but if no one sitting around the conference table saw (or produced or wrote) the programs, with no tape to refer to, these performances are just history.

A composite reel is like a "Whitman's Sampler" of the on-camera roles that show you to best advantage. It is essential that you obtain copies of any speaking parts you play on soap operas, episodic series, films, and on-camera commercials in which you have lines or play a significant role. If you have a VCR, tape every show you appear on or enlist the aid of a friend to do it for you. Commercials can be requested from the ad agency once they have been aired. (Whether or not you will have to pay for your copy will frequently depend upon the producer's generosity.)

We suggest you enlist an expert to help you select your best clips. While you should be developing your critical sense, it is extremely difficult to look at one's own work objectively; a second, professional, opinion never hurts.

EDITING

Once you have gathered your material, you'll need to go to an editing studio to assemble your reel. Your original film clips, taped shows, and commercials will be transferred to 3/4" professional-quality tape. From this reel you'll create your 3/4" master — the composite reel — which will allow you to make copies as needed on standard ½" videocassette tapes. Most casting and production offices and talent agencies are equipped with standard VCRs.

Videotape editing is costly and time-consuming. Don't bring your clips to the studio and expect the engineer to create video magic. Know exactly how you want your segments pieced together. Time the segments with a stopwatch. The tape should not exceed ten minutes; five to seven minutes is preferred. Professionals in a position to hire you will know within the first few minutes whether you've got what they're looking for.

Begin with your name and contact information, either your answering service or your agent's name and phone number. Follow with a shot of a recent 8 x 10" that looks exactly like you.

First use a soap opera or prime-time scene where the focus is on you. If it contains some humor that's even better. It is important that the scene show you in a relationship. Then try to choose two or three short scenes that demonstrate a range of type or physical appearance — for example: a doctor, a construction worker, and a playboy; a landlady, a gypsy, and a psychiatrist; a runaway, a candy striper, and a cheerleader. Or you might show different locales, such as a hospital, a nightclub, the beach. The more variety you exhibit, the more interesting the tape will be and the more it will hold the viewer's attention. Remember, agents and casting directors try to find time during harried work days to watch your tapes. Help them by making the experience as entertaining as possible. They should, at least, be able to see your face clearly.

Commercials should be included after the dramatic scenes. Finally, a recommended ending for the tape might be a reprise of your opening shot: your name, contact information, and your headshot. If you have done your homework properly, editing charges should be within the $200 to $300 range.

THE NEWCOMER'S VIDEOTAPE

Most beginning performers don't have the kinds of clips mentioned above because they haven't played major roles with enough on-camera footage. However, actors who have appeared in student films (such as those produced by students at the film departments of UCLA or NYU) may have done a well-written, well-produced scene that proves their potential in that medium.

If you are trying to put a tape together and have no professional credits, look for an inexpensive, but reputable, production house with facilities for taping a short scene or a duologue where you can use the camera as the person you are talking to. The material you choose could be from a role you've played, a part you've worked on with your drama coach, or a piece you've written yourself. It should be contemporary, not classical, and always originate from a place of emotional truth. There should be energy, humor (if possible), and stay within a comfortable age range. Movement should be minimal and always motivated. Remember, on camera, less is more. The scene should end with a closeup on you, and fade to black.

Lighting and audio must be of top-notch professional quality. Enhance your personal appearance with the help of a makeup artist, hair stylist, and wardrobe consultant. Look at the playback. If you're not totally satisfied with what you see, do it again.

Renting studio facilities is expensive. To save time and money, prepare for your studio taping by taking a course in video technique, taught by industry professionals, which will allow you practice time. Members of the Screen Actors Guild Conservatory and AFTRA's Audio-Video Center may sign up for classes, direction, studio, and rehearsal time at no charge.

DUPLICATING AND DISTRIBUTING TAPES

There are no standard prices for tape duplication. Compare the prices at a number of facilities, many of which advertise in the trade papers. Label the tape boxes clearly with your name and contact numbers. Affix your picture postcard as well. Remember to label the tape itself, in case it gets separated from its cover.

Keep records of whom you sent your tapes to and when. If you want the tape returned to you, provide a stamped, self-addressed return mailer. It's a good idea to telephone after a couple of weeks to find out if the staff has had a chance to view your tape, whether you should pick it up, or whether they'd like to interview you as a result of what they've seen.

Always try to keep a couple of dupes on hand, so that you or your agent can speed one to the producer who must "see film on you within the hour!" Frequently the tape is as important as a live audition. Dan Lauria, one of the stars of ABC's Emmy-winning series *The Wonder Years,* tells how he landed the role of the father without appearing at the final callback:

> When I had to go to the network for *The Wonder Years*, I was in Vancouver doing a *Wise Guy* episode. They [Neal Marlens and Carol Black, creators of the series] brought an episode from *Head of the Class*, in which I had played an alcoholic father, to the network and used that as my audition.

KEEPING YOUR TAPE CURRENT

The tape is a record of your achievements on film and video. So as your career progresses, your tape will need revision. Don't keep a clip that shows you as an ingenue or juvenile when you've matured to leading lady or character actor status.

Remember to put "videotape available on request" on your résumé. The videotape has become an essential tool of the trade. Don't leave home without it.

THE AUDIOTAPE

If you have a distinctive speaking voice with flexibility and range and have mastered Standard American speech; if you are a whiz at dialects; if you can come up with all sorts of trick voices and can do them consistently on cue, you may wish to be considered for voice-overs — announcers or characters who are heard but not seen on thousands of TV and radio commercials.

A small cadre of performers have been extremely successful in this area. To compete with the likes of Lauren Bacall, James Coburn, Whoopi Goldberg, James Earl Jones, Sally Kellerman, Frank Langella, Jack Lemmon, Robert Mitchum, Martin Sheen, James Stewart, Donald Sutherland, or Kathleen Turner will require an audiotape. Ordinarily, this is compiled of commercials you have already broadcast. If you're just starting out, you'll have to put a tape together from material that other actors have performed, or you may write your own copy *if* you are good at that. Listen to commercials, select those you feel you should have auditioned for, tape them on your tape recorder, write out the lines, practice, and then go to a professional recording studio to have a tape put together.

Sound studios advertise in all the trade papers. The membership departments of the unions usually know of studios that offer special rates to members. Interview engineers at sound houses just as you did photographers. It's important to feel comfortable and confident when you are putting a tape together: it will be another substitute for you in a casting person's office.

Always start with the material you do best. The entire tape should be no longer than three minutes, so equip yourself with a stopwatch and train yourself to bring in sixty, thirty, or twenty seconds' worth of copy exactly on time.

Larry Keith, actor and former president of SAG New York, tells everyone that voice-overs allowed him to survive until his juicy, long-running role as Nick Davis on *All My Children* came along:

> I auditioned for over a year before I won my first audition. It was for a cake mix. I did two spots, for which I was paid two times the $80 session fee, or $160. And then, a while later, a check for $2,500 arrived, for all the uses. And I thanked my stars for SAG's contract! It was months before I won another audition. I was so low I couldn't see beyond the gutter. Which is how I happened to find a five-dollar bill in the street — that's where my eyes were. I took it as a sign that my luck would change — finding money on Park Avenue. And, sure enough, it turned out that the spot I had just auditioned for was eighteen spots for a soft drink! And I started to make a living.

INDUSTRY GUIDES

Union members can, and should, be listed in two directories, *Players' Guide* and *The Academy Players Directory*.

Players' Guide is the annual directory for stage, screen, and television. Since 1942 it has been distributed to casting people in every phase of The Business. Your entry includes your photo, name, union affiliations, contact (if you are signed to an agent), and service phone number. Most people also include their significant credits. Deadline for submissions is early in February of each year. The most recent cost of a new entry is $80, renewals with no copy changes are $40.

For additional information, contact: *Players' Guide*, 165 West 46th Street, New York, NY 10036.

> You'd be amazed how many film directors sit with me thumbing through the Guide, sometimes for hours, and say, "Oh, Shirley, what about this actor?" It's terribly important.
>
> —SHIRLEY RICH, *veteran casting director*

The Academy Players Directories are published by the Academy of Motion Picture Arts and Sciences. Sole criterion is that you be a member of SAG or AFTRA. The directories are published three times each year. There are four editions, or categories: leading men and juveniles; leading ladies and ingenues; character men and boys; character women and young girls. Entries include only the performer's photo, name, contact phone number, and agent. Credits are not given. Filing periods are in January, May, and September of each year. Listings cost $20 per issue or $60 per year.

For additional information, contact: Academy of Motion Picture Arts and Sciences, 8949 Wilshire Boulevard, 4th floor, Beverly Hills, CA 90211-1972.

If you decide to place your photo in any of the talent directories, be sure it is as good as the photo you are sending out to casting people. That means a *current* picture. The agent or casting director who sees your photo and calls you, then doesn't recognize you when you walk into the office (in your photo you have hair like Michael Bolton, but now you look like Yul Brynner), will wonder, "How long ago was that picture taken?"

FINDING YOUR LEADS

Actors learn about job opportunities by reading the trade papers. *Back Stage: The Performing Arts Weekly,* in its more than thirty years of publication, has become the prime source of casting information for the New York actor and for the performer seeking work in regional theater. The paper now publishes a Los Angeles edition as well, *Back Stage West.* Editor-in-chief Sherry Eaker writes a column, "Center Stage," that highlights the theme of each issue. She oversees all casting news and checks out as many as 170 notices per issue.

> When I started out at *Back Stage* in 1977, the thrust of the paper was casting news. We are no longer just a New York casting paper; we are a national performing arts publication. The main thrust of the paper will always be casting; however, every week we have a feature pertaining to some aspect of the industry, another opportunity for performers, playwrights, and directors to take advantage of, and it is always accompanied by a list, so you have the how-tos and the who-tos.
>
> —SHERRY EAKER

At the start of each season *Back Stage* lists anticipated productions; there is a monthly list of incoming films, with as much information about the production and casting staff as it is possible to garner. Each year issues are devoted to particular aspects of The Business: off-Broadway theaters; regional theaters and how to apply or audition for them; dinner theaters; opportunities in cabarets, in theme parks and amusement parks, at outdoor drama festivals, and even on cruise ships. In time for summer casting, the paper publishes a directory of theaters, both union and nonunion, lists the plays they are planning to do, and gives contact information.

In addition, there is news of special interest to performers: columns on the latest activity at Equity, AFTRA, and SAG, columns from regional correspondents, from playwrights, from choreographers and directors, along with advice on monologues, auditions, and vocal mastery. Helpful to new talent is the paper's practice of reviewing new acts and small productions that will never be covered by the major critics. A favorable *Back Stage* review can often fill a tiny nightclub with local industry people — exactly the audience a fledgling talent is seeking.

> Someone once described *Back Stage* as a very actor-friendly paper. We are helping the actor look for the work. How to audition, whom to contact. And we always try to keep an "up" sort of attitude in the paper. . . . The purpose is to serve the actor. There are actors who have made it who don't need to read *Back Stage* yet still read the paper to keep up with the industry. Gregory Hines told my publisher he still reads it to keep up with all the theater news.
>
> —SHERRY EAKER

Back Stage is on sale every Thursday. Single copies are currently $2.25. Subscriptions are available. It might be a good idea to subscribe before you travel to New York or Los Angeles, to familiarize yourself with what's happening in The Business.

For further information write: *Back Stage*, 1515 Broadway, 14th floor, New York, NY 10036.

Drama-Logue is to many actors the West Coast equivalent of *Back Stage*. It was founded in 1973 by Bill Bordy, an actor who found looking for work in Los Angeles so difficult that he decided to establish one central source people could turn to.

> The only advice I ever got was "Read the trades." Once in a while I'd see a little notice that so-and-so was casting a show. It never said what kind of show, whether it was union or not, or what sort of people they were looking for. By the time you drove all the way over to wherever the audition was held, you found out there was nothing in it for you, or they were charging a fee to audition!
>
> —BILL BORDY

Drama-Logue's staff covers theater, film, TV, and cabaret on the West Coast — San Francisco and San Diego as well as Los Angeles. There are pages and pages of casting notices, plus interviews with prominent personalities — actors, producers, directors, and, probably most helpful to talent, casting directors. It seems that everyone who teaches a course, runs a workshop, or takes a photo places an ad in *Drama-Logue*.

Drama-Logue is available each week on newsstands throughout the Los Angeles area and in the major production centers. Single issues currently cost $1.85.

For subscription information write: *Drama-Logue*, Box 38771, Los Angeles, CA 90038-0771.

Ross Reports Television was first published in 1949 by the late Wallace Ross. There is an enormous amount of useful information in this pocket-sized booklet. New York's advertising agencies, independent casting directors, TV commercial producers and packagers, talent agencies, and literary agencies are all listed, with information as to whether they accept pictures and résumés, videotapes, and audiotapes, or will even answer your phone calls. Also included are the names of production personnel and casting directors for all the daytime serials (on both coasts) and for musical and variety shows (such as *Saturday Night Live*) that employ dramatic talent.

The West Coast section lists all network prime-time programs and includes a directory of casting personnel, program packagers, and production facilities. Easy-to-read symbols show at a glance which programs or offices have had personnel changes during the previous month.

Ross Reports, as everyone calls it, is published during the first week of every month. We suggest you buy one at least every other month, for there are constant personnel changes. Single copies are available at the Drama Book Shop, 723 Seventh Avenue, New York, NY 10036, at the membership department of AFTRA, or through the publisher, Television Index, Inc. Yearly subscriptions are available. A free copy of the current issue is given to the first 350 AFTRA members attending each semi-annual membership meeting.

Television Index, Inc. has recently introduced *Ross Reports, USA* ($4.95), which lists all the agents in the nation, state by state. For further information write: Television Index, Inc., 40-29 Twenty-Seventh Street, Long Island City, NY 11101.

Theatrical Index is a weekly listing of play production — what's opening, what's on, what's in previews or rehearsal, and what's announced or projected for the future. For each show, the producer, the playwright, and the director are named, as is the casting director. Frequently there will be a brief outline of the play and capsule descriptions of available roles. Off-Broadway information is included, divided into the same categories.

For the use of union members, *Theatrical Index* is posted on the bulletin board of the Equity Lounge, at 165 West 46th Street, New York, NY 10036.

Single copies are $8. Information about subscriptions is available from the publisher, Price Berkley, 888 Eighth Avenue, New York, NY 10019.

Variety, Hollywood Variety, and *The Hollywood Reporter* may be the most famous of the industry's trade papers. *Variety* is available each Wednesday at newsstands in the theater district. Its news is essentially about the business aspects of show business worldwide; its pages carry data on the grosses of movies, plays, records, nightclub acts, and television deals. It also reports on which executives have moved to new offices with more or less power.

Variety is fun to read occasionally, if only to acquaint yourself with industry jargon — "Sticks Nix Hick Pix" is one of its more famous banner headlines — and to acquire a sense of the tempo and scope of The Business on an international scale. It is of minimal use to actors looking for jobs. A limited amount of space is devoted to casting news of theatrical productions.

For subscription information, write: *Variety*, Inc., 475 Park Avenue South, New York, NY 10016.

The daily *Hollywood Variety* and *The Hollywood Reporter* offer inside information on the intricacies of The Business, chronicling the comings and goings and wheelings and dealings of studio executives, stars, and agents. Grand for gossip and an occasional read, they are of little real help to performers eager for jobs. They are readily available at newsstands (and in the swanker hotel lobbies) throughout Los Angeles.

Less well known, but extremely useful, is *The Motion Picture, TV, and Theatre Directory*, a guide to industry products and services. Between the listings of accountants, cameramen, and screening rooms, you'll find names and addresses of advertising agencies, casting consultants, and producers throughout the United States and Canada (as well as in Great Britain, Europe, and Japan). The directory is published semiannually. For information write: Motion Picture Enterprises Publications, Inc., Tarrytown, NY 10591.

ANOTHER IMPORTANT SOURCE
To find out which advertising agencies create commercials for which products, consult the *Standard Directory of Advertising Agencies*, better known as the Agency Red Book because it is bound in bright red. Published three times a year, in February, June, and October, it is as thick as the Manhattan telephone directory and contains information on thousands of advertising agencies — their more than 60,000 clients, the account executives, creative directors, executives, even the ad-campaign budgets. The latest copies of the Agency Red Book are available at public libraries and at the offices of AFTRA and SAG. For further information, contact the publisher: National Register Publishing Co., 3004 Glenview Road, Wilmette, IL 60091.

OTHER PUBLICATIONS
Advertising Age, AdWeek, Broadcasting, CableVision, and *Shoot!* are similar to *Variety* and the daily Hollywood trade papers in that they report each week on the business of advertising. You won't learn about casting from reading these trades, but you may find that an agency that appreciates your work has just won a new account. Good for occasional reading.

American Theatre surveys live theater throughout the United States and frequently publishes the complete script of a new play in its pages. The magazine is published ten times a year by Theatre Communications Group, 355 Lexington Avenue, New York, NY 10016.

Theater Week, Premiere, and *Entertainment Weekly* talk about what's happening in The Business, but their contents are geared to the audience's interests, rather than the professional's. They're fun to read, nonetheless, and can clue you in on celebrity gossip and goings-on.

Soap Opera Digest and other publications that synopsize the daytime TV storylines can be particularly useful to actors who want to work on soaps. Their condensations are helpful in clarifying the complicated relationships between characters.

HANDY TOOLS
If you don't know the territory, you need a map. As we have already suggested, you should be able to get these from the Convention and Visitors bureaus. Color-coded tourist maps such as *Flashmaps: Instant Guide to New York* simplify the grid system and help you locate addresses. In California, everyone swears by the Thomas Brothers' Los Angeles County *Popular Street Atlas.*

When you begin seriously to make the rounds (which we discuss in Chapter 4), you'll be able to plan your day efficiently if you invest in a *Geographical Casting Guide* — there's one for Los Angeles and one for New York. These guides may be purchased in New York at the Drama Book Shop (723 Seventh Avenue) and in Los

Angeles at Larry Edmunds's (6658 Hollywood Boulevard) or Samuel French (7623 Sunset Boulevard).

You've accomplished the first steps. You've had your pictures taken, ordered copies of your photo, résumé, and postcards. You've assembled your video and audiotapes. You have your calling cards.

Now, let's discuss whom you're calling on.

CHAPTER 3

BUYERS AND SELLERS

I have always felt that casting and agenting is a symbiotic relationship. We need each other.

—MARK TESCHNER, *casting director,* General Hospital

From your study of the trade publications you will acquire a collection of leads: names and addresses of producers, directors, talent agents, casting directors, and managers. You could, of course, sit down and in one colossal burst of energy send your photo and résumé to every one of them. That would be a "mass mailing." A more efficient way to proceed, however, would be to learn first what it is that all these people do and what they are looking for.

In their enthusiasm and innocence, newcomers tend to lump all casting people into one omnipotent group, a sort of modern-day Emperor Nero — thumbs up, you're in; thumbs down, you're dead. In reality, the people you hope to impress with your talent can be separated into two categories: they are either buyers or sellers.

TALENT AGENTS

Whether they confine their efforts to theater, films, television, or commercials, or are active in all these areas, agents are *sellers*. They are in the business of selling the efforts of their talented clients to the *buyers* — casting directors, producers, and directors engaged in a particular project.

> A good agent is someone who cares about The Business and the actor's place in it. We do find the young talent in New York. We nurture them and get them going. Those that get the right breaks will hopefully progress up the ladder. The best part for me is seeing them on a stage in that wonderful role in which all their potential is realized.
>
> —TEX BEHA, *partner, Paradigm Talent Agency*

Actors, regardless of age, are frequently heard to moan, "Oh, what I really need is a good agent to get me a job!" That is fallacious thinking that derives from a fantasy in which actors, totally passive and dependent, wait for the phone to ring, wait for the Big Break, wait for someone — a *deus ex machina* in the person of an agent — to hand them their careers. But the agent cannot get you a job. The only one who can do that is *you*.

What agents *can* do is find out about jobs through their long established contacts with producers, directors, and casting directors, and through descriptions supplied them, at some cost, by an organization known as the Breakdown Service. The agents then try to find clients who are right for the roles being cast.

> We are more aware and encourage our clients to pursue jobs on their own. Downtown theater and low-budget films and writing your own vehicle, which is the way of the world now.
> —MARK REDANTY, *head of New York office,*
> *Bauman, Hiller and Associates*

An agent can submit you, via picture and résumé, to the person or persons casting the project. If the person to whom your name is submitted agrees to see you, the agent can then arrange an appointment for an interview or an audition. If you win the job, the agent may then be able to negotiate salary and other terms, such as billing. The agent will then be entitled to receive 10 percent of your earnings for that job, after you have been paid.

This last is an important point. Agents work only on commission. Ten percent is the legal commission an agent may charge a client. *Never have anything to do with any person representing him- or herself as an agent who asks you for a fee, or any form of payment in advance.* The agent gets paid only after the client gets a job, performs the job, and has been paid for the job.

How Agents Work

Talent agencies are doubly regulated: they are licensed by the state, and they are required to sign franchise agreements with each of the unions in which they endeavor to find work for their clients. To obtain a franchise, the agent must have a certain amount of previous experience and a reputation in The Business. The credentials are defined by the unions. To further ensure union members' protection, agents' offices are periodically inspected.

Talent agencies are franchised by the unions in order to be able to submit clients — union members — for work in theater, films, television, and commercials. Some agencies specialize. An office may work only on commercials, for example. Others, usually those offices with several subagents, are active in all fields.

Some agencies work only with signed clients, a select number of performers whose work they know very well whom they submit for all the jobs they may be right for. Other agencies handle only freelance talent: they will submit any performer whose work they know for any jobs they think the actor may be right for. The actors they submit are not signed with any other agencies for that field of work.

There are also agencies handling both freelance and signed clients. When none of their signed clients are suitable for a role, they suggest freelance performers whose work they know.

A performer may sign with only one agent at a time in any field. In other words, you may have one agent for commercials; another agent for theatrical work; a third office for films. If the office is large and active in all areas, you may be represented by three people within the same agency. The agreement you sign must state whether that is so. If you hear an actor say, "I'm with the William Morris office," that means the performer has a contract with a large, powerful agency and is represented by its staff in all areas.

Once you have signed with an agent, you do not freelance in that area. You may, and should, continue to look for work on your own, but you refer your contacts to your signed representative.

> I encourage my clients to keep 3 x 5" file cards to keep track of the people they have met, producers, directors, whoever, and send them reminders occasionally as part of their business.
>
> —TEX BEHA

MUST YOU HAVE AN AGENT?

In New York the answer to that question is, "Not necessarily." It is possible to work as a freelance performer in New York. In fact, many people believe that it is to the beginning performer's advantage to do so. The agents you meet will almost invariably see you differently. One office may think you're perfect for roles described as the young executive type. Another office may categorize you as the down-to-earth, rural, homespun sort. You, of course, are positive that you can play both types of roles marvelously, as well as countless others. What you are seeking, then, is representation that will be aware of all the things you do well. Until you meet that savvy agent, it's up to you to keep in touch with all the offices interested in freelance talent.

In Los Angeles, on the other hand, you definitely need representation. You need an agent for commercials and an agent for theatrical work, which in Los Angeles means TV and films rather than stage work. The system in Los Angeles is such that you can barely gain admission to a studio lot unless you have a definite appointment arranged by your agent with a casting director or producer.

WHO BECOMES AN AGENT?

We polled agents across the country. The majority of them have had previous experience within the industry and have worked as subagents for larger offices. Many of them have been in business for a long time.

> I was a director/writer/composer/lyricist. Martin Gage was in town, interviewing assistants. I got an appointment, not wanting the job, just wanting to meet Martin because I needed an agent, and got hired!
> —PHILIP ADELMAN, *vice president, The Gage Group*

Fifi Oscard, whose office employs a number of subagents, went to work for no pay at a highly respected agent's office after her children started school. She described what happened after that:

> Then another agent, Lucille Phillips, offered to pay me a small salary. I went to work in her office. Later, when she retired, I took over the business. We are really looking for the same things now as we did then — a "look," something that makes you respond. A few years ago a kid walked in the door, and there was something about him that just blew everyone

away. It was Matthew Broderick, and we just loved him, immediately. We represented him until he went out to Hollywood to make a few films.

Los Angeles-based Richard Dunn, whose staff of four represents more than seventy signed clients, went from acting to a job as an NBC page, which led to a spot as a producer's assistant. He became a casting director, then a director and producer of such shows as *Guiding Light*.

Monica Stuart of the William Schuller Agency was a successful teenage model. She turned to agenting when she realized that she was never going to be tall enough to make it as a high-fashion model. Her background was "perfect for an agency that now handles about two hundred kids."

What Do They Want?

We asked the agents what they look for in new talent. *Charisma, personality, uniqueness*, and *ability* were the words they used most frequently.

> When I meet with a prospective client I look for several attributes: emotional availability and vulnerability. Someone who can reveal the experience of a life being lived and whom I trust to take me on a journey to explore the complexities of the human condition.
> —Ricki Olshan, *Don Buchwald Associates*

> Talent turns us on, and we can spot it coming through the door. We look for honesty, self-confidence (but not cockiness), intelligence, consideration of others . . . and a measure of insanity helps.
> —Peggy Hadley, *Peggy Hadley Enterprises, Ltd.*

> When I am asked what I look for, I will say: "I don't know. When I see it I will know." That is where an agent's personality and taste come in.
> —Carole Ingber, *Carole Ingber & Associates*

The agent can pay the rent and phone bill only if and when the clients are working. Of course, every agency wants the next new person who comes into the office to be a potential money maker. Yes, indeed, they do want to see dollar signs.

We also asked agents what turns them off. The answers were almost unanimous: greed, overt aggressiveness, egomania, ignorance, stupidity, a sloppy appearance. They don't want to meet:

> Actors who tell you they want to be "stars," and actors who really don't want career guidance, but just want you to produce auditions.
> —Peter Strain, *president, Peter Strain & Associates*

> I don't like actors with swelled heads, especially those who have no reason to be so egotistical. They are usually self-defeating and don't get very far.
> —Mark Redanty, *Bauman Hiller and Associates*

The turnoffs are people who don't take as much interest in their careers as their agents do. I am thinking of people who are constantly late for auditions, are frequently ill-prepared, and whose social calendar is more important than making auditions.

—RICHARD SCHMENNER, *Paradigm*

What turns me off is anyone with an oversized view of himself and the attitude that I owe it to him to get his jobs.

—MEG MORTIMER, *Ambrosio/Mortimer and Associates*

THE RIGHT AGENT FOR YOU

Every performer would love to be represented by an agent who is dedicated, powerful, and willing to invest limitless time on the client's behalf. This may not always be an attainable goal, particularly when you are new to The Business. Certainly no reputable agent will want to represent a client whose work he or she does not know and appreciate, or whose potential he or she doesn't believe in.

You and the agent should be clear with one another about the contacts you are expected to make on your own. Be realistic. There will naturally be a greater incentive for the agency to make phone calls on behalf of other clients whose earnings may be ten times what you can command at present. Therefore, it is smart business practice for you to continue your independent efforts to make yourself known to the potential buyers of your talents. The fruits of your own efforts will affect the representation you get down the road.

Do find out whether the agent wants to hear from you about job ideas, or whether he or she prefers you to wait quietly for his or her calls.

Flip through the pages of *Players' Guide* and *The Academy Players Directory* to see whether the office handles clients whose talent conflicts with your own. If you fear that there are too many people like yourself in their "stable," discuss this with the agent. It may mean that you should seek representation elsewhere, but it could also mean that you and the agent have different ideas about the way you register. Clarify how the agent sees you. Are you the upwardly mobile executive or the homespun hero, or both?

On the other hand, a stable of talent like yourself may mean that the agent hopes to corner the market for a particular type, so that if young bride A is working, young bride B will be the next choice for a job, or young bride C, and so on. These are subtleties that must be discussed openly.

I think there is a prevailing attitude that has always been in existence. We have to be really careful as actors that we are not pulled into the psychology that we are working for the agent. The agent works for the actor. It is particularly difficult to keep that in mind when you are a fledgling . . . even during your career.

—MARILYN SOKOL, *Obie-winning actress/singer/comedienne*

SIGNING WITH AN AGENT

We assume that you have determined that the agency is franchised by SAG and/or AFTRA and Equity. We assume, also, that you feel comfortable with the idea of this person, or this office, representing you.

> I think that, in a town of illusion and fantasy where it is sometimes diffi-
> cult to separate truth from fiction, all actors who are approached by an
> agent or a manager should do their homework and check the credentials
> of that person with the unions and the Conference of Personal Man-
> agers, but also find out who their clients are. I think that an actor will
> have a sense or a "vibe" that someone is not legitimate, and you have to
> trust that, because all they really have to go on is their instincts.
> —MARK TESCHNER, *casting director,* General Hospital

First-time agreements, which are standard agency contracts approved by the unions, may be for a period of one year. That is considered sufficient time for you and the agent to test the relationship. However, each agreement contains an "out clause": this is (1) for you, if you begin to suspect that the initial interest has cooled too quick-ly, and (2) for the agent, if in some way you fall short of his or her expectations. After ninety-one days, if you have not had fifteen days of work through the agent's sub-missions, either of you may abrogate the agreement.

TWO EXEMPLARY AGENTS

For many of us in The Business, two people personified the ideal representative. Pas-sionate theatergoers, Juliet and Lester Lewis were smart, ambitious, dedicated, tire-less, and possessed great style and a highly developed sense of humor.

Juliet and Lester ran an office that employed four subagents. They were not only married to The Business, they were married to each other for more than forty years — which also makes them unique. Lester recalled getting his start in 1932 when his brother sold a few jokes to George Burns "at $25 a joke — a lot of money in those days". He met Juliet, they married in 1941, and they became business partners in 1943. "In the early days of TV," he explained, "we produced a show called *Hollywood Screen Test,* which gave Jack Lemmon, Grace Kelly, Cloris Leachman, and Martin Balsam their first crack at television. Then Betty Furness came into my life and asked me to represent her when she'd done a few commercials for Westinghouse."

Ms. Furness became the first superstar spokeswoman. Lester realized that in the commercials business a smaller agency could compete against the huge agencies like William Morris. The Lester Lewis office represented more than a hundred clients in commercials. You may be familiar with some of them: Jan Miner (Madge the Manicurist for Palmolive); Bob Elliott and Ray Goulding (Bob and Ray); Shari Lewis, Bethel Leslie, and Michael Wager. Juliet used to say: "There's a chemistry and a delectable charge that comes from a really talented actor sitting across my desk. But, of course, it is a matter of taste, too. And we do make mistakes. I turned down [Oscar-winner] Eva Marie Saint for *Hollywood Screen Test."*

Juliet and Lester shared an appreciation of the history and continuity of The Busi-ness, which they imparted to their clients and staff. They made a unique contribution to The Business through their generosity to the young people coming into it. Perhaps that is why they were the very first agents to be honored with a caricature at Sardi's Restaurant, prominently placed on the celebrity-laden wall in that renowned show business hangout. Over the years, the Lewises entertained many friends and clients there, and Juliet recalled the time Vincent Sardi said to her, "Juliet, the only office with a bigger monthly bill than Lester's is Paramount Pictures." She replied, "Please, don't tell him, you know how competitive he is."

> My mentor, Lester Lewis, gave me the best advice. He said if the actor doesn't feel comfortable in a meeting he's certainly not going to feel comfortable in an audition. So you should always be yourself.
> —JOANNE COLONNA, *Paradigm, West Coast*

PERSONAL MANAGERS

The personal manager is another type of *seller* who works with a very small group of signed clients. Managers are not franchised by any of the unions or regulated in any way. The Conference of Personal Managers, serving as a sort of board of ethics and standards, aims to advance the reputation of the group.

Managers frequently work with agents, again with a small number they are close to, or they may sometimes go directly to casting directors, producers, or directors to get their clients' work seen. But a manager may not sign the deal; only a franchised agent can do that.

> Managers are supposed to rely on agents to get appointments with casting directors. But if you believe in somebody and you can't get an agent to support your belief, then you have to go after it yourself.
> —JEAN FOX, *manager, Fox-Albert, New York*

Personal managers can be extremely useful in guiding a career. They are expected to have a great many contacts with important, powerful people, such as packagers, studio heads, and executive producers. They charge a higher percentage of a client's salary than do agents — as much as 25 percent, over and above the agent's commission. (Both the manager's and the agent's commission are calculated on the *gross* payment to the actor.)

> I guide my clients in every aspect of their lives. I direct them to appropriate professionals, such as agents and publicists. I advise on dress, makeup and comportment, and draw on my experience and expertise to lead them on the road to success.
> —SUZANNE SCHACHTER, *president, Suzelle Enterprises*

> It may be a questionable expense, but I intend to take a very active part in developing my career. I feel that I can't call my agent everyday to ask what's happening, but I can call my manager and talk about what's going on with me, me, me.
> —BRUCE NOZICK, *actor*

If a personal manager expresses interest in you, make certain that he or she is experienced enough to have amassed impressive connections. Ask for a client list so that you can try to find out whether the manager has a successful track record.

Dale Davis, whose clients include Dixie Carter, Jeffrey DeMunn, and Elizabeth Franz, says:

> We are always interested in actors who are willing to take chances, to project a sense of danger, to cause goose bumps.

Like the agent, the manager should never demand any payment in advance. Managers' payments are commissions on work you have performed through their offices and for which you have been paid.

Initial agreements are generally for a term of one year. The client agrees to pay a certain percentage of gross income to the manager. The manager agrees to provide advice, counsel, and direction in the development and advancement of the client's career and to use reasonable efforts to contact others who can help further the career. The manager also agrees to advise and counsel in all matters of presentation, public relations, and general promotion of the client's career.

Manager Bill Boyle's standard letter of agreement was particularly appealing because it contained this clause: *Conflicts: I realize that during our relationship we may from time to time disagree and even quarrel. After such times, we will actively go out of our way to genuinely make peace with each other.*

Any agreement you sign with a personal manager should be approved by an attorney — yours, not the manager's. Reputable managers will be known in The Business. When in doubt, inquire at union headquarters, ask a good agent, or get in touch with the Conference of Personal Managers, 1650 Broadway, New York, NY 10019. Their West Coast office is at 4527 Park Allegro, Calabasas Park, CA 91302.

THE PERSONAL PUBLICIST

Publicity is a means of bringing yourself to the attention of others. The publicist is also a *seller*, working to develop and sharpen your image, draw attention to your activities and achievements, and invite opportunities for advancement by making people aware of you. Publicity often determines whether an actor gets noticed or not. A good publicist, like a good agent or manager, can be an actor's best friend.

Publicists can act as your advance staff and do your boasting for you while you stand back and smile modestly. And they can give you feedback on your appearance and demeanor and explain the best techniques for dealing with the press.

> Personal PR people hold several aces: they have extensive media contacts and writing ability.
>
> —ANNE MARIE RICCITELLI, *director of public relations, ABC, New York*

Such expertise is expensive. Publicists' monthly retainers range from $500 to $3,000. Mailings, phone calls, business meals — getting the client to the right people at the right places — are additional expenses. There should be enough interest in the actor's career to justify the cost as an investment rather than an expense.

If you want to move from soap to prime time, it is important to have a publicist.

—MYRNA POST, *publicist*

Your agent, manager, or fellow actors may be able to refer you to a capable publicist. Interview a number of people until you find the one whose track record, media plan, and personality most appeal to you.

Unfortunately, PR has its charlatans. Beware of publicists known as "flacks," whose techniques include staging of publicity stunts and simulation of romances. They are far too flamboyant and would destroy your credibility. Your goals should be recognition and career advancement, not notoriety.

—ANNE MARIE RICCITELLI

HOW TALENT CAN BE DISCOVERED

The alert agent or manager does a great deal more than sit in the office, scan the Breakdown Service listings, make telephone calls, and hope for an exciting new performer to drop off a photo and résumé. The good agent — the one you hope to sign with — is energetic in pursuit of talent. That means going to showcases to see new talent at work and attending the graduation exercises of respected acting schools. It means leaving the confines of the city to see performances in regional theater, in summer stock, and at drama festivals.

We discovered a skinny, tall girl in an amusing improvisational group at the White Barn Theater, Mary Steenburgen. She was so poor she was working as a waitress at the Magic Pan restaurant. We sent her to Paramount to meet Warren Beatty, and while she was sitting in the office, Jack Nicholson saw her. He asked if she was there to see him. She said no, she was there to see Mr. Beatty. He asked if she'd mind seeing him after she saw Mr. Beatty! Out of that came a role in the film *Goin' South*.

—FIFI OSCARD

My favorite story is: when [the late] talent agent Stark Hesseltine and I went to the junior play at the American Academy of Dramatic Art — I think they were doing T.S. Eliot's *The Cocktail Party* — a young, reddish-haired man in the background had very little to do, and he found a way to fill his moment. We were both riveted to him. Stark sent his card back, requesting a meeting. It was Robert Redford. There was something about his presence — doing what he was supposed to do — taking over in the best sense.

—JANE ALDERMAN

A performer could not ask for more than the chance to be discovered working in a professional situation. For Marin Mazzie, her role in *Carousel* at the Barn Theater in

Augusta, Michigan, provided that opportunity. The star of the show was the young TV and film actor, Tom Wopat. His agent traveled to Michigan for the opening, and was captivated by Marin's performance. The agent went backstage to see his client, made certain to meet Marin, and offered to represent her as soon as she came to New York. She made the trip at the end of the summer season, was represented by the J. Michael Bloom Agency, and appeared in *Big River*. In 1994, she received a Tony nomination for her performance as Klara in *Passion*, the Tony-winning Stephen Sondheim musical.

> I dislike the word "discover." I think an actor's talents are not well hidden from any pro. Discovering them is like sighting the World Trade Center. Somebody is bound to discover them. It's just a matter of timing.
> —RICHARD DUNN

> My favorite discovery story dates back about eight years ago, when I saw a performance of a Shakespeare play at Yale Repertory. It was not a good performance, but one young actor, covered in chain mail and speaking through a mask, made me sit up and pay attention. He had two lines only, but they were the only two lines delivered with urgency and truth the entire evening. I dropped the actor a short letter and said I would like to see him in something where I could actually see his face and hear more than two lines. He responded, and to this day we have a very successful working relationship.
> —RICHARD SCHMENNER, *Paradigm*

How Talent Is NOT Discovered

Talent is not discovered or eased along the path to stardom by means of the "casting couch."

> There are the people who, when you ask what time they'd like to come in and see you, say "Six o'clock in the evening." Then you know that they have a very wrong focus.
> —CARMEN LaVIA, *Fifi Oscard Agency*

> Oh, that old myth about the casting couch! And that you have to "put out" to get work, and that someone's sexuality is going to be used for or against them. It is just a myth. It is not true, and what actors do is use it as an excuse.
> —JOSEPH HARDY, *producer*

Legitimate talent agents and personal managers do not advertise in the Want Ads of newspapers or in the trade papers. Any ad that solicits "new faces" for commercials, for modeling, or for films, and then implies that experience is unnecessary and suggests that high salaries are waiting to be paid to the first people who answer the ad, is a phony.

Beware of any person representing him- or herself as an agent or manager who asks you to read sample copy for a dramatic scene or as a commercial test, who then agrees that you have "talent" but that it needs to be "developed," and who next suggests that you attend a particular school or study with a particular teacher to whom he or she recommends all "clients." Such a person is either a phony (getting a kickback from the recommended school or teacher) or a very stupid operator. In either case, such a person can be of no value to you in your career.

RIPOFFS

There have been get-rich-quick schemes since the dawn of civilization. That great 19th-century showman and entrepreneur, P.T. Barnum, declared "There's a sucker born every minute." And W.C. Fields drawled, "Never give a sucker an even break." The Business, where there is so much money and celebrity to be won, is a particularly fertile area for take-the-money-and-run gimmicks that may appear legitimate on the surface, but are fly-by-night operations. The old saying "Buyer Beware" becomes "Actor Beware" and "Parent of Little Stars Beware." Let us examine some of the more common fraudulent schemes.

PHONY GUIDES

There are always ads or solicitations for publications promising to do more for the newcomer than the established guides can do. Clever entrepreneurs will offer to get information about their "personal" clients to "influential" people. Such ventures are usually rip-offs of some sort. A newcomer may enjoy feeling that some star-maker is taking an interest in his or her career. But the venture is just a money-maker's scheme — for the person collecting the checks. Newcomers must face the fact that they are the only ones who can create interest in their career. And they have to do that by working hard for themselves.

The advent of cable TV brought a new wrinkle to the familiar scam. "We have now entered the electronic era," one ad began, "the day of the two-dimensional photo and résumé is obsolete." These promoters promised that, for a hefty fee, they would telecast performers' pictures on the public access channels during the day for casting people to view in the privacy of their offices. An eager, unsuspecting performer might not stop to realize that casting people are extremely busy working during the day — especially seeing talent, in person, by appointment. The only audience for such a broadcast would be the talent's family. The promoters found few customers and went out of business.

One "production company" was headquartered in a very posh section of southern California. They rented a gorgeous home and tacked up posters of successful Hollywood stars to program wanna-bes to think they, too, could be like the legends on those walls. Innocent applicants who filled in the "New Faces Data Sheet" had no idea that this firm's principals were wanted in seven states for fraud and theft.

DECEPTIVE ADS AND SERVICES

Even a reliable trade paper such as *Back Stage* cannot always know when an ad is not legitimate.

We pride ourselves on the fact that we try our hardest to keep scam artists out of *Back Stage*. But when these scam artists approach performers on the street, or call them at home after getting hold of their résumés, and offer actors a way to get their union cards, all we can do is wave a big red flag and advise them to be aware and stay away!

—SHERRY EAKER

An actress we know responded to an ad in *Back Stage* for a film to be shot in New York: "Actresses/dancers to do extra work in *Native of Beijing* in New York." Within ten days she received a phone call from a man claiming to be with a talent agency. He said she had been referred to him by a fellow employee in his office who had received her picture. He wanted to set up an appointment for the following week. She was confused, but thought it couldn't hurt to check it out. Here is her account of the meeting:

"The office was located in a nice-looking building. When I got off the elevator, I had to walk down a corridor that seemed vacated by other entertainment agencies. His was the last office on the hall. The general appearance was disorganized, pictures and résumés stuffed in one huge file behind the reception area, separated by torn cardboard. Pictures on the wall were discolored and outdated. The whole atmosphere looked unprofessional. I told the receptionist I had an appointment, and she had no idea he even made appointments. She stuffed my photo and résumé under a pile of others. After an hour and twenty minutes I finally got to meet with the agent. In his cramped, dirty office, he came across as rather charming, with a pleasing voice and warm smile. He told me about himself and how prestigious his agency was, showed me a binder filled with faxes from movie companies looking to audition certain types, and explained what a working relationship with him meant.

"Each week I would submit twenty-five headshots. He would send me out at least ten or more times a week. I would call him every day between 2 and 6 P.M. I would stop by once a week to look through legit requests.

"In all this time he never asked me to read. Nor was he interested in seeing me in anything in the near future. Yet, there he was, ready to sign me!

"He suggested I could take a day or two to think about it, because he could sense I was not ready to make any commitments. He then explained that if I did decide to work with him, he would need $375 to do a mailing. After all, I was a new face and people needed to start to see it. A mailing was vital if I wanted to work professionally. He would put me in touch with important people he had been working with for years.

"I asked if I couldn't pay him once I got a job. He said the mailing needed to be done A.S.A.P., and all his clients pay up front. He gave me his business card so I could call him within the next few days. Before I left I inquired about the film mentioned in the ad. He said someone would call me about that within a few days, leading me to believe I would be used. I have yet to hear from him, or anyone in his office about the film, or other things."

Rightly skeptical, the young woman asked the advice of industry professionals and was spared laying out all that money for a "mailing." But imagine how many young hopefuls fall for this gimmick every day. We hope it never happens to you.

Beware, also, of companies offering photo and résumé "counseling," especially if they advertise in the regular daily newspapers. These outfits show sample formats of résumés, promise lists of casting directors, sheets of nonunion casting calls and a typical cover letter — information which is readily accessible. In conjunction with their photo advice, however, they recommend the services of a particular photographer, for a sum (usually $250) which must be paid in advance. The actor must sign an agreement which states that a reshoot is guaranteed if the subject is not satisfied, but only if requested in writing, or by phone, within three days of receiving the proofs. Photos, if not picked up within thirty days, will be discarded and payment forfeited. The actor is responsible for makeup and hair styling.

These rules seem forthright and clear. However, this organization also purports to act as a talent representative. And in that capacity their rules are:

1. Client call-ins are limited to one day a week.

2. Clients are given a specific time to stop by for "casting submissions."

3. Clients are given an exact number of photos and résumés to submit.

4. Since they are not franchised, the firm will gladly take 15 percent of your salary.

5. Clients are given a permission to look at "open call sheets." Yet this information is readily accessible!

The firm also warns that if they book you for a job and you don't show up, they will not consider you for any future work!

RIPOFF PROTECTION
There are countless talent-agency, acting-school, and modeling scams, and new ones are concocted daily. Remember that jobs for performers on network television shows are *not* advertised in the Help Wanted or Classifieds section of a daily newspaper. Remember that legitimate agencies are licensed by the Department of Consumer Affairs and franchised by the unions. Their licenses are always displayed prominently in the office. You can always call any of the talent unions to find out if the people offering to build your career, make you a star, put your name in lights, and so on, are all they claim to be.

Remember, too, that *no legitimate agent or manager asks for payment in advance.* The talent gets paid first, after the job has been done. Only then do the agent and the manager receive their percentage of the performer's salary.

CASTING DIRECTORS
The casting director is a talent *buyer* and your major link to the people who are in a position to hire you. It has been said that the best casting directors are those who have acted, for they are aware of the problems that the actors have.

> An open mind is the most valuable tool that a casting director has. That makes the difference between being creative and being a hack.
> —GENE BLYTHE

Ideally, casting directors go to see as much work as possible, remember all the good actors, and are willing to believe that a mediocre performance is not necessarily the actor's fault, but can be the result of bad direction and poor casting.

The casting director is engaged in a never-ending search to find the right actor for the right job. Constantly under the gun to meet a production deadline, the casting director needs to have a broad knowledge of actors and the talent pool and to have a computer-brain of information.

It also means that after eight or nine hours at a desk looking at pictures, interviewing actors, and hearing them read, evenings are spent going to plays, showcases, cabarets, and comedy clubs, and watching movies and television. The casting director is always seeking the talent no one else has yet found.

> I try to come up with something new and original in every piece of casting I do. When I am at a movie, I am constantly making notes. It's not like I am watching the movie for enjoyment. It's like, "Oh, I have to remember that actor and put him on my new faces list." I spend my nights flipping television channels because I am afraid I haven't thought of every actor who could be right for a part.
>
> —MARY JO SLATER, *president, Slater Casting*

Casting directors frequently have only two weeks to cast twelve characters. That means there's no time to do any prescreening and there are approximately a dozen people to please — including producers, writers, directors, network programming executives — each of whom has a different mental picture of what actor is perfect. This is where the casting director has nightmares.

> I have trouble sleeping at night because I keep thinking there is an actor out there I have forgotten. I use the *Players' Guide* and the *Academy Players Directories,* and I have a program on my computer keeping track of when I saw the actor, what I saw the actor do, age, etc., so I can keep my mind fresh with new ideas.
>
> —MARY JO SLATER

The casting director's greatest reward is completing a job, looking at the results, and saying, "Yes, that was the person for the role." There's also the knowledge that whatever happens to the actor from that break, that job could be his or her launching pad. One respected casting director who loves discovering new talent and illuminating their path reflected on the nature of the job this way:

> You can't always predict at a screen test what will happen. Sometimes you see a spark in someone on camera, or you see something that is ready to explode, and you must let it happen. There is almost a psychic need to get inside the head of an actor, as well as a need for incredible perception of what an actor can do. You can't always tell from the audition alone, just because of nerves. So I am a firm believer in the interview process. It's important to look deeper, to see something of who the actor

is, to try different approaches to reach beyond that nervousness, to get to the divine spark.

A casting director may have a permanent position on the staff of an advertising agency, a network, a continuing show, or a busy packager or production company. In such capacity casting directors actively seek out talent and will frequently travel far from their home base to get a glimpse of it. They will be in touch with coaches at professional schools and directors of college theater programs. They will maintain contacts with agents and talent scouts across the nation and even pay attention to productions in foreign countries. *Interesting* talent is what they are after — the stars of tomorrow, able to grab an audience's attention and hold it, for thirty seconds, for two hours, or for the duration of a story line.

> I tell young actors: you can get along without a manager, you can even do without an agent, but to get a job you need to see and be seen by the casting director!
> —TONY NICOSIA, *director of auditions and casting,*
> *Actors Equity Association, New York*

INDEPENDENT CASTING DIRECTORS

A freelance expert who knows the available talent pool and will also go exploring for new performers, the independent casting director is employed on a per-project basis by the producer of a film, play, commercial, or other vehicle requiring talent. An independent casting director may be involved in the initial casting of the core characters for a series or soap opera and then decide to hand the day-to-day casting chores to a staff casting director.

Possibly the major difference in the way freelancers work is that they are less likely to invest as much time in developing young people and will not set aside time to meet actors unless there is a particular role for them to play.

Freelance casting directors complain that actors who don't fit the type or age range they are looking for, but who nonetheless plead to "drop off a photo" or "just say hello," are wasting both the casting director's time and their own — as well as the photo and résumé, which more than likely will be tossed into the wastebasket. On the other hand, there are times when a casting director believes strongly that an actor who doesn't fit the published description may be right for a role, as Meg Simon discovered when she was on a talent search in Chicago. She had seen more than 2,000 actors, was enthusiastic about one in particular, told him to come to New York, and, sure enough, he got the part!

HOW CASTING DIRECTORS WORK

Whether on staff or independent, casting directors who work in television, theater, film, and commercials synthesize their personal impressions about each character, gathered from careful examination of the script and ideas they receive from the producer, the director, and the writer. Then they make recommendations.

We generally got a script about seven days before the production start-ed, and had maybe three days of casting. The process involved the pro-ducer, the director, and the casting director. Ideally we'd show them from three to five actors for each role. As the casting director, I must feel confident that any of those people can do the part. Sometimes I'd get a script Friday morning and have a reading that afternoon at 3 P.M. That means I had about two hours to get my thoughts together and get the actors in for the parts. I've even cast on Sundays at times.

—MOLLY LOPATA, *West Coast casting executive*

I find out about major contract players from my producer. I read about the roles in the script breakdowns. Each week I meet with the directors to discuss the noncontract players who will be needed. My assistant is told by them about the types and number of extras we will need. We try to be a month ahead in terms of casting. That is not always possible.

—BETTY REA, *casting director,* Guiding Light

I take the tapes from the first casting session and show them to the pro-ducer and the creative team. There can be an enormous amount of fast-forwarding if they are unsure what it is they are looking for. Criteria can change on the spot. But the fact is, they know what they want and my job is to satisfy them.

—ARISTA BALTRONIS, *casting director, Grey Advertising*

I have seven or eight days to prepare. I read the script, I jot down ideas, I personally contact the files. I usually bring in at least two or three new people for each episode, whether or not I think they're right for the parts, so I can hear them read my words. The worst time I ever had was when we went through fifteen actors for a one-line paramedic role — to make sense of complicated medical jargon and still bring personality to it. When New York actors come to L.A., because of their training those are normally the kinds of roles I can zip them into. Right away they get a terrific credit, and it helps me out tremendously.

—GENE BLYTHE

I may read 250 actors for one role. The philosophy is that if there is someone who might be remotely right, I would rather take the extra five minutes to read them than not at all.

—MARK TESCHNER

Feeling the constant pressure of time, casting directors must deal with certainties: they must have someone on their list of recommendations that everyone will agree on for each role.

We casting directors look to the actor to solve our problem. We want them to be good. The worst thing in the world is when you have seen 180 people and feel that you have not found it! We really love going to the producer and saying we have five to ten really good choices.

—MARK TESCHNER

Please remember, a casting director is *not* to be called a casting agent — that is a contradiction in terms. The correct terminology is *talent agent,* and *casting director.*

THE HEAD HONCHOS

Whatever the casting director's recommendations, the final casting decisions must be approved by the executives in charge of production. In films, they are the producer, the director, and the writer. Sometimes all those positions may be held by the same person. And, in films, the entire production frequently relies upon the bankability of the star. All the rest is after the fact.

In soaps, if the show is owned by the network, the top people will be the daytime program executives, the producers, and the head writers. If the show is owned by, say, Procter and Gamble, there will be a Procter and Gamble executive producer assigned to the show — then there will be the producers and the head writers.

In commercials, approval comes from the agency producer, the production house director, the account executives, the art director, the copywriter, and the client.

In theater, the decision makers are the producer, the director, and the playwright.

In made-for-TV films, they are the producer, the writer, the director, and the network executives in the motion pictures division.

In a new series, the final casting decisions are up to the network entertainment division executives — these are heads of programming, development, and casting — as well as the series producer and the creator.

In episodes for an ongoing television series, they are the executive producer, the line (episode) producer, the director, and the writer.

> You always know you have the right person when you have everyone in agreement. It is ultimately the producer's choice, but if the producer doesn't please the writers and their vision of the character, it is not going to be well-served.
>
> —JO ANN EMMERICH, *executive producer,* Loving

Having separated the buyers from the sellers, it's time to set about meeting them.

CHAPTER 4

LOOKING FOR WORK

Techniques are the key to the door that lets you into the room of inspiration.

—JOSÉ FERRER

The business of being an actor, whether you are employed or not, is a full-time job. Serious pursuit of your career demands diligence in developing your talents, looking for jobs, being able to perform on cue, and packaging yourself correctly. It is a total commitment.

POLISHING YOUR SKILLS

Of course you can be born with a talent for acting, just as one may have a natural aptitude for sports, music, or even finance. Yet in those fields we readily acknowledge that to compete as a professional requires training: singers vocalize morning, noon, and night; musicians practice scales for hours; athletes work out under the guidance of a demanding coach; executives hone their necessary business and communication skills at seminars and management workshops. And actors take classes.

> Even working actors are still going to class, to experiment, to make mistakes, and to learn from those mistakes.
> —JUDY HENDERSON, *casting director*

> The teacher has to inspire. The teacher has to agitate. You cannot teach acting. You can only stimulate what's already there.
> —STELLA ADLER, *famed acting teacher*

A good class develops and invigorates the "acting muscles": imagination, humor, sense memory, emotional range, style, movement, timing, improvisational facility, vocal variety, and speech. Class is where you stretch, where you learn how to analyze, understand, and enhance an author's material. You refine your technique, so that when a director tells you, "Do it again," you can repeat the moment — up to Take 45, if necessary.

An actor will frequently give a marvelous instinctive reading. The director will say, "That was a marvelous reading. I want you to do it again for Sam, the producer, who is coming in in ten minutes." And when the actor has to do it, he is petrified. He has absolutely no idea what he did, because it was all instinctive. He has no idea what gave him that marvelous inspiration.

—FLO SALANT GREENBERG, *acting coach*

Why does Ben Vereen need a coach? Because he considers himself a musical star and never took acting seriously—he only worked instinctively. Now that he has come back from the dead, he wants to do Shakespeare and wants to develop his speech and his acting.

Diahann Carroll also never trained as an actress. And then she started getting straight jobs — I coached her for *Claudine*, which got her an Oscar nomination, and *Agnes of God*, which she starred in — twenty years after her debut in a musical — playing a psychiatrist, a part originated by Elizabeth Ashley! And from that came *Dynasty*.

—ALICE SPIVACK, *acting coach to many stars*

Helen Hayes, renowned as the First Lady of the American Theater, bemoaned the fact that, as a young performer, she had absolutely no idea of what she was doing or how she did what she did. She strained for effects, giving performances that were hardly recognizable from one evening to the next.

"It is remarkable," she writes in *On Reflection*, "that it took me so long to protect myself. . . . For a while I had heard and ignored the shrillness of my voice. I also spoke too slowly at times. The quality of my performing would decline during the run of a play."

And then she saw a play starring Minnie Maddern Fiske, one of Broadway's most celebrated leading ladies. Fascinated by the actress' seemingly artless performance, she sat through the show again the following evening and the night after that, and she realized that Mrs. Fiske (as she was known) "gave exactly the same performance every single time. There wasn't a smile or a shrug that was a fraction of a second early or late. A crumb was brushed off her jabot at precisely the same moment she was fashioning a particular syllable. All the incredible spontaneity was calculated to a sigh."

Flawless technique enabled Mrs. Fiske to give the illusion that everything she did was inspired by the moment. "Then," Miss Hayes recalled, "I knew I had to take acting lessons."

Classes do more than help you to refine your technique. They also put you in touch with other talented, creative people like yourself. They are the beginning of your own network — colleagues who know and respect your work, who feel comfortable with you, and who may remember you when they are involved in a future production. Class is where you may find the ideal stage partner, the other half of the act you've always wanted to do.

Acting instructor Catherine Gaffigan includes this advice in the guidelines she has written for her students:

> Though deep friendships often develop (appropriately), the partnership arrangement in this class is a business relationship and should be treated as such. Your acting partner is not assigned to be a surrogate parent or a lover or to meet your emotional needs. Potential intimate relationships are wisely put on the back burner for the present.

The actor in New York or Los Angeles has the opportunity to study with some of the finest talents—Oscar, Tony, and Emmy winners—in the business. F. Murray Abraham, Betty Buckley, Helen Gallagher, Uta Hagen, Anne Jackson, and Michael Moriarty are but a few of the dedicated professionals who have much to give and who enjoy sharing their skills. Award-winning director Robert "Bobby" Lewis, one of the founders of the Actors Studio, told the students who were ready to worship at his feet:

> You know, in a good class the director learns something, too. I expect you all to teach me a great deal.

But the instructor's reputation should not be your prime concern. There's no benefit in studying with the chic teacher, or the one whose class is supposedly most difficult to get into, unless that person is someone whose work you respect, with whom you feel a connection, who demands the best of his or her students and seems genuinely interested in inspiring them. Try to audit a class first or at least talk with the instructor. Check out the achievement level of the other students. Acting is like tennis: you get more out of it when you play with someone who's a bit better than you. If you are the best one in the class, leave.

Classes in basic technique or scene study are generally operated on a month-to-month or thirteen-week basis. Schools offering a complete theater training course will usually require that you sign up for a semester.

SPECIAL TRAINING

In addition to your acting or scene-study class, you'll need workshops in soap opera, commercial, and film technique. While a knowledge of acting technique is essential, these jobs call for different skills. It would be counterproductive to take classes in commercials and soap opera concurrently. Begin with the field that you feel offers you the most immediate opportunity. When you become expert in one, move on to the next.

SONG AND DANCE

The performer who can sing and dance becomes a triple threat, because our theater currently produces more hit musicals, which employ so many more actors than do straight plays. And hit musicals enjoy long runs. John Cullum, Sandy Duncan, Joanna Gleason, James Naughton, Jerry Orbach, John Schneider, and Tom Wopat are all musical theater performers who have gone on to leads in TV and films. Angela Lansbury's long list of award-winning performances includes her starring roles in the musicals *Mame* and *Sweeney Todd*.

Learning to sing can be expensive. Singers usually take classes in vocal technique as well as theatrical performance. The trades frequently carry notices of group workshops, which are less expensive than private classes. Consider bartering lessons — offer your skill in another area to a colleague who sings.

Body movement is an essential element of the actor's training. Movement is a function of character — as the writers of books explaining body language have made clear. A dance class, therefore, may be more valuable than calisthenics for career purposes. And if you supplement your ability to move well with a knowledge of dance steps and combinations, you'll enhance your chances of work.

Some time ago, agents were besieged with calls for "actors who could dance" in a grand ball sequence on *As the World Turns*. The shows were complicated and required five days of taping. Two couples who seemed to understand exactly the kind of romantic period quality that the director wanted to achieve became the focal point of each ballroom scene. None of the quartet had ever met or worked together previously, but they were ideal dance partners, and the director quickly made use of what they could bring to the scenes.

For dance classes, which can double as excellent fitness sessions, one can buy a card admitting you for a length of time or for a number of lessons. This is a relatively inexpensive aspect of your training.

YOUR SPEAKING VOICE

The number of aspiring actors with slovenly speech is appalling. Relying on microphones to do the work for them, they have no breath control or tone support. The muscles that should be working to produce great or, at least, audible sound are flabby.

Ask yourself: do strangers (not your family or friends, who talk the same way you do and know what your sounds are supposed to mean) frequently ask you to repeat what you've just said? What's your name again? What was your address?

Acting is, after all, a business of words as well as of moving images. You have to make a lot of phone calls in this business, and before you can get a job you need to ask for an appointment. And keep in mind that the hero must say, "I love you," the heroine must answer, "I love you, too," and the audience has to hear and understand every word.

In Comden and Green's *Singin' in the Rain* and Kaufman and Hart's *Once in a Lifetime*, which dealt comically with Hollywood during the advent of talking pictures, there's consternation at the studio when it is evident that the he-man has the voice of a wimp and the *femme fatale* squawks like an irate peacock. Does your voice match your look? If the voice you hear when you replay a recorded tape is not a sound anyone would care to listen to for more than three seconds, run, do not walk, to a speech coach.

Start practicing on your own, too: read aloud, slowly, for ten minutes three times a day. Practice, practice, practice.

Cleanse your speech of localisms — intonation and pronunciation that announce even to a casual listener that your flat "A" is from Chicago, your "Ayuh" hails from up North, your "Y'all" comes from down South, your nasal twang resonates from the Southwest. Aim for the general American sound of announcers on national commercials, or your network newscasters. Actors who speak in any kind of dialect should be doing so only for the purpose of characterization.

> If you're going into all aspects of the business, you should be able to do Standard American speech. If we get someone with too Southern an accent, unless they're playing a Southern part it's going to be out of sync with the family they're supposed to be in.
>
> —BETTY RAE, *casting director,* Guiding Light

One of the many reasons British actors are so well regarded on this side of the Atlantic is that they are taught that the actor's voice is an integral part of his or her instrument. They are trained to read the words as the author wrote them, and it is a pleasure to listen to them. Every word is as clear as crystal. Practice. Practice. Practice.

The late Edith Skinner, coach of Laurence Olivier, has produced an audiotape, *Good American Speech*, which you can usually find at theater bookshops. José Ferrer, who had one of the most expressive voices in the theater, told an interviewer:

> You can never speak admirably enough. You can hit this note, but there are notes still higher that you can hit, and this is why I am spending a fortune training my voice. My voice will never satisfy me. I see only its faults. I see how much better than my voice Gielgud's is, and how much better than my voice Laurence Olivier's is.

KNOWING YOUR FIELD

The life-stories of well-known performers and the literature of the theater should be familiar to you. If you don't already have a library card, get one. It costs you nothing. Read plays — in their entirety, not just the scenes that may be assigned to you. You may discover a role that seems to have been written just for you. Read about the history of acting, actors, the theater, the cinema. Learn as much as you can.

> People come to me and say, "What should I work on?" I say, "Don't you read?" Musicians have jam sessions all the time. Why don't actors do that? Read plays, and when you find plays that interest you, start to work on them. We cannot stop practicing. You don't stop learning to act until you are dead.
>
> —UTA HAGEN, *at a seminar for Equity members*

Thanks to the generosity of producer, theater owner, and former actress Lucille Lortel, your library card also admits you to the Theatre on Film and Tape (TOFT) archive at the Lincoln Center Library for the Performing Arts at 65th Street and Amsterdam Avenue, in Manhattan. It is the world's foremost collection of films and videotapes of live theater. The archive includes Broadway, off-Broadway, and regional theater productions. There are also related items such as interviews, documentaries, lectures and awards programs.

> Thank God for Betty Corwin and the Lincoln Center Library! She's maintained all the tapes of Broadway shows, through private funding, for all

these years. Without the *Company* tape, I'd never have been able to recreate Michael Bennett's work, his brilliant conceptual staging.
—DONNA MCKECHNIE, *the original Cassie in* A Chorus Line

KNOCKING ON DOORS

Here is where the actor must switch from sensitive artist to energetic business executive. You are a door-to-door salesperson, and what you are selling is *you*. Obviously, the more doorbells you ring, the greater your chance of making a sale. And the more cards you send, the more familiar your face will become.

> The best thing is to send your picture, a postcard every month. Every day I go through the postcards and if I see actors that I keep recognizing and there's a job coming up, a lot of times I'll say, "Bring in this person."
> —LESLEE FELDMAN, *commercial casting director*

> Keeping in touch with everybody, sending out the cards, the notes, making calls — it seemed there was so much to do. I was up till all hours. And then I realized my Dad had office hours, so I set office hours for myself — every morning, from ten to twelve! Managing the time makes it easier to do New York.
> —PATRICK PAGE, *actor*

SENDING OUT YOUR PHOTOS

You will need a supply of 9 x 12" manila or colored envelopes with a flat cardboard insert. You don't want the post office to crumple your picture along with the rest of the mail. Always write "Photographs. Please Do Not Bend" on the envelope.

With each photo and résumé include a *cover letter*. This is a short note introducing yourself. Keep it simple. Mention the name of the person who may have suggested that you contact the agent or casting director and request an appointment. Now is the time to use every connection you have: parents, relatives, mutual friends, acting teachers, your college alumni. But do make sure your referral is legitimate. You're trying to establish credibility, remember.

> My office gets hundreds of photos and résumés. Sometimes they have no phone number, no address, not even a note. If people don't ask me for an appointment, I can't guess why they're sending me pictures.
> —LEONARD FINGER, *casting director*

The Cover Letter Your stationery, while it need not be engraved by Tiffany, should nevertheless be attractive. Do not used a lined sheet of paper torn from a spiral-bound notebook or even a small legal pad. You are presenting yourself — via your photo and résumé and everything that goes out under your name — for consideration in your chosen career. You are advertising yourself. This is your first business call on a client.

The letter should be typed (or word-processed) neatly. If that's not possible, a handwritten note will do, provided that your script is legible. Trying to decipher a scrawl is a turn-off. So is misspelling, improper grammar, or words used incorrectly. One actor's letter contained the line: "This is a funny antidote I heard the other day." If you don't know that you are telling an anecdote, should an agent be willing to risk credibility by submitting you for work?

> Forget sparkles, sprinkles, and all that. I will read it as long as it is legible. Sometimes I will look at a picture and there will be nothing on the résumé but something in the cover letter that will strike my fancy, and I will take a chance. They have to start somewhere.
>
> —CAROLE INGBER, *agent*

Make sure you've spelled the recipient's name correctly. Mari Lyn, for example, is not Marilyn, Mary Lynne, Mariann, Mary Lou, or Merry Lynn. Be certain of the sex of the person: Lynn and Carmen could be women, but, as it happens, they are *Mr.* Stalmaster and *Mr.* LaVia. It's your business to find out such things.

> I got a note from a young actor saying, "Dear Ms. LaVia, so nice to meet you at so-and-so's party last week!" Now, what am I supposed to think of that actor? Would I ever call him? Not on your life!
>
> —CARMEN LAVIA

Your initial task will be to send a photo and résumé to every franchised agent and subagent whose name you have read in *Ross Reports* or in special issues of the trade papers.

Next, go through your list of leads and find the casting directors who regularly cast series, soaps, and any other shows that use dramatic talent. Send them your photo and résumé with cover letter.

Advertising agency casting departments and production houses with on-staff casting directors should also receive a photo and résumé with cover letter. If you have an audio- or videotape, say so in your cover letter. Do not send these recorded materials unsolicited.

After about two weeks, send a postcard as a reminder and ask again for an appointment. Be pleasant and positive; remind them that you sent your material to them a short time ago and ask when it will be possible to meet.

A telephone follow-up is *not* advisable in this instance. Agents are trying to get work for clients they represent; casting directors are trying to accommodate agents and see people for specific roles. They don't really have the time to talk to people they don't know. They will call you if they are interested.

If you feel that you must call, be able to state succinctly what you want to ask or to say about yourself. This is not the time to stammer, be shy, giggle, or sound desperate. You will get one of three answers: Your picture is on file — don't call us, we'll call you; call back in about two months; we see people at four o'clock on Thursday.

Always note the response you get in your records and date it.

Keeping Track   It is vital that you keep a file of all the people you try to see. Whether you use index cards, a personal computer program, or an accountant's notebook, what matters is that you know at a glance when you sent a photo, to whom, and whether you received a response. As your career progresses, you will refer to the records for follow-up notes and phone calls and to remind yourself what happened at each exchange.

It is easy to forget that agents and casting directors are human beings with legitimate concerns beyond whether or not they are going to see you on Tuesday. Make a note that one casting director's son runs a French restaurant, or that another's husband had a book published, or that a third has been elected to an honorary position. It's something you might talk about next time. In doing so, you become a human being to all the people you speak to. There is more to life, after all, than the next appointment, although it may not seem so to you at the moment.

FINANCIAL RECORDS

Because their income profile is so different from that of the general public, actors seem to be prime targets for income tax audits (which is ironic, considering how little money the majority of performers earn). We cannot overemphasize the necessity for keeping precise records — not only on your income, agents' commissions, and tax deductions, but on every expense. Start now to train yourself to keep a daily account book, noting phone calls, meals (how much, with whom, where), clothing purchased for business occasions, travel, mailing expenses. The list will seem endless, but you will find that it soon becomes a habit. Keep your receipts in order, too. As we noted earlier, paying by check is a way of recording expenses. As a careful record keeper, you will be able to deal sanely with changes in federal, state and local tax regulations.

Precise employment records are necessary not only at income tax time, but also in case you apply for unemployment insurance compensation. In this freelance business, a performer may possibly work for twenty or more employers in a year. It's in the performer's interest to know exactly what the employment dates were. Other people have been known to make mistakes, and their errors can cost the actor money. Insurance requirements differ from state to state and have been seen to change frequently, depending upon the general employment picture.

THE OPEN CALL

While conducting your general mailing effort, you continue to read the trades for specific casting news. Auditions known as *open calls* are held by casting directors, producers, and/or directors when they need people for "atmosphere" and when they are looking to cast a very special role and have been unable to find anyone that the writer, the producer, and the directors can agree upon. An open call means just that: Is there anybody out there who can do this job?

Cast lists and character descriptions are almost always provided for open calls. Read the description carefully and try to look like what the production people say they want. Bring your photo and résumé. Have a monologue prepared in case they show interest and want to see your audition skills. This is a chance to sell yourself; bring everything that you think will help you make the sale. You may not need it, or even get to use it, but you must be prepared.

A common occurence took place in the summer of 1993, when Paul Newman was seeking a youngster to play his five-year-old grandson in a film that Newman was also directing. The film shoot was on-location in Poughkeepsie, New York, so the casting director suggested they hold an open call there. The notice was carried in the local newspaper, listed insignificantly among the week's events. On the appointed morning, there were 500 blond, blue-eyed five-year-old boys and their mothers (some sisters and some fathers, too) waiting for the doors to open.

Often considered a media event for the studio, the network, or the project which initiates it, the open call (sometimes known as the "cattle call," a term we hate) requires that you just show up at the designated address between certain hours. When it was announced that a new Scarlett O'Hara was being sought for the CBS mini-series, over 400 women, ages twenty-one to sixty-one, stood in line at Atlanta's Civic Center, anxious to meet the director and be "discovered." Two actresses were called back, but neither was cast. The role eventually went to a British actress with some rather good film credits on her résumé. Not since the director Otto Preminger scoured the countryside for an innocent girl to play Saint Joan and found Jean Seberg in Iowa has an unknown been cast from an open call to carry a film. (And the experience nearly destroyed Miss Seberg.)

Several years ago an ad in *The Hollywood Reporter* announced an open call for a young actress to play Marilyn Monroe before she became Marilyn Monroe. The ad gave the address, the hours, special instructions about bringing a picture and a résumé, and said that no prepared audition material was required. The first 1,500 actresses would be seen. According to a casting executive overseeing the call, only 500 women showed up, most of them physically wrong for the role — plus one young person wearing an oxygen mask, who tried to tell him that Michael Douglas was intercepting her mail.

One reason casting directors are not enthusiastic about open calls, aside from the eccentrics, is that amateurs flock to such events out of curiosity. An open call was held for a role on *General Hospital* in the early 1980s. The ad appeared in *Back Stage*. The criteria were clear: a beautiful, upscale, Grace Kelly type, twenty-five to thirty, not over 5'8". The notice said the actress should have some experience and be willing to relocate to California if selected. Interview times were 10 A.M. to 1 P.M. and 2 P.M. to 6 P.M., at ABC headquarters in New York City. It was a frosty February day, but at 6 A.M. young women started lining up outside the building. Wearing short skirts, high heels, and borrowed fur coats, they shivered in anticipation at the chance for soap stardom. ABC pages, carrying cardboard signs listing the qualifications for the part, paraded up and down in front of the building. No one left the line. Some of the actresses had driven up from Philadelphia, southern New Jersey, even as far away as Washington, D.C.

One thousand women passed through the revolving doors. Twelve were asked to go to another room and read the script. None were chosen. Few were prepared or experienced enough to handle the creation of a character on a network soap opera.

Recently, a leading studio took some flak for trying to institute an open call policy to meet actors who were without representation. One actor explained how he felt humiliated, for the experience lasted only a few minutes during which he was hastily handed a script to read, for a role inappropriate to his type, in front of casting directors who, he intuited, did not want to be there. Yet, while he may have had good reason to feel he was given short shrift, the casting directors were trying to see as many people as possible, given their time frame. The fact is, reading for top casting executives for two minutes is better than never getting the chance at all.

Despite the negatives — the long lines, the people who should have stayed home, and the impersonal treatment — there are happy endings. One young woman who stood in line with her friends at the open call for singers for the San Francisco production of *Phantom of the Opera* had never sung professionally, though she had won vocal scholarships in her home town. Her fine voice attracted the attention of the casting director, who asked her to return for a call-back. Director Harold Prince was impressed by her range and ability, approved her for the chorus, and subsequently chose her to understudy the smaller women's parts. She's on her way.

Debra Monk, Tony-winning actress, remembered an open call she went to for director Tommy Tune:

> There were 800 people there, and I got down to the final eight. When I was through, Tommy came over to me, put his arm around me, and said I was wonderful. I knew I wasn't selected, but I remember how good I felt that he took the time to make me feel that I had talent.

Before he was twenty-five, Billy Porter was on Broadway in *Miss Saigon* and *Five Guys Named Moe* and was cast as the Teen Angel in Tommy Tune's revival of *Grease*. He also won the $100,000 Star Search prize for his singing ability and talent. He dispensed this good advice:

> I tell actors all the time to go to the open call. Don't wait for your agent. I am with William Morris, and I still go to open calls. If I sit around and wait for them all the time, I will never work, because then I'm putting the power in someone else's hands. You have to own yourself.

TALENT SEARCHES

Far more structured and specific in nature than the open call is the talent search. ABC Daytime Programs recently launched a nationwide talent search to discover the best actors from culturally diverse backgrounds and to find performers with disabilities. Because New York and Los Angeles are home to ABC's four daytime programs, those areas were not included in the search. Opportunities for leading roles on daytime dramas were therefore presented to actors in regional markets, who ordinarily would be unaware of them. Actors were submitted by agents, and appointments were set up. Actors without representation were able to submit themselves. Each actor was asked to perform a two-minute monologue. Finalists were assigned a specific soap scene and were videotaped.

It is important for the success of the talent search that pictures and résumés be reviewed in advance of appointments. We cannot emphasize strongly enough how important the photo and résumé are. They must be current, professional, and well-packaged. If a videocassette is acceptable to send, it must be well edited and demonstrate your best work.

ELIGIBLE PERFORMER AUDITIONS (EPAS)
In a continuing effort to provide open access to employment, the Actors Equity Association contract requires producers to set aside time for open casting. These are the Eligible Performer Auditions, or EPAs, and they must be held before any other auditions and before any cast members (other than stars) are signed for the production.

> Yes, they may know who they want, but they can change their minds if they see somebody terrific! Just recently, the actress who plays Bloody Mary in the new national tour of *South Pacific* was hired from an EPA.
> —TONY NICOSIA, *director of auditions and casting,*
> *Actors Equity Association*

Members have the right to be seen for every Equity production. However, nonunion performers who meet the eligibility criteria — continuous work for a certain number of weeks at a salary at least equal to Equity's "Theater for Young Audiences" level — may apply for Eligible Performer status. Payment of a $20 annual fee (to cover administrative expenses) for the identifying card allows them to audition in the system.

For the EPA, the actor comes prepared with an audition selection, a monologue of two minutes or less. There is no limit to the number of people who may sign up, but only the first 115 are guaranteed to be seen per day. There is no carryover of names. If you don't make it on the first day, you must come in early the next day and sign up all over again.

> Now, there is no reason to rush into joining Equity. If you are eligible, you can audition. But you can also do nonunion work, which union members cannot do, to gain experience and training, build a résumé. We want qualified members.
> —TONY NICOSIA

THE LORT LOTTERY
Twice each year, access to jobs in regional theater is provided by a five-day EPA known as the LORT lottery. Representatives of the League of Regional Theaters (LORT) travel to New York, Chicago, or Los Angeles. They screen 400 actors in each region for the first three days, then spend two days auditioning selected performers, who receive four minutes each to perform their monologues.

These are not general auditions. There are specific roles to be filled for named productions. However, the actor who does a sensational audition will surely be remembered for the next season's casting — provided he or she keeps in touch.

Admission to the LORT lottery is gained by sending in a postcard. But dates, times, and details of the lottery process are changed each season. For the latest information you are advised to read *Back Stage* or call Actors' Equity.

OTHER OPPORTUNITIES

Plays for Living,® a division of the Family Service of America, has for almost fifty years employed professional actors to perform original half-hour dramas that illustrate a particular compelling social or health problem: alcoholism, a child's inability to read, stealing, lying, illiteracy, AIDS, racism, and the like. The plays are presented to parents' associations, professional associations, and corporations in school auditoriums, churches, or meeting halls throughout New York City. The casts are small and usually double- or triple-cast to alleviate actors' conflicts with paying jobs. Actors receive a small honorarium and are usually invited to share the coffee and cake served after the performance. Audience discussion follows, but by then the cast is on its way home. While the payment is minimal, the experience of adjusting to different theaters and audiences is invaluable. Some of the material is excellent for audition scenes.

Send pictures and résumés to: Plays for Living, 49 West 27th Street, Suite 930, New York, NY 10001-6936. There are licensed affiliates throughout the United States and Canada; there may be one near you.

The Bedside Network is a forty-five-year-old volunteer service started by performers after World War II to provide recreation for hospitalized veterans by presenting radio and television scripts. Performers serve as professional directors, while the patients become proficient enough after an evening's rehearsal to perform the script for their fellows. They also tape musical and variety shows. It's one of the favorite activities of AFTRA and SAG members.

For further information, contact: Screen Actors Guild, Vets Bedside Network, 1515 Broadway, 44th floor, New York NY 10036.

The In-Touch Network is a special closed-circuit radio station for the blind which is heard nationally, as far as Hawaii. This is a volunteer activity. Volunteers spend an hour or two reading into a microphone — daily newspapers, news magazines, stories, almost anything of interest. This presents a marvelous opportunity for actors to improve their skill at cold reading.

To learn more about the In-Touch Network, write to Executive Director Bruce Masis, 15 West 65th Street, New York, NY 10023.

MAKING THE ROUNDS

Trying to see agents and casting directors by knocking on doors has become difficult. Small offices, frequently staffed by women, must take security precautions: doors are locked to those without appointments. And yet we think it is always worth a try. If you are going out on an open call, an interview, or an audition, do take along a batch of photos and résumés, with cover letters, in manila envelopes. Call upon all the offices in the area. Even if no one will see you, you can always leave your photo and résumé. Do not forget to note these deliveries in your records.

Some time ago *Back Stage* printed this account of what some actors making the rounds will do to make a lasting impression.

Balloons, gift baskets,
Tricks and treats,
Candy, cakes, cookies,

All kinds of sweets,
Pieces of puzzles,
A token, a ring,
Chests without shirts,
A telegram they sing,
Soapboxes, matchbooks,
Pens, pencils, and pads,
Buttons, cartoons,
Magnets, *Back Stage* ads,
Champagne and wine glasses,
Sent by the score. . . .

What Actors Will Do to Get a Foot in the Door
by Mari Lyn Henry

For years actors have spent large amounts of money on products designed to leave a favorable impression on talent agents and casting directors. Boxes of Godiva Chocolates, Hershey's Kisses, peanut butter cups, lollipops, and candy corn have been sent with photos and résumés, plus brief notes seeking interviews and/or auditions. According to agents and casting directors on both coasts, performers who use those enticements are rarely, if ever, called.

Agents Jerry Hogan and Karen Kirsch of the Henderson-Hogan Agency, Inc., recall the time a pharmaceutical bag was delivered to the office, "with an official pharmaceutical label, and containing little jars filled with jelly beans," says Kirsch. "There was a postcard of the actor. We didn't meet the actor, nor did we eat the jelly beans, for fear they might be poisoned." Some egos are so fragile that any rejection might set them off, or their perception of the "power mongers" may be so distorted, that her concern about the jelly beans is not a case of overreaction.

There are other considerations, too. Most of us are on diets, some of us are hypoglycemic or on special food plans.

Kirsch also cites the actor who sent organic popcorn, followed by a mailgram. What truly amazed her was the fact that the actor had some impressive credits.

Mary Jo Slater, of Slater Casting, remembers the actor dressed in a baker's outfit who managed to get past the security guard when she was casting *One Life to Live*. "He delivered a cake, and his 8 × 10" was the decoration."

A case of champagne "impressed the hell" out of agent Michael Thomas, and embarrassed him as well. "If actors can afford it, great! It's the poor starving ones who seem to do the most, which only makes us feel sad," says Thomas.

A few years ago, the ABC casting department received two wine glasses every week for six weeks. Then came the champagne and the pictures and résumés. But the actress who sent them was never seen. Persistent, yes. Practical, no!

One story of tenacity that did pay off is told by Fifi Oscard, owner of the Fifi Oscard Agency, Inc. "Many years ago a salesman for the Kimberly Clark Corporation visited me every day with a long-stemmed rose and a martini. He was so intent on launching a career. Finally, I started sending him out. Not only did he book some terrific accounts, he became one of the highest-paid voice-over performers in the industry!"

A young man in a bunny suit got through security to serenade me with a singing telegram about his credits and the reasons I should hire him. He had a wrapped parcel in his hand, which he presented at the end of the song. Before I could unwrap it — to find his framed photo and résumé — he fled.

Karen Kirsch wishes she could figure out why a young woman dressed as a mouse came to deliver a singing telegram about herself. "She wanted to do musicals. Her picture and résumé with no credits were also delivered. She couldn't act and really couldn't sing."

Aside from the rented costumes and singing résumés, casting directors have also been the recipients of soap boxes, with photo affixed; magnetic letter openers with name and contact info; a sneaker with a letter about "getting a foot in the door"; cartoons about the work search; self-published newsletters giving an update on their auditions, callbacks, and interviews; mock *TV Guide* or *Soap Opera Digest* covers with the actor's photo; stuffed mechanical dogs that squeak and bark; Bart Simpson back scratchers.

Let's suppose one does get in the door, with or without a gimmick. The responsibility to the work, to the audition material, now becomes the priority.

Didi Rea, who formerly headed the Edith Rea Talent Agency, was auditioning actors for a regional theater production of *One Flew Over the Cuckoo's Nest* when one actor delivered the line, "Hi, you guys, how's every little thing?" followed by a very hard smack that literally flew her across the room with the breath knocked out of her.

Michael Thomas recalls "an Ivy League type who disappeared behind a door before his scene, stripped down to jeans and a torn T-shirt, and delivered the most sexually graphic scene from an Erskine Caldwell short story."

Mary Jo Slater will never forget the actor who played the *Rocky* theme on his boom box while doing one-handed push-ups for three minutes.

Then there is the story of the Method actress who auditioned for the role of a junkie. She dragged herself down the hallway to the casting director's office, slid down the wall, and became hysterical.

Nick Wilkinson, ABC's West Coast director of casting, tells about the Theatre Communications Group audition "where a young actor, instead of two contrasting monologues, felt just one magic moment with Shakespeare would give me everything I needed to realize what a gem of an actor he was. He stripped down to a black unitard, and on a folding chair proceeded to stand on his head and intone, 'To be or not to be . . .' Unfortunately, his hands slipped and he took a tumble mid-sentence, never to regain his composure. When I asked him what compelled him to attempt this ill-fated mission, he responded, 'The only way to make Shakespeare matter in our world is to strip down to the truth of the words and turn them upside down.' He was never heard from again."

Actors can make the most favorable impression when they simply tell the truth. Several agents and casting directors shared their negative reactions to false credits on the résumé and to those actors who drop big industry names in order to be seen. "So and so said I should contact you . . ." or "Joe Blank said I was a perfect soap type."

Politics has always played a role in who gets in the door. It is impossible to deny an appointment to the CEO's daughter's sorority sister who wants to be an actress, the wife of the Wall Street connection, the star's relative, or anyone connected with the power. But ultimately, if there is no talent, discipline, dedication, the career will fizzle and fade.

Perhaps the most memorable example of an actress' determination to be seen for a role occurred at National Airport in Washington a few years ago. I was holding an open call for an ingenue role on one of our soaps. A young woman who had missed the audition drove to the airport, had me paged on the shuttle, and when I responded to the page, appeared at my seat so she could meet me.

When I had heard myself paged, I immediately imagined a family member was in danger. So, when I saw her, I admit I was unimpressed. Sensing this, she got off the plane. But she had made sure that the stewardess delivered to me her 8 x 10" and résumé.

Reflecting upon the incident later, I did call her, and she flew to New York at her own expense, where I had arranged an audition with the show's casting director. She didn't get the part. But she did earn a degree in Theater from NYU and is now starring in features and on Broadway.

When an interview is granted, some actors make the mistake of taking over the meeting. Pat House, owner of Actors Group, Inc., resents actors who use her time to do a monologue about themselves: "I end up feeding them reactions, like 'uh huh' or 'I see'. The interview should be a dialogue."

Mark Teschner, casting director of *General Hospital,* gives an excellent example of overdoing self-promotion. Several years ago an actress paid for tear sheets, which she had plastered outside the studios, bearing the question, "What Soap Will This Vixen Appear On?"

According to agent Bret Adams, one actress trapped a casting director in the ladies' room because she was unable to get an appointment with her. When this kind of desperation sets in, perhaps it is time for the performer to reevaluate the priorities and head for a saner place. It's most important to realize that agents and casting directors want to see a together, poised, healthy, self-aware, responsible human being walk in the door. Interview time should be quality time.

"I think", says Adams, "that many actors make the mistake of thinking that the longer they take in an interview, the better it is."

Instead of spending hard-earned money on gadgetry and gourmet delights, limo rides to showcases and tons of printed promotional propaganda, use it for the best picture — no Don Johnson stubble, bare chests, or provocative cleavage, please! — as well as an organized, truthful résumé, on wardrobe for the office visit, further training, and aerobics to keep in shape. Take advantage of networking opportunities and union-sponsored activities. Remember that once you get your foot in the door, you have to deliver the goods. Robert DeNiro never put his face on a matchbook!

COMPUTERIZED CASTING?

Within the past few years computerized casting has progressed from an idea ahead of its time ("Role Call") to something with real potential. Companies offering this variation on *Players' Guide* charge a set-up fee, which includes your photo and résumé information (which may be updated periodically). For an additional fee you may include clips of video and/or audio work to showcase your talent. The entire database is on a disk, which casting directors can view on their computer screens at home or in the office.

We polled agents, managers, and casting directors on both coasts for their reactions to computerized casting:

> Computerized casting will never compete with the creative process of looking at two actors doing a scene and creating characters, interacting with each other. The live moments do not happen on a computer. I couldn't get a gut reaction from a performer on a computer screen or a TV screen.
>
> —JUDY LEVERONE, *manager*

> I think it is a great idea. But I don't think you hire somebody without meeting them in person. It will help in the initial phase, but this biz is about how a person relates to you face to face. Plus, you don't know how long that person has worked on the scene you are seeing.
>
> —JEAN FOX, *manager*

> I don't think anyone uses computerized casting services. I think, in our end of The Business, casting directors trust the judgment of the agent, and if they go into the computer they are going to miss out on new people. I am computer unfriendly, anyway. My computer beeps at me all the time.
>
> —CAROLE INGBER, *agent*

> World Talent Bank is a very good tool for me, especially in commercials. I can use their database, and I not only get the picture of the actor, I get the résumé. It is a quicker reference than the *Academy Players Directory* or *Players' Guide*. If I need a juggler, for example, I can key into the jugglers in the database and see the picture and the background. It doesn't cut out legwork; it's just another tool at my disposal. Every month I get a new laser disk. It doesn't replace anything. Nothing will ever replace the hands-on approach.
>
> —JUDY HENDERSON, *casting director*

INTERACTIVE CASTING

Thanks to fiber optics technology, broadcast executives in one city can interview talent in offices anywhere else in the world. They can direct auditions, talk to the director in a studio control room, and see at a glance how the talent responds to direction, to the material, to other members of a cast. Certain casting directors feel that this can be a time-saving, money-saving, way to put actors and roles together.

I had an interactive callback session with L.A. I think actors in New York
will get more of an opportunity to audition for pilots and episodic shows.
—CAROLE INGBER

When you want to get your foot in the door, stick with the tools of the trade. Keep
current. Keep visible. Remember what you're doing here.

Remember that you're in it for the long haul. Work works. Timing works. Preparation works.

Maybe a short note that says something like, "I know you're busy, but. . . ." Or,
as one casting director put it: "KISS: Keep It Simple, Sweetheart!"

CHAPTER 5

GETTING YOUR ACT TOGETHER

Actors work and slave — and it is the color of your hair that can determine your fate in the end.

—HELEN HAYES

Did you know that studies have proved that within the first thirty seconds your appearance will indicate your social standing, your occupation, marital status, lifestyle, age, education, and financial stability?

Can you look at yourself objectively? If the package is you, the question is: what are you selling? What kinds of parts are you really right for?

When you look in the mirror, what do you see? Is that the real you? How connected are you to that person? Are you imitating some image you've seen in a magazine, or on a movie screen? A passing fad? How are you presenting yourself?

Ask yourself these questions: How do I want to be perceived? What impression do I want to make when I walk in the door? And when I walk out the door, what impression am I leaving them with?

In the glory days of the big Hollywood movie studios, those questions were answered for the performer by the studio production department. Rita Gam, who frequently refers to herself as the last of the MGM contract players, remembers that she and her roommate, Grace Kelly, were pampered, protected, coached, and styled for their screen debuts:

> We were taught to ride, to speak, to dress, how to be interviewed, how to move, how to stand up, how to "make a moment."

Talented designers, also under contract to the studio, created clothes to enhance, and eventually exemplify, the performer's image. The exaggerated shoulders and smooth, lustrous fabrics Adrian used for Joan Crawford's glamorous leading-lady persona are quite different from the unstructured, lace-collared, short-sleeved rayon frocks she wore as an ingenue.

Hair stylists, such as Sidney Guilaroff, created individualized coiffures. Makeup artists designed a special look. Claudette Colbert, Rosalind Russell, Myrna Loy, and Joan Crawford were all fair-skinned, dark-haired leading ladies, but no two of them wore the same hairdo, eye makeup, or mouth shape.

The image-making process operated for male performers as well. Think of some leading men of the period: James Stewart, Gary Cooper, Cary Grant, or Fred Astaire. None of them would wear the same cut in a jacket or slacks. Their sweaters, shirts, and ties would be different, as would their colors and fabrics.

That exquisite packaging which was the hallmark of the Hollywood studio glamour factory is now largely a memory. With the demise of the studio system, today's actors must develop an image themselves or seek expert guidance in the creation of it.

> I want to see that the actor is "together" when he walks through the door. It is not my job to teach him how.
>
> —BEVERLY ANDERSON, *agent*

Renie, the noted costume designer of the '40s and '50s who clothed such superstars as Greta Garbo and Clark Gable, gave concise advice on style which still seems appropriate today, even though her words were published in 1959:

> A good objective, wardrobe-wise, is to be interesting, individual, and truly one's self. You should wear clothes that make you happy.

Here are a few of Renie's tips:

1. Color and line are the governing factors in everything you wear that shows.

2. As you grow a bit older, an entire new color scheme can make you look more interesting than ever before.

3. Line means the changing line of style, and your best line is probably one that doesn't hug you too tight. To be elegant, be conservative.

4. A lot depends on the shape you're in.

5. Watch your posture! Learn how to get up gracefully from a table. Never slouch. Make your movements leisurely and sure, and look years younger.

6. Good shoes are not necessarily the most expensive. Heels can do wonders for the "feminine" leg.

7. Before you purchase slacks, shorts, or other sports outfits, install a full-length mirror with a rear view.

8. Buy clothes that match you and conform to good style in your community (New York vs. Los Angeles).

9. Best of all, take a good look at yourself. Everybody does!

Let's examine the components of your package, from top to toe.

HAIR CARE, SKIN CARE, AND MAKEUP
The eye immediately focuses on your hair, its color, condition, and style. Skin care is the most effective way to retard the aging process, protect the skin from the elements, and stay youthful and vibrant. Properly applied makeup can enhance and define your features.

GLORIOUS HAIR

Your hair color should complement your complexion, while the style frames your face and enhances your image. Stylists and colorists, like the image consultant, are trained to look at performers in terms of recognizable types. Let them know how you seek to present yourself. They will know what you're talking about and will undoubtedly offer helpful suggestions.

Alan Adler, hair stylist and perm specialist, and Tom Frasca, colorist, are a team whose theatrical clients have included Jill Clayburgh, Terri Garr, Kate Capshaw, Faye Dunaway, and Mary Steenburgen. They are located in New York's Gerard Bollei Salon. They firmly believe that actors exude a sense of drama, and their hair color and style should complement them visually, going beyond trends to project their individuality.

Frasca points out that when brunettes find they suddenly have to use more makeup, they may actually need to warm up their hair color.

> Some of the hair starts to get lighter; the effect becomes ashen, resulting in a flatter color. Perhaps a shade lift, to bring back color to the chestnut browns, burgundies, or mahoganies, whatever it takes to remove the ashiness. The skin tone will be enhanced, and daywear will look better. Retouching is necessary when too much of the contrast shows.

To cover gray or darken hair, he recommends semi-permanent, nonperoxide colors. Lightening, which requires peroxide or bleach, can create dimension and play up strong features — a benefit for men as well as women. For example, to draw attention away from a weak chin, highlight the hair around the eyes. When long hair is worn in an upsweep, lightening the underneath hair makes it look as though you are surrounded by backlighting.

> One of the biggest mistakes is to choose a hair color that doesn't harmonize with your skin tone. Yellow skin tone and red hair don't work well together, unless you choose a red with an orange base. Pale-skinned brunettes need a red with a blue base. Whatever the shade, hair color should look as though it happened naturally, on the beach, not as if it came from a bottle. Hair with highlights photographs better than one flat shade. When the contrast with your natural color becomes noticeable, it's time for a retouch — that's about every four to eight weeks.

Once the color is accomplished, Alan Adler suggests ways to improve the style. He feels that if you have great hair, you shouldn't get it cut too short. Keep hair longer in back, shorter in front. If your face is round, hair on the sides looks silly. If your face is oblong, long hair will only make it look longer. He advises a cut every four to six weeks to be on top of it.

> Think of hair as fabric, exposed to the sun, shampooed with detergents, dried with heat, and damaged by tight hats and rubber bands. Hair needs to breathe or it breaks. Fiber loses its shine, no matter how much conditioner you apply. To restore that luster, use *humectants*. These are

conditioners that add moisture you do not wash away. Use a small dab in the palm of your hand and work it first into the oldest hair — the ends — then through your scalp. Always brush hair before shampooing to loosen the scalp and work out the oils. Limp hair will wake up with a little sculpting lotion. Or add a body wave on top to avoid flatness.

Options for Versatility   Actors who start to lose their hair frequently rush to cover their baldness with a part-time toupee or permanent hair transplant. The toupee wearers should realize that nature has now given them two looks: leading man and character. We know an actor whose postcard showed him with and without his hairpiece. The clever caption read, "Toupee or not toupee."

Similarly, women who think their hair is the wrong length, texture, or fullness have the opportunity to use wigs, extensions, and hair weaving. Use whatever helps to connect you with your image, whatever works with your face shape. Because inclement weather can cause those "hair days from hell," take a curling iron or portable hot roller kit, purse-sized spray net, clips, scrunchies, brush, and/or styling comb, and head for the restroom to make the necessary repairs before an interview or audition.

A HEALTHY COMPLEXION

Women *and* men should cleanse, condition, and moisturize their skin regularly. Many dermatologists consider *exfoliating*, which rids the skin of dead cells and impurities, the single most beneficial thing we can to maintain a healthy complexion.

Know your skin type: sensitive, dry, oily, or a combination of these. If you have allergies or problems with acne, have your doctor prescribe a regimen for you. Otherwise, any drugstore or cosmetics counter will display a selection of brands for you to try. Many are supposedly allergy- and fragrance-free. What's most important is what works for you. Give each new item a fourteen-day trial. Buy small sizes to ensure freshness.

Cleanse your face at least twice daily, when you wake up and when you go to bed. Remove the dirt, grease, and makeup. Be sure you rinse away the cleanser, too; otherwise, you get that dry, tight, itchy feeling. Next, splash on a toner or freshener. Replace the moisture your skin tends to lose each day with a lotion or cream. If your skin is dry, use a richer night cream; otherwise, a moisturizer will do.

Using exfoliants, or facial scrubs, need not be a twice-daily process — once or twice a week will do. You can use a soft-friction cream, usually an almond paste that you dilute with water. Rub it gently all over your face and feel the tingling sensation. Regular use of exfoliants removes dead skin cells, diminishes blotchiness and gives your skin a healthy glow.

Your skin can benefit from a weekly facial mask — there are many varieties sold in drug stores as well as at cosmetics counters. A professional facial every other month will cleanse the pores and retard the aging process. Periodic collagen treatments will maintain the skin's elasticity.

You should always drink plenty of water, maintain a sensible diet, and exercise. During the day, always wear a moisturizer with an SPF (sun protection factor) of 15 or higher if your skin is sensitive or fair. Also wear tinted glasses to protect your eyes and to prevent your developing squint or frown lines. Just think, there may come a day when researchers will have developed gene therapy to retard and even reverse aging. Until that day comes, however, you should be aware that signs of aging are caused mainly by sun damage. Dermatologists are finding that exposure to the sun's rays is more harmful than originally suspected. A ninety-year-old Buddhist monk who never smiles, frowns, or exposes himself to the sun can appear at least forty years younger, but the rest of us have to rely on common sense and wide-brimmed hats.

There's another factor in sun protection: actors should *never* suddenly show up on the set with a sunburn. If it's necessary for purposes of plot or character, the makeup artist can always apply a dark basetone, but as a rule, producers don't want the leads in their period piece to look like they just got back from a Caribbean vacation.

MAKEUP TECHNIQUE

As Paula Begoun states in her exhaustively researched guide, *Don't Go to the Cosmetics Counter Without Me*:

> Knowing *how* to apply makeup is the key to looking your best. Spending more money does not mean you will look more beautiful.

Whether your face is oval, round, square, oblong, triangular, heart-shaped, or diamond-shaped, the idea is to apply cosmetics so expertly that you don't look painted. There are professional makeup artists working at department stores and cosmetics boutiques and as private consultants who teach application techniques. The most successful sessions are those where the makeup artist does one side of your face, and then you apply the same cosmetics to the other side. Doing the work at that moment reinforces the lesson. You will feel more confident when you go home and have to start from square one.

MAC cosmetics — the initials stand for Makeup Art Cosmetics or Makeup Against Cruelty — is a line of skin care and makeup products created in Canada that contains only natural ingredients, no chemicals, and is packaged in recyclable containers. (They make a nonglare base tone which is particularly good for use on camera.) At the original MAC shop in Manhattan's Greenwich Village, you can arrange for a makeup lesson or application. Their products are also sold in Henri Bendel, Bergdorf Goodman, and Nordstrom's.

Basic Application   Always cleanse the skin and apply moisturizer before you begin. Match the foundation, or base tone, to your skin and apply lightly. There should be no difference between the color of your face and neck. Some people like to dust a translucent powder over the foundation to set it. (The MAC Company's Studio FX is a combination foundation and powder in a compact; it produces a matte finish that matches your skin tone.) Blusher, or rouge, in cream or powder form, gives your face a healthy glow and helps to define shape. Apply the color sparingly on the apple of your cheeks, and blend up into the temples. Blush must never overpower the face! The lighter your skin tone, the lighter the shade of blush you need. Sheer tones enhance pale skin; cognacs and burnt sienna work well with ruddy complexions. Warm apricot and dark rose matte blushes complement black skin.

Eye Emphasis Brush your brows to neaten their shape and cleanse them of powder. Use a matching pencil, lightly, to fill in their shape. Eyebrows should never be darker than your hair. Consider your face shape. Women with square faces can have a slight curve in the brow to help soften the angles of the face. Round faces can have a slightly sharper brow line, with a little more arch. Women with oval faces (the most normal shape) are flattered by a rounder line.

Eye shadow will enhance and intensify the color of your eyes. Beige powder on the lid gives a very natural look and yet acts as a highlight. Darker shades at the lash line will define the shape and size. Taupes, browns, and grays complement all eye colors. Any hint of blue, green, or violet must be blended in perfectly.

Eye liner makes the lashes look fuller and lets the eyes stand out. Black gives most definition and looks most sophisticated. Brown is softer, more natural. Follow the curve of the upper lid at the root of the lashes. Do not extend the line beyond the outer corner of the lid. Use a light line on the lower lid. Don't join them at the corner; that closes the eye and makes it look smaller.

Next, apply two coats of mascara to your lashes. Avoid the heavy, beaded look. For your health's sake, replace your mascara every three months: bacteria collect on the wand. Do not buy refills. False lashes are an option to create the illusion of rich, full lashes.

Luscious Lips Your lipstick color should complement your skin tone and your wardrobe color. An orange dress and a fuschia lipstick are not a happy pair.

A lip liner or lip pencil lets you create a perfectly defined mouth and even allows you to extend your lip line subtly, correcting or enlarging the shape and size. A neutral brown liner slightly deeper than your natural lip color will work with virtually any lipstick color you own. Outline your mouth, fill in with your lipstick, and blot.

ADVICE FOR MEN

The same daily skin care, exfoliating, and moisturizing program is advisable for men as well as for women. Men who tend to have a heavy beard are smart to carry an electric razor whenever they have a late afternoon interview or audition so they can shave away the five o'clock shadow. Actors who wear a mustache should use an eyebrow pencil that matches their hair color when they want to achieve an even, overall tone.

THE POWER OF COLOR

There is no point in selecting a wardrobe until you understand how vital the power of color is in your total package. Casting directors and agents want to see you in a color! If you have money for only one outfit, be sure it is in your color palette.

According to color specialists Judy Lewis and Joanne Nicholson:

> Every woman can wear all the colors in the spectrum. It is the *shade* and *clarity* of the colors she wears that matters.

All of us have specific colors — whether they are dramatic, understated, or neutral — that look better on us than on others. Wearing the right colors next to your skin can have a rejuvenating, uplifting, and healthier impact on your overall appearance. You will know the colors are wrong if you suddenly look older, sallow, or blotchy, or your cheeks are drained of color.

If you have pale skin and dark hair, the jewel-tone colors — sapphire blue, emerald green, ruby red — and the icy pastels of the winter season will bring out your natural blush. Skin tone with a beige, pink, or ivory undertone wears the summery pastels extremely well. Yellow or peachy undertones suggest deeper pigmentation and the ability to wear clear spring colors or the golden-based hues of autumn. Some skin tones are balanced and can wear both cool-based and warmer colors. Remember, there are no absolutes. Wearing what makes you feel good when you put it on should be the rule of thumb. But bear in mind that you must wear the color; the color must never wear you.

The color you choose to wear to an interview can have a psychological impact on the interviewer. So choose carefully to avoid sending the wrong vibration. For example, red is associated with passion, ambition, desire, aggression, and self-sacrifice. It is the "I am" color. If you are meeting someone for the first time, be careful about the red you select. Avoid reds with too much yellow; they can overwhelm you. Reds with more blue in them — such as the wine colors, raspberry, and cranberry — or more brown — such as brick and terra cotta — will be less intimidating. Red is also effective as an accent color — scarf, tie, belt, or pocket square.

Green has a cooler energy and, like the color of the forest, is calming, nonthreatening, balanced, and restful to the eye. The deeper shades of green — jungle, emerald, and hunter — are terrific to wear to the interview and on camera as well. Blue is the color of trust, loyalty, and inspiration. Corporate executives in navy blue suits inspire confidence. If you want to appear honest and wise, wear blue.

Yellow is so bright and dynamic that it can cause anxiety and hyperactivity. It is more effective in a print design. Large doses should be avoided, unless you have a tan to balance the color. Orange may be the color of geniuses, extroverts, good negotiators, and safety on the construction site, but it cannot be worn by everyone. White is reflective and can upstage your face.

Black, technically, is the combination of all the colors and not a color at all. It is distancing, lacks vibration, absorbs color and light and can drain it from your face. Gray represents passivity and noncommitment. These shades keep your energy contained and can rob you of vitality.

Season after season, many *haute couture* designers stay within a very narrow range of color choices. Most of the time store windows show beige, sand-washed shades, and earth tones. You can always pick up neutrals and give them zest with a touch of color. Even a black and white combination can be enlivened with shades of red or hot pink in accessories.

Color triggers memory more readily than your name. If you see a casting director or producer making notes during your audition, it is probably a record of the colors you're wearing. After auditions, clients will frequently say, "You know, I really liked the girl in the purple jacket," or "Remember that guy with the red vest?"

An actress confessed that she wore a rose-colored blouse to a commercial audition, got a callback, wore the same blouse to the callback, and got the job. The connection and self-confidence she felt wearing that blouse impressed those who hired her.

You can learn more about your best colors by hiring an image consultant (discussed below) or by making an appointment with a professional color analyst. To find one with the proper credentials, contact the Association of Image Consultants International (AICI) at 1-800-383-8831.

DEFINING STYLE

In their book *Universal Style*, Alyce Parsons and Diane Parente have identified seven basic styles. We link them with name performers to give you a better sense of the look.

1. Sporty (friendly and casual): Tom Cruise, Tom Hanks, Katharine Hepburn, Jane Fonda

2. Traditional (conservative and businesslike): Dan Rather, Ted Koppel, Margaret Thatcher

3. Elegant (refined and stately): Cary Grant, Diane Sawyer, Audrey Hepburn

4. Romantic (soft and feminine women): Grace Kelly, Princess Diana; (handsome, sensitive men): Kevin Costner, Tom Selleck

5. Alluring (glamorous and sexy women): Ann Margret, Tina Turner; (sexy men): Luke Perry, Ed Harris

6. Creative (original and artistic): Robin Williams, Goldie Hawn, Arsenio Hall

7. Dramatic (fashionable and sophisticated): Al Pacino, Michael Douglas, Diana Ross

For example, if you are a *sporty male*, your wardrobe colors are earth tones such as tan, khaki, olive. Your favorite fabrics are easy-to-wear Oxford cloth, corduroy, or denim. The fit is loose, comfortable. Your hairstyle is short, loose, and carefree. Your shoe is a penny loafer or a sneaker. Your preferred daytime attire: sport jacket, button-down shirt, casual slacks.

In your closet hang some plain shirts, chinos, jeans, a jeans jacket, cable-knit sweaters, tweed sport coat, possibly a baseball jacket. For accessories you probably wear a chronograph watch, aviator sunglasses, wool knit and repp stripe ties, woven leather belts, argyle socks, and suede bucks. The labels you'd wear include Perry Ellis, Banana Republic, Boston Trader, Eddie Bauer, J. Crew, L.L. Bean, Nautica, and Gap. The overall message you want to communicate is that you are casual and approachable. And that is what you want to impart at the interview.

For the *feminine actress*, your primary style is defined by pastel wardrobe colors: pink, blue, lavender. The fabrics are fluid, lightweight challis, chiffon, and rayon. The fit is loose and flowing. Your hairstyle is soft, with face-framing curls, and your makeup is delicate, luminous. Your preferred daywear: a dress, with a pair of pearl earrings.

In the feminine closet hang suits designed to give the look of a two-piece dress, the tunic jacket/pleated skirt, or the sweetheart neck. Jackets can be slightly fitted at the waist, or loose. Skirt shapes can be wrap, side-drape, dirndl, gored, tiered, or full circle. Blouses can be gathered, or tucked, with rounded, ruffled, and lace collars. Shells are lacy. Sweaters are detailed with open work, embroidery, and applied trims. Shoes will be T-strap, bowed pumps, open-toe pumps, and soft ties. Belts are soft leathers and fabrics tied in a sash or bow, or adorned with open-work buckles. Jewelry includes cameos, pearl necklaces, heart pendants, lockets, and charm bracelets. Designer labels would include Gillian, Laura Ashley, Cachet, Jessica McClintock, and Valentino.

> Representing the realistic nineties, the styles have matured and are simplified. Traditional is less stuffy and more current; elegant has relaxed and become more youthful; alluring is less obvious, more restrained; dramatic is more approachable; and sporty is more polished and grown-up.
> —ALYCE PARSONS and DIANE PARENTE

For further information about *Universal Style,* write to: Parente and Parsons, Box 202, Ross, California, 94957.

> Ultimately, style is not what you wear but how you wear it.
> —CHITA RIVERA, *Tony winner*

> The way you dress is one of the biggest statements you make in life. Like it or not, you define your character and your opinions with it — politically, sexually, financially, religiously — with what colors you like, what shape you like.
> —BJORK, *pop singer*

> Style is in the end what goes on in a person's head and heart.
> —GIORGIO ARMANI

CHOOSING THE RIGHT ENSEMBLE

You do not need a closet bursting with clothes. Most fashion consultants will recommend buying the basics, and varying the look with accessories. A few well-fitting, quality pieces will do your wardrobe more good than several "on-sale" items that don't go together.

Basics for Women   Every actress should own a lined blazer, single or double-breasted, in a lightweight, year-round fabric such as 100 percent wool gabardine, twill, or crepe. Black, navy, khaki, cream, camel, and warm or cool shades of gray are the most versatile colors. Some solids such as jungle green or burgundy are optional and should last more than one season. When buying any jacket, avoid exaggerated proportions. You always want to look long and lean on camera.

Look for classic pleat-front trousers in wool gabardine or gray flannel. The shape and length of your skirt should be long enough and wide enough for you to feel comfortable. When you shop for skirts and slacks, bring the jacket with you, to ensure the right proportions and compatible colors. Do not invest in a mini skirt, even if you have great legs, because when you are seated it's impossible to keep from pulling it down, and that makes you look uncomfortable.

A long-sleeved white shirt has become indispensable, but choose simple, man-tailored styles without bows or oversize collars. Not everyone can wear bright white: it is reflective and can steal the focus from your face. It's best for people who have white teeth and large eyes, with a great deal of white around the pupil. If your eyes are small and your teeth are not pearly white, we suggest off-white or ivory.

Shells, blouses, shirts in crisp cottons, sheer linens, washed silks, and rayons in your best colors will add warmth to your ensemble and provide a variety of looks for your core wardrobe. The "little black dress" for evening can be accessorized and modified by adding color in a scarf, jacket, or belt.

Do not wear black next to your face. Allow a skin break between your chin and bust line. Wear jewelry such as gold, or warm metals, to give your skin a glow. And always wear makeup to add some drama.

Basics for Men In addition to the sporty clothing most men own, basic wardrobe elements include the medium- or dark-gray suit, pastel shirts (white may look best in life, but it's reflective on camera), and regimental stripe repp ties. The navy-blue blazer and gray flannel slacks are classics and know no seasons. Red ties always look good. Black shoes, either lace-up or step-ins, black socks, and belt.

It would be ideal to have a dozen shirts in all colors, like ivory, pale gray, sea-foam green, pale pink, and powder blue, plus patterns such as tattersall checks. If your budget can afford six shirts, include a couple with conservative stripes, plus two blue and two white.

BEFORE YOU BUY

Always do a closet review before you go on a spree. Discover what can be salvaged with a new hem, lining, alteration, buttons, trim, or even a new color. If there are items in your closet that you haven't worn in more than a year, give them to a homeless shelter. Get rid of what is no longer relevant or stylish, or doesn't fit. If you are squeamish about doing this, hire an image consultant who specializes in this area to assist you. It is an investment that can ultimately save you shopping time and credit card charges.

You should also know about *S & B Reports*, a monthly guide to New York City sales and bargains, showroom sales, retail sales, factory outlets, consignment shops, and discount services. Yearly subscriptions are $49. The same company publishes the *Outlet Shoppers Guide*, which contains information about 300 outlet centers around the country, and *Shop by Mail*, a mail-order guide to 850 companies.

For information write to: Lazar Media Group, Inc., 112 East 36 Street, New York, NY 10016.

YOUR HANDS, SMILE, AND VOICE

We cannot ignore three very important and frequently overlooked elements of your package. The first is your hands. They are your visual means of expression as a performer. They also do a lot of work during a normal day — carrying packages, making phone calls, reading newspapers, doing dishes, darting all over the computer keyboard. And they are quick to reveal age. Care for them with regular manicures. For women, pale pink or nude nail polish is the color of choice for TV commercials and soaps. Men can use a buffer to create shine and a rosy color. Apply hand lotion after putting your hands in water. We recommend wearing rubber gloves when you do dishes or similar work with your hands.

Other than your eyes, the one feature of your face that is always in motion is your mouth. What impression do you make when you open yours? Are your teeth straight? Is your jaw aligned? Advances in cosmetic dentistry make it easy to have a dazzling smile. Actress Lauren Hutton has shown that spaces between your teeth, which may interfere with your glamorous image, can be masked instantly with a removable flipper. Put your money where your mouth is in the most literal sense. Actors have lost roles because of their teeth, and one young actor won a role on *One Life to Live* after he had his large teeth filed to look more in proportion to his face.

Faye Dunaway, following her Lincoln Center debut, was summoned to a casting director's office for an interview. She was very insecure and never smiled. Asked why she seemed so uncomfortable, she admitted it was because of her "little pointy teeth." The casting director recommended a dentist for caps, and the rest is history.

The last element is your vocal means of expression: your voice. And that is not so immediately whipped into shape. What do you sound like? Does your voice match your look? We pay so much attention to externals, but unless you have a resonant, well-modulated voice on the telephone and in person, these efforts are pointless. Breathy, high-pitched, whiny, inaudible monotones announce the amateur. Take a lesson from Eliza Doolittle: She would never have been the Fair Lady if she hadn't learned to match her voice and her look.

THE IMAGE CONSULTANT

In the Fashion Supplement of *The New York Times*, William Grimes wrote:

> A good fashion sense is like a good sense of humor or a clever, fresh way of phrasing things.

News anchors, politicians, corporate executives, and professionals with high visibility depend upon the expertise of trained image consultants who have extensive backgrounds in fashion, retail, marketing, and communications. Their areas of expertise include personal shopping, color analysis, presentation skills, menswear, cosmetics, skin care, etiquette, and style. An image consultant will be able to zip through your closets and eliminate the unnecessary, the unflattering, the unwearable. The consultant may also discover a sensational treasure you've forgotten about, put shirts and skirts together in snappy combinations you somehow never thought of, suggest changes in trim, hemline, and even color. Most important, the consultant knows what you need and where to find it.

HOW THEY WORK

Your initial consultation with an image consultant may last more than an hour or even two. You discuss your experience, your career, what package you want to be selling. The consultant will analyze your color palette. The consultant can zero in on color choices that enhance your skin tone, your eyes, your hair. Having your colors done will forever take the guesswork out of shopping.

The image consultant may suggest a makeup artist, hair stylist, dermatologist, personal trainer, photographer, even a plastic surgeon, if necessary, and will assemble the wardrobe essentials for the looks that are right for The Business. These will include a general interview outfit; a good commercial outfit; industrial, glamour, and upscale looks — all with appropriate shoes and accessories. You'll always be confident that you look your best at interviews and auditions. You'll have someone to count on to help you prepare for a photo session, or a super-important callback when you've been asked to wear "something else."

Image consultants are listed in the Yellow Pages of the local telephone directory. You can also contact the Association of Image Consultants International, a world-

Noelle Neal

BEFORE

Actress Noelle Neal was helped by an image consultant in terms of hairstyle, makeup, and wardrobe. BEFORE: Photo by Drew Yenchak/Lighthouse Photography, Inc. AFTER: Photo by David Rodgers.

AFTER

BEFORE

Kathy Poling

AFTER

David K. Varnay was the image consultant who encouraged
Kathy Poling to see a plastic surgeon for rhinoplasty, and then
worked with her to change her hairstyle and wardrobe,
increasing her marketability. BEFORE: Photo by Tim Tew,
Studio Tew. AFTER: Photo by Sally Russ.

wide, nonprofit professional organization of men and women in the fields of fashion,
image, and related industries. Members have been professionals for a certain length
of time and adhere to a code of ethics.

For additional information, write: AICI, 1000 Connecticut Avenue, N.W., Suite 9,
Washington, D.C. 20036.

Remember that there's no single recipe for creating *the* image. Everything
depends upon your physical type, coloring, individual flair, and personality.

YOUR DIET

As you approach excellence in face, figure, interview technique, and overall appearance, remember to take care of the inner person. Shiny hair, healthy skin, strong
teeth, sparkling eyes, and an inexhaustible supply of energy come from proper nutri-

tion. A schedule of interviews, auditions, classes, and rehearsals requires stamina. A balanced diet, rich in fresh fruits, vegetables, and grains, is essential. Candy bars or pills are not the answer for quick energy.

> All the makeup and skin-care products in the world can't cover up an unhealthy lifestyle of no exercise, smoking, and a high-fat diet.
>
> —PAULA BEGOUN

Plenty of people, including the biggest names, brown-bag it through the day, toting fruits, nuts, raisins, strips of raw carrot and green pepper, wedges of cheese. They do this not because they are hypoglycemic or diabetic or to save the (high) cost of lunching in restaurants, but because they know how important it is to take good care of themselves. This is especially true when you spend a full day at the studio or on location. It's impossible to predict what kinds of foods are available in the vicinity. Catered shoots — which the crew always loves to dig into — may not supply what you should be eating.

You are your business, after all. Keep the package in perfect condition.

CHAPTER 6

SURVIVAL STRATEGIES

Oh, you're an actor! What restaurant do you work at?

Of the thousands of performers looking for work, almost as many thousands spend some time working at jobs outside the industry. To pay the rent, utilities and telephone bills, nonworking actors need survival jobs. We'd prefer you to think of these secondary occupations as survival strategies. Consider what they can do for you above and beyond helping you to keep the wolf from the door.

THAT'S NOT MY TABLE

Restaurant work seems to be what everyone thinks of first. There's no commitment, no long-term responsibility, and at the end of the evening you can gross a fair amount in tips. Swell. It's like a summer vacation job or working your way through college again.

> I can get a waiting job in about two seconds. I wish I had that confidence in getting acting jobs.
>
> —BRIAN LEDER, *actor*

> Waiting tables is hard. The key is to pretend you're playing a waiter!
>
> —BILL PENNELL, *actor*

If you are able to get a spot at Orso or Joe Allen — restaurants that cater to a theatrical clientele — you stand the chance of meeting, or at least seeing, some of the casting people and agents whose offices you want desperately to crack.

> Please do not talk to me when I eat. I go to a restaurant to relax or to talk business.
>
> —MARY JO SLATER, *casting director*

Many performers have been surprised to learn that at Joe Allen applicants audition for those choice table-waiting positions. There are a great many actors "between engagements," and the restaurant is in business to satisfy customers, not to provide actors with a neat way to make contacts.

If the tables you are waiting on are not at a theatrical restaurant, ask yourself, "Is waiting on tables really what I came to the Big City to do?" The job is, after all, menial, demanding, and tiring. We think you need more than that. You can go for alternatives that are rewarding, nourishing, that offer an outlet for your creative energy, and give you a positive sense of self.

What kind of job should you want? The umbrella description is this: Work that allows you to enjoy a sense of accomplishment and to have a measure of control. Work that will not turn you into a drone with tunnel vision. Work that will add to your personal experience, pay you a decent wage, and not tie you down to a schedule that's so tight you're merely trekking back and forth from job to home to job. If "tied down" describes how you're spending your time, you don't have a survival job, that's your life.

What skills do you bring with you? Are you computer-literate? You can register with any temporary agency in the city and even request assignments at offices related to The Business. You will work on the days you choose, at networks, advertising agencies, production houses; you'll see what goes on in the industry and possibly learn while you earn. Or you can work the late shift at publishing houses and banking institutions, earning as much as $18 an hour.

Do you have a good eye, and can you spell? Magazines may employ you as a freelance proofreader. You will be in a pleasant environment, exercising a technique that you need as an actor, getting pay and appreciation.

Office temporary agencies that like to hire actors — who are, after all, so presentable, outgoing, charming, and disciplined — advertise in the trade papers.

ON YOUR OWN

You can exercise greater control over your life by creating your own survival business. We've all read stories of the personal exercise trainers, gurus who serve a select group of executive clients. As a personal trainer you can schedule your time so that interviews and auditions never conflict with your work. Like actress Lyndi Patton, you might become an exercise instructor:

> To supplement my income I started teaching dance classes and began teaching people privately in their homes. My business is called Tone At Home. My background is in dance and exercise therapy. Just by doing the personal, at-home classes, I could pay for my acting and dancing classes, and I didn't have to be up all night waitressing. I could look good and feel good the next day.

Lyndi's Tone at Home business led to a series of fitness videos sponsored by a leading magazine, and doing those tapes expanded her camera experience.

Jacklyn Zeman, before she signed her contract on *One Life to Live*, was the manager of a slenderizing salon:

> I scheduled my hours around my interviews, kept myself in shape, and became a very good manager.

We know an actor who is an excellent masseur. He has a license and a portable massage table; he has no trouble finding clients whenever he needs to replenish his bank account.

What are your hobbies? Photography? — why not take photos of other performers? Astrology? — you surely know what a constantly absorbing subject that is. One actor did "charts," free of charge, for casting people he wanted to meet, but he also sold his knowledge of the future on a consulting basis to the public. What about Tarot? Channeling?

An enterprising young actor created a singing telegram business, which gave him the chance to perform every time he made a "delivery." With his fine voice and ebullient personality he got a lot of positive feedback, and built a list of enthusiastic clients in the business who call upon his services repeatedly. He has also established himself as a charming, talented, reliable performer, which has led to acting jobs.

Another runs a business that supplies party personnel — bartenders, waitresses, even omelette makers. Everyone who works for him is an actor. Parties are always fun and usually take place in the evenings or on weekends — no conflict with job-seeking.

Another actor fills the time between interviews with a job at a concert artists' bureau. "It allows me to get the nurturing I need."

One actress wrote on the back of her résumé that in addition to acting jobs, she was available for carpentry work! Do you have any idea how welcome a skilled, responsible, neat, craftsperson is?

Another young woman had acquired a knowledge of plants and flowers while she was working her way through college. When she came to New York she found part-time employment in Manhattan's flower district and became an expert at flower arrangements. Her extravagant bouquets were presented to all the celebrities participating in the Actor's Fund galas. She now has an impressive list of corporate clients, restaurants, and caterers. She notes: "Selling to clients is like acting, only you don't get the rejection!"

Another actress started a business designing hair ornaments. Some of Fifth Avenue's most exclusive stores have been her clients.

Robin Strasser, the definitive Dorian on *One Life to Live*, refused to learn to type because she didn't want to fall back on it. Instead she went to work in a boutique: "Selling clothes, to me, was a lot like acting."

If you know word processing, but don't want to tie yourself down to an office, you might consider creating attractive résumés for other performers. More than one alert actor has developed a part-time business answering the fan mail of one or more working performers — an occupation that keeps you right in the middle of the scene you want to be a part of. A young man who appears in a recurring part on *Loving* performs this service for several leading players on the show.

Freelance writing is another of several jobs you can do at home, in your otherwise free time. We know an actor who creates the copy for several of the catalogs we find in the mailbox.

Richard Frank, a graduate of the Juilliard acting school, turned his free time to good use by designing *The Starving Actor's Coloring Book*. When John Allen was starting out, he realized that there was no guide to nonunion summer theaters. He compiled such a reference, found ten friends willing to lend him $250 each to get it printed, and sold it himself to other aspiring actors he met at auditions.

Two actresses we know used the time between soap opera jobs by creating a theatrical tour business, employing other performers as guides. Out-of-town visitors were thrilled to be in the company of the very people they watched on TV. If you're knowledgeable about the city, you might enjoy working as a sightseeing guide and getting paid for speaking to audiences that will listen eagerly to every word you say.

> As a native New Yorker, I am in love with this city, and I know a lot about its past. Working on the Circle Line allows me to plan my schedule, perform in front of an audience, and sharpen my microphone techniques. And it's out of doors.
>
> —BERNARD FERSTENBERG, *actor-lecturer*

For the more than thirty years before he became an Oscar-winner for his performance in *Prizzi's Honor*, William Hickey had been teaching other actors while pursuing his own career. Tim Monich's specialty is speech: he helps foreign actors lose their accents and teaches American performers how to imitate foreigners. Alice Spivack became a dialogue coach, a survival strategy that has taken her all the way to Australia working on a film.

A few seasons ago, macramé was fashionable — wall hangings in hotel rooms and restaurants, hanging knotted plant holders filled with pots of ivy. Plenty of actors did very well tying those intricate knots. Are you interested in crafts? Do you knit, crochet, do needlework? You can teach, take orders for hats, vests, pillows, and possibly participate in crafts fairs all over the area.

What about training to be an image consultant? A makeup artist? A food stylist for commercials?

Did you ever think about the selling potential in that favorite secret recipe? Are you an adventurous cook? Perhaps the catering business beckons!

> Catering is hard work, but you make good money. I work for Glorious Food. There are 600 waiters, and they are mostly actors, writers, designers. You are constantly meeting people who may help you later on. It was through someone at Glorious Food that I started my Rita Hayworth show.
>
> —QUINN LEMLEY, *actress-singer*

Since you are already your own door-to-door salesperson, have you thought about becoming a part-time distributor of cosmetics, vitamins, pantry items? An actress we know was initially very tentative about showing friends the vitamins she'd bought from another performer. To her surprise and delight they became her first regular customers. Now her survival strategy allows her to rent a car and a summer house, plan a vacation, and best of all, thanks to her success she exudes confidence when she walks into an office.

You might think about telephone sales (now called telemarketing), or coaching. Selling a product is just a step away from being a product spokesperson — sometimes called a demonstrator. You may see one working in a department store showing you how to use the newest silver polish or hair ornament. Spokespersons may also tour the country representing a new product. They can talk to customers in shopping malls, lecture to organizations, or appear on local TV shows.

> I also travel around the country demonstrating Karaoke software. A
> friend of mine was hiring and had to find singers. It is a weekend job, so
> I have flexibility. And it pays you well.
>
> —QUINN LEMLEY

Your survival strategy should be geared to enhancing your estimation of yourself. The nature of the business requires that actors become adept at communicating on a person-to-person level. It's necessary to develop a manner that others perceive as charming, outgoing, pleasant, energetic, and confident. Try to capitalize on those attributes in your second occupation. And if at the end of all this you decide that you still want to be a waiter, be an energetic, smiling, attractive, marvelous one. Don't just wait, *serve!* Use the chance encounter with executives as an opportunity to show that you are a terrific, attentive, excellent waiter. If you are good enough, they will want to know who you are and whether you can act.

Think about it — you could be a taxi driver, going mad in traffic, never having time for lunch or a phone call, or you could take that same driving skill and become a chauffeur for a limousine company catering to celebrities. That, again, would put you in a place where opportunity can find you. You might even start your own limo service, using actors as your drivers.

Whatever you can do that is positive will serve you in every aspect of your existence. Work you loathe, work that is unrewarding, will taint your entire being.

> I came to New York in the 1970s, from the graduate program in theater
> at Southern Methodist University in Dallas, with no Equity card or
> agent. I found a cheap apartment, took temp jobs and waitressed.
>
> —DEBRA MONK

During her experience waitressing, the seeds of *Pump Boys and Dinettes* were planted. She collaborated with Jimm Wann, Mark Hardwick, and Cass Morgan, and together they appeared in the off-Broadway hit for two years. They also launched regional companies of the show. And all without an agent.

HELP FROM THE UNIONS

Equity, SAG, and AFTRA contribute funds to the Actors Work Program, brainchild of actress Joan Lowell. Members seeking training for a variety of new skills are first interviewed by a professional career counselor who then helps the performer to plan a second career.

> I have interviewed over 2,000 people. I know the actor personality. Actors
> are unique. They have drive, energy. They are communicators. And they
> are so versatile. I force them to focus, to channel energy, to set goals.
>
> —DR. RONDA ORMONT, *career counselor, Actors Work Program*

The Actors Work Program began as a service for mature members who were getting beyond the truly productive years as far as roles were concerned. Now, new members are taking advantage of the service.

Second careers are essential. We can see that it's happening throughout our economy.

—Joan Lowell, *actress, founder, Actors Work Program*

Thanks to a roomful of new computers, training in word processing — and the instrument to practice on — is available right on the premises. Career seminars are offered throughout the year. Funding for special education is frequently provided.

> One of our people decided to become a nurse. She graduated at the top of her class. She has been sent to Washington to meet with Hillary Clinton. And she says, "In my new role as a nurse I am doing so much more to help people." If you can develop another interest, another career, then you can cope with auditions. You can say *no* to a role you don't like. You can let your agent negotiate a better salary, because you're not afraid of losing the role just because you asked to be paid what you think you're worth.
>
> —Joan Lowell

Their high rate of success has made the Actors Work Program a model for more than nineteen other social service agencies. Headquartered in the Equity Building at 165 West 46th Street, the service is available to union members at no cost.

EXAMINE YOUR PRIORITIES

Some time ago, one of the New York newspapers, in a feature describing the offstage lives of actors who were a long way from being bankable names, told of an actress who began each day cleaning offices in a shabby part of the city, working with broken equipment, all alone. The description of her daily routine was unbearably sad. How, we wondered, could this young woman hope to succeed? Each day began on such a note of despair, it would take superhuman resources to rise above that daily dose of negative energy.

That is not the way to be an out-of-work actor. That's punishing yourself. That's not what you left home for. And if that is all you can do, stop and rethink your plan.

> Some people get trapped in a rut. If you are catering all the time or working in a restaurant, what is the point of being in New York? You are here to be an actor. You still have to study. You always have to keep reinvesting in yourself. It is an expensive proposition to be an actor. But there are ways to do it.
>
> —Quinn Lemley

You may need to take a year off from The Business, save every penny you can, see everything you can, learn. Then when you've restored your own confidence in yourself, think about beginning again. You don't have to be twenty-one to begin an acting career or even to continue it. You can begin at any age, so long as you give yourself a real chance.

CHAPTER 7

UNDERSTANDING THE UNIONS

I am very fond of Mr. Ziegfeld, and enjoyed working for him, but my duty is to stand by the actors and see that justice is done.

—EDDIE CANTOR

Professional actors belong to three unions: Actors Equity Association (AEA, or just "Equity"), Screen Actors Guild (SAG), and the American Federation of Television and Radio Artists (AFTRA). These are, in turn, members of an umbrella organization, the Associated Actors and Artistes of America, known as the Four A's, chartered by the AFL-CIO.

In simplest terms, Equity has jurisdiction over performers and stage managers in live theater. SAG covers performances — movies and commercials — on film. AFTRA's jurisdiction includes live and taped television shows, soap operas, and commercials, radio, and recordings; its membership, in addition to actors, singers, and dancers, includes announcers, disc jockeys, talk-show hosts, stunt people, sportscasters, and news persons.

In an arena that prizes individuality, where a performer's personal magnetism can be so captivating that it overrides lack of technique or inspires an audience to forgive banal writing or insipid production, where the "powerful chemistry" between two performers can translate into a surge in ratings, the idea of performers belonging to a union may seem downright absurd. What, after all, can such free-spirited, highly distinctive artists have in common with those more or less anonymous people who deliver packages or work in offices and on assembly lines?

One essential feature unites them — they all work for their living. And the work they do can be quite specifically defined. Moreover, the people who employ them, simply by virtue of the fact that they control jobs, are powerful and may even belong to power-enhancing organizations of their own. So, like seamstresses, bolt tighteners, and countless others, actors (and singers, dancers, announcers, and news persons) have found that by forming a union they gain a measure of clout.

Through the process known as collective bargaining, representatives of performers (unions) and employers (producers, networks, and ad agencies) arrive at agreements regarding performers' wages and working conditions. The resultant contracts establish the minimum salaries — or *scale payments* — for performances on stage, film, records, television, or radio. There are also agreements covering what is known as nontheatrical employment, such as industrial shows, educational or documentary films, and material recorded for purposes other than commercial broadcast.

Today's union members are the beneficiaries of the gains their predecessors risked their careers to obtain. The high unemployment rate notwithstanding, union scale — $504 for a day's work in film; $435 for a principal role on a half-hour soap opera, and $580 for an hourlong soap opera; $414.25 for shooting a TV commercial; or $950 as the weekly salary for a Broadway show — would appear to be acceptable compensation. With health insurance, pension coverage, and cost-of-living adjustments (COLAs) — all history-making benefits when they were first achieved — it's easy for new arrivals to think there's nothing a union can "do" for them.

Veterans become indignant at this attitude. On hearing the newest young leading man boast that his slightly over-scale salary was evidence that the producer valued the "pizzazz" his performance would add to the show, the matriarch of one of the long-running soaps, whose distinguished career has encompassed theater, films, and television, raised her cultured voice so that everyone in the commissary could overhear: "Darling," she purred to the young man,

> You would be working gladly for $5 without the efforts that all of us have put in for years. You think they're paying you all that money because they're in love with your blue eyes and your talent? Don't be a fool. They're paying you because a lot of actors who worked for a lot less money than you fought to get those minimums up to a decent level. You are riding on the shoulders of all those other people, and don't you ever forget it!

With her passionate words as our cue, let's take a brief look at the way things used to be and how they've changed.

A BRIEF HISTORY

Professional theater has been part of American culture since colonial times. European settlers brought the theatrical tradition from their homelands. President George Washington enjoyed the theater — *The School for Scandal* was his favorite play — and his regular attendance helped to popularize playgoing. By the end of the eighteenth century, touring companies headed by actor-managers — performers who had risen through the ranks to head companies of their own — entertained audiences in most of the cities east of the Mississippi River. Years of tradition had defined the way an acting company operated and the actor's place within that unit. One could sign a contract with these employers and be certain of what was expected.

In the boom following the Civil War, the development of transportation opened up the country west of the Mississippi, and the theater surged along with the rest of the nation's businesses. Hitherto independent theater owners and managers formed associations. Instead of traveling informally from one locale to the next, touring companies were now routed along circuits dominated by theater chains. Stars such as Edwin Booth, John Drew, and Sarah Bernhardt toured the country in lavish productions, receiving such acclaim that by the end of the nineteenth century acting had become recognized as a glamorous, rewarding profession.

In 1896, an important booking office known as the Theatrical Syndicate was organized to supply shows, systematize the production and financing of attractions, eliminate wasteful competition, and prevent booking tangles. By the turn of the century, the Syndicate could dictate which productions would play in what theaters, which actors would appear in them, and what the financial terms would be. The actor-managers, such as Joseph Jefferson, Richard Mansfield, Fanny Davenport, Minnie Maddern Fiske, David Belasco, and James O'Neill (father of playwright Eugene O'Neill) now had to contend with a new species of theater citizen: the efficiency expert/manager, who knew nothing of theatrical tradition and cared less.

To these businessmen, actors were not the backbone of the theater. They were merely one of many cost items on an income statement, to be obtained as cheaply as possible. So tyrannical did the Syndicate become, and so severe its terms, that the great Sarah Bernhardt bought herself a tent and toured the country playing in it, rather than accede to their demands.

There was no standard contract. The managers wrote a different agreement with each performer, demanding concessions and inserting loopholes. There was no minimum wage. There was no pay for rehearsals and, because they were free, there was no limit to them. Eighteen weeks of rehearsal was not unusual for a musical show; ten weeks was the average for a straight play. Actors worked seven days a week, doing as many performances as the managers wanted.

Under his contract with the Shubert organization, one unfortunate actor rehearsed twenty-two weeks and played only four nights. Incredible as it may seem, he appeared in three plays: the first ran two days while the other two ran one night apiece. According to his contract he was entitled only to payment for the performances played — four days out of twenty-two weeks.

According to the late Conrad Nagel, a film and stage star:

> Stock companies doing doing ten performances a week — seven evening shows and three matinees — while rehearsing the next week's play each morning, were not unusual.

Salaries could be paid any day of the week following performance — whenever the manager got around to it. Holidays, as now, were peak attendance periods, yet managers paid half-salary for Christmas week, Easter week, and Election week, regardless of business or whether or not there were any elections.

The centuries-old custom of two weeks' notice was abolished. Managers could label actors "unsatisfactory" and fire them on the spot. Shows could be closed with no warning to the cast. More than a few managers were in the habit of leaving town while a performance was in progress, taking the entire week's receipts with them. The abandoned actors, unable to pay their hotel bills, had to sneak out of town on their own — which may explain why so many innkeepers on the touring company circuit posted the warning, "We do not rent to theatricals!"

Many managers refused to pay transportation from New York to the opening town, or from the closing city back home. So, if a show opened in Wilmington, Delaware, and closed in St. Joseph, Missouri, the actors had to buy their own tickets to Wilmington and from St. Joseph back home.

The West Coast company of Victor Herbert's *The Enchantress* was stranded in Los Angeles. Among the ads for "Snooky-Ookum" dolls and Teddy Bears (which were hawked between the acts), the November 8, 1913, issue of *Billboard* carried the notice that the production was abruptly canceled and that the cast of sixty-seven performers and stage managers had "to look otherwise than to the management for railroad tickets back to Broadway."

Performers were also required to supply their own wardrobes, a particular hardship for the women in a company. The cost of elaborate costumes, which they could use nowhere else, could be greater than the salary they received if the play closed early in the run. The actress Clara Morris wrote that at the start of her career, in the 1870s, she was particularly proud that she was "gifted with her needle" and found ways to rework the fabric of her gowns again and again; no one in the audience realized that she was, in effect, wearing the same dress she had toured in during the previous season.

Dressing rooms, usually in the cellar or at the top of the building, were filthy, unheated spaces. They rarely had running water or sufficient space to set out makeup and change one's clothes.

A UNION OF THEATRICAL PERFORMERS

That was how matters stood in May of 1913, when 112 performers, men and women, met in a hotel ballroom near New York's Columbus Circle and agreed to form the Actors Equity Association. They adopted a constitution, elected officers and a council (among whose members were such stars as George Arliss and Charles Coburn), and set about trying to achieve a standard contract which covered seven key issues:

• Free transportation from New York back to New York

• A limit on free rehearsal time

• The re-establishment of the two weeks' notice clause

• Protection from dismissal without pay for actors who had rehearsed for more than one week

• No increase in the number of extra performances without pay

• Full pay for all weeks played

• Adjustment of the situation regarding women's costumes

Negotiations with the managers dragged on for six years. The managers were determined not to give in on any item. Finally, in the summer of 1919, the membership — now grown to more than 2,500 — voted to strike. In this drastic action they had the support of featured players and chorus people as well as the leadership of major stars — among them Eddie Cantor, who was rehearsing for the *Ziegfeld Follies*, Ethel Barrymore, Pearl White, Marie Dressler, and the beloved comedian Ed Wynn, then starring in *The Gaieties of 1919*.

On August 7, the cast of *Lightnin'* informed the management of their theater that they would not perform that evening. There was more than ordinary drama in the announcement. *Lightnin'* was actor Frank Bacon's first Broadway success, after more than twenty years in stock companies and on the road; as star, author, and part-owner of a hit show, he was seeing his first real chance to make some money and enjoy a strong career. If the strike failed he would surely lose everything and have to return to playing the provinces. Yet he ordered the walk-out without hesitation. He said: "When this whole thing began, my wife said to me, 'We'll stick to our own people. I can still cook on a one-burner oil stove, if necessary.' So, we're stickin'."

It was Bacon and the cast of *Lightnin'* who led the enthusiastic parade of 2,000 actors, dancers, and musicians marching down Broadway from Columbus Circle to Madison Square. The stagehands brought up the rear, carrying a banner: *Nations arbitrate, though managers won't.*

Sympathy and support for the performers came from unexpected places. Land-ladies of theater-district rooming houses, where so many chorus dancers lived, stopped asking for the weekly rent while the dancers were on strike. Taxi drivers pasted *Equity for Actors* banners on their cabs. Merchants on 45th Street donated 10 percent of their gross to the Equity strike fund, and Broadway-area shops offered discounts to striking actors. One cigar store owner posted this sign in his window: *Striking actors get your cigarettes here, pay me when you win.* The management of Gimbel's, the big department store on 33rd Street and Sixth Avenue, phoned Equity to offer jobs to any actors who needed them.

When a fifteen-car motorcade driven by leading men and filled with "the prettiest strikers in history" rode through the Financial District, the Curb Exchange (now the American Exchange) declared a recess and gave them an ovation. This audience understood that entertainment was the fourth-largest industry in the United States. They told passersby, "Their cause is just."

Frank Case, proprietor of the Algonquin Hotel, offered free space to the Equity Publicity Committee and their clerical staff. For the duration of the strike, he had their meals delivered to the meeting room. He not only refused to accept payment for the food, he also donated $1,000 to the Equity strike fund.

Through it all, the managers refused to recognize Equity or the contract. Secretary of Labor William Wilson sent two assistants to New York to persuade the managers to negotiate. New York's governor, Alfred E. Smith, met with both sides in an attempt to get the managers to settle. Their efforts were fruitless.

And then Samuel Gompers, president of the American Federation of Labor, returned from the Versailles Peace Conference. Whisked to a special Equity meeting, he announced to the members and the waiting reporters that all the power of the American Federation of Labor was lined up behind the actors. The actors were ecstatic. And the managers suddenly paid attention. Minutes before midnight on September 6, 1919, the first Equity contract was signed. The strike was over.

The actors' strike of 1919 lasted thirty days. Before agreement with the managers could be reached, the strike had spread to eight cities, closed thirty-seven plays, prevented 167 from opening, and cost actors and managers about $3 million. During the strike, membership in Equity increased to more than 14,000.

SCREEN ACTORS GUILD

Twenty years after the first Equity Meeting, a handful of film stars met at the Masquers Club in Hollywood to discuss what could be done to improve their working conditions. Hollywood was turning out 600 films a year. To do this, everyone had to work six days a week, with no limit on hours. Actors could finish a day's shooting after midnight and be told to report back on the set at 9 A.M., which meant arriving at 7 A.M. for makeup, hair dressing, and wardrobe. Allowing for travel time often meant a 5 A.M. wake-up call. Meal periods occurred at the producer's convenience.

There were no uniform requirements for compensating actors for travel time to and from locations. There were no restrictions on weather-permitting calls. There was no arbitration machinery for handling contract disputes. Under the studio system, a handful of moguls controlled the industry. Contract players were property to be developed, groomed, and improved — and lent out to other studios at a profit.

One actress who had been under contract to Metro-Goldwyn-Mayer said:

> I was only in five pictures at MGM. By being lent and sent around to other studios and independents, I made two dozen pictures in five years. My hair changed color in every picture. We had nothing to say about our appearance. We weren't asked. We were told.

In March of 1933, the moguls decreed that contract players would have to accept a 50-percent reduction in salary (nonstars earned about $75 a week), and pay for free-lance actors would be cut 20 percent. With no organization to turn to, they had to take the cut. Talk about a union became serious.

Articles of incorporation were filed on June 30, 1933. The eighteen founding members named Ralph Morgan their first president. Within the year membership rose to 2,000. Eddie Cantor — as big a star in films as he was on Broadway and radio — was then elected president.

Lyle Talbot, one of the first members, remembered Cantor's impact:

> He gave us a big boost. I'll never forget the day we got a phone call from Eddie in Washington, D.C., telling us that we had been recognized as a labor union. He was a wonderful man, and very important in getting this guild off the ground.

Getting the contract took four years and many meetings for which actors parked their cars blocks away from meeting places so as not to be seen and penalized by the producers. Their contract proposals covered the following:

- An eight-hour day, with fifteen hours of rest between calls

- Regular one-hour meal periods

- Sundays and holidays off

- Overtime pay

- Payment for transportation expenses

- Contracts in writing, with a copy of the contract given to the actor

• Continuous employment pay (Several nights might elapse between calls for the same part, during which time the actor had to be available and could not accept work from anyone else, yet was paid only for days actually on the set.)

In May of 1937, the producers finally accepted the guild's demands. The membership of 5,000 had voted to strike the studios. President Robert Montgomery, also a major star who had been instrumental in establishing the guild, declared "the victory of an ideal." Scale was $25 per day.

FROM AFRA, TO TvA, AND AFTRA
The last of the major talent unions to organize, the American Federation of Television and Radio Artists (AFTRA), is the result of a merger between AFRA — the American Federation of Radio Artists, chartered by the Four A's in August of 1937 — and Television Authority, TvA, which had been established in 1950. The merger was effected in 1952.

In her entertaining book *Tune in Tomorrow*, veteran radio actress Mary Jane Higby recalled that, in the early days of radio, performers received $5 for an hour-length program which they might have rehearsed for two days. Sometimes performers were expected to work merely for the glory of doing the show. When Barbara Luddy, a noted radio actress, asked the producer of *Hollywood Hotel* how much she would be paid for her appearance as the female lead on the show, she was told, "You're not getting paid, you're getting billing!" It took great courage for her to face a powerful producer and maintain that she could not afford to work for nothing.

> Movie actors were frequently "invited" to appear on radio shows to talk about their latest film. Then they'd do a dramatization of the picture, with four or five actors working for free.
>
> —CONRAD NAGEL

In New York and Chicago, small bands of performers, proficient at reading a script and delineating a character, gained a foothold in the industry and manage to do quite well. Some extremely versatile actors played two and even three roles in the same show. However, as more and more radio stations were licensed, more and more performers joined the talent pool, and producers, whose ranks were also growing, realized that someone was always willing to work for less money. Before long, according to Ted de Corseia, one of those first performers:

> Every agency was trying to do it a little bit cheaper. We'd spend the whole day rehearsing, with no meal breaks, or even time for coffee, and end up with a check for $11.88 for the show and for the repeat [the rebroadcast of the same show three hours later for stations on the West coast].

In his articles in *The New Yorker*, in 1948, James Thurber stated the matter succinctly:

> . . . Before the American Federation of Radio Artists and the Writers' Guild were formed, the broadcasting industry took easy and cynical advantage of actors and authors.

Fortunately, many stars, who had been down the same road with Equity and SAG, were among the earliest supporters of the idea of a union. At the first meeting of what was originally called the Radio Division of Actors Equity, some nominees for the board of directors were Eddie Cantor (who later served as AFRA's first president, as he had with SAG), Don Ameche, Jack Benny, Bob Hope, Bing Crosby, Edgar Bergen, Rudy Vallee, Dick Powell, Martin Gabel, and Helen Hayes.

Hearing that New York, Los Angeles, and Chicago performers had embarked upon the formation of a radio union, performers working at stations across the country wrote to the nearest headquarters requesting help in organizing their area. Within the year there were AFRA locals in cities across the country.

Management seemed to understand that AFRA's proposals for a code of fair practice benefited employers as well as talent: with standardized payment, rehearsal rates, and times, they could, in a sense, stop worrying about whether they were getting the biggest bargain and concentrate on getting the best work done. The first contracts between AFRA and the networks were signed in July of 1938.

HOW THE UNIONS WORK

Equity, SAG, and AFTRA are unique among labor organizations in that they are governed by the members. There are differences in their specific structures, but essentially they are run by councils or boards of directors whose elected members are volunteers and serve with no remuneration. The policies determined by these bodies in weekly or monthly meetings are then executed by a staff of paid executives.

Contract demands are formulated by volunteer committees made up of performers active within each field. Their proposals for wages and working conditions are presented to the union's highest governing body, the annual convention or meeting of elected delegates. At the convention the proposals are accepted, rejected, or modified. The executive staff then attempts to negotiate the union demands with management.

While the unions cannot get any performer a job, they protect all performers in their relations with employers. By negotiating and then policing their contracts, the unions guarantee minimum salaries and the conditions under which performers will work.

As we've seen, working conditions include such things as length of rehearsal, meal periods, place of rehearsal (you cannot be made to rehearse in an unheated barn in the wintertime), time between calls, manner of transportation, and performer safety. This last is a newer concern, as movies and TV films (and even daytime serials) seem increasingly to search for outrageous situations and locales in which to deposit their leading characters. The pressure upon performers to be courageous good guys and perform their own stunts can be heavy, so trained persons are required to be on the set to perform all of those feats.

Union representatives regularly visit studios, production centers, and location shoots to make certain that contract provisions are observed and that union members who have paid their dues are being employed. The field reps also deal with any member complaints about the day's work. These are handled with absolute secrecy as to the identity of the performer; no actor who voices a legitimate complaint need ever fear reprisals.

In long-running situations, such as theatrical productions and TV serials, an elected cast member, the deputy, serves as liaison for the cast, the union, and the management. Members bring concerns about the show to the deputy; management, when it feels a performer is acting irresponsibly, brings that to the notice of the deputy.

The union contracts also guarantee that you will be paid within a certain time after your performance; otherwise a late payment penalty is invoked. You should not ever have to call an employer to find out when or if your "check is in the mail."

In certain instances, AFTRA and SAG receive and distribute the payments for session fees and reuse. "Residuals," the payments for rebroadcasts of programs and commercials, now form the bulk of the earnings of SAG and AFTRA members. While it may seem obvious nowadays that recorded material is a performance, winning reuse payments was difficult. Management people had argued that if session fees were set high enough, performers should not expect to be paid for work they'd already been compensated for. At that time it was inconceivable that programs would be rerun for decades, as they seem to be now. There was not today's density of commercials: ten-, twenty-, and thirty-second spots, making air time for more (rerun) commercials, were nowhere on the horizon. But then it *was* already known that certain former stars whose films were televised constantly on Saturday mornings received not one cent from those uses, and were even living in poverty. George Reeves, the actor who played the first Superman in the half-hour weekly series, filmed in the early 1950s, suffered from this; when the children of America were watching him years later (as they are to this day), he received no residuals, no income, from any of the stations carrying his show. Meanwhile the stations were charging sponsors top dollars to advertise on the program. At the same time, he was so identified with the role that he was unemployable!

The point was won, and today the life of a performance in commercial or program material is protected through a system of use and reuse fees. The unions maintain departments devoted to processing of residual checks and monitoring reruns of recorded material. Recent developments in the fields of cable, pay-TV, and videocassettes mean that the principle of payment for performance will be increasingly important.

Hardest fought for, and possibly their most significant achievement, were the unions' health and retirement plans. These are totally financed by employer contributions based on a specified percentage of each performer's salary, original payments, and reuse fees. The retirement plans thus manage to offer a modicum of financial security to retired performers, based upon their earnings and length of employment. With group medical coverage (and life insurance), for which members qualify by earning a certain amount of money within the union's jurisdiction each year, performers are freed from the terrible fear that unexpected medical expenses will bankrupt their families. The funds are jointly administered by representatives of industry and the unions.

The unions also regulate the business relations between actors and talent agents. Union members may not be represented by any person or firm not franchised by the union in which the agent hopes to be able to get the actor work.

National and local publications inform members about all union activities. The publications also publish lists of franchised talent agents, incoming productions, and even performers who have residual checks waiting. They also frequently call attention to pending legislation that will affect performers.

ADDRESSING ISSUES

Union concerns reach beyond money matters. It was a committee of SAG that first monitored TV commercials and then agitated for a change in the way women were portrayed in them. "We do other things besides the laundry," their report stated.

Equal Employment Opportunity committees of the three unions have pressed for better minority representation in casting. In this they fortunately have had the support of many in management. Micki Grant became the first black actress to play a feisty young woman attorney, after the casting director of *The Edge of Night* asked the producer of the show: "Does this character have to be white? Male?"

To alert management to the creative possibilities of nontraditional casting, SAG has engaged an affirmative-action administrator who presents seminars to advertising agency executives and clients' representatives across the country and screens for them a reel of award-winning commercials whose principal players are either senior citizens, disabled or handicapped people, or members of ethnic minorities.

Recently, the results of a year-long survey which monitored ten years of programming and recorded the invisibility of senior citizens, women, nonwhite, and handicapped people, made front-page news. In response, the ABC Broadcasting Companies initiated a nationwide talent search in regional markets.

Still another SAG committee, reporting on ripoffs by phony talent agents, provided sufficient documentation to the office of the Attorney General of New York to effect a crackdown on the offenders and create the office's warning brochure for the industry.

Through its Memorial Foundation, AFTRA offers several scholarships to eligible members and their children. These grants were established in the memory of past union leaders. Some are expressly for persons interested in the performing arts, labor relations, or music; others are available for any course of study.

With each new contract negotiation, the unions press for greater access to casting information and for member preference at auditions. Equity has required that theatrical producers hold EPAs (Eligible Performer Auditions) at which a representative of the production must be present to receive photos and resumés from Eligible Performers — union members or nonmembers — who have sufficient experience to qualify as professionals.

INCOME TAX ASSISTANCE

One of the most successful membership activities is a program initiated by the late Michael Enserro, a fine character actor. He saw that people in the business had special problems in making out their income tax forms because of the sporadic nature of their work, because they worked for multiple employers during the year, and because they had unusual deductions. He set out to provide help in the form of Volunteers Providing Income Tax Assistance (VITA). At first, Enserro was a one-man committee, working each spring at Equity's offices. Now, the work he began is carried on in his name, at Equity and AFTRA, by a growing committee of trained volunteers, headed by actor Conard Fowkes. Appointments with VITA volunteers are available from the first of February each year.

CREDIT UNIONS

As we noted in Chapter 1, performers have historically had difficulty establishing credit. Banks, in particular, looked down upon them as irresponsible and refused to consider them for loans. Twenty-five years ago, one of the leading actors on a daytime serial, who'd always paid in full for everything when she bought it and had been advised to establish credit, was told by a bank officer that, since her show could be canceled the next day, she could not borrow $800. The program is still on the air.

In 1961, Conrad Bain — you may remember him from *Diff'rent Strokes* — and Theodore Bikel — who is now the head of the Four A's — were the instigators of an effort to protect their fellow actors from this prejudice. Through their efforts, and with the support of the membership, the Equity Federal Credit Union was established. Within a few years, AFTRA in New York and, later, AFTRA and SAG jointly on the West Coast, followed Equity's example.

The Actors Federal Credit Union (the New York AFTRA and Equity credit unions have merged) now offers checking accounts, and its own low-rate Visa card to members who maintain a qualifying balance. This recently was welcome news to one of the cast members of *One Life to Live* who, despite her steady income and much higher-than-average salary, was rejected by two major credit card companies. She joined the Actors Federal Credit Union and received her credit card with no trouble.

> Of course, actors are still interviewed for loans. We do have to know that the money can be repaid. But at least you are interviewed by someone who understands the sort of life you lead.
> —ARTHUR ANDERSON, *a past Credit Union president*

Enlarging the scope of member services whenever possible, the Credit Union now offers the possibility of low-cost mortgages, car loans, and even an investment advisory service.

LOCAL AUTONOMY

Union branches, or locals, are free to engage in whatever membership activities the members vote for and are willing to finance. AFTRA locals in Boston, Chicago, Miami, Philadelphia, and Washington/Baltimore distribute talent directories to the industry. Locals in San Francisco, Portland, Atlanta, Cleveland, Miami, and New York, maintain Casting Hot Lines. SAG and AFTRA in New York have each invested in top-of-the-line audio and video equipment that members, who pay a small annual fee, may use to improve their skills. The fees cover the cost and maintenance of the equipment. Member volunteers teach others the fine points of soap opera, voice-over, and commercial technique.

In other cities, union members are able to arrange for seminars, weekly rap sessions, workshops, showcases, or outings that allow members to get to know one another and to network.

And, of course, all of the union offices offer the essential members' bulletin board, where one can learn about apartments, equipment, classes, scenes, possible roommates, car rentals, jobs, lessons, or even whose adorable pet needs a new home.

MEMBERSHIP IN THE UNIONS

We have gone into some detail about what the unions have been able to achieve for the members. There is a reverse side to this picture: what the members are obliged to do — not for the union, per se — but for the professionalism of the whole.

Actors must do their jobs to the best of their ability. Actors must be on time, must be prepared to work, and must abide by the contracts they have signed. Actors must know what their responsibilities are. Actors must comply with union regulations. Actors must let the union know where they live and can be reached (so they can receive those hard-won residual checks in the mail).

It's fine to know that an employer can be penalized for late payment of your session fee or for failure to break for lunch within five hours of your original call. You should know that performers also can be disciplined, and have been, by their peers. Stars have been fined for failure to honor contracts. Actors who have jeopardized productions have been called to account for it. Like civilization as a whole, The Business is a complicated mechanism, delicately balanced. It only works when we all respect one another and do our jobs.

To do your job, you have to know what it is. Get all the information your union has to offer, study it, and abide by it. When you don't know something, ask. And, if you feel strongly about it, contribute. Join a committee. Volunteer.

Larry Keith, who was president of the New York branch of SAG for five years, had this to say:

> I wanted to help. I felt it was important for me to do so. The business had been good to me. And I am very glad, because I know there were times when what I said helped us to avoid confrontation, which would've hurt everyone.

BECOMING A UNION MEMBER

The simplest way to join Equity, SAG, or AFTRA is to get a job in their jurisdiction. A signed contract with a legitimate producer, saying that you are engaged for such-and-such a role in such-and-such production at whatever salary, immediately confers upon you the status of professional. You will then be required to pay the initiation fee and six months' dues.

However, there are other ways to get your union cards. Let's see what they are.

American Federation of TV and Radio Artists　AFTRA is an open union. Any actor can sign the membership application and pay the initiation fee, which is established by the local. In New York and Los Angeles, the largest locals, the initiation fee is $800. Dues are paid semiannually, on a sliding scale, based upon the previous year's income. As a new member you would pay the lowest amount, which in New York is $35, semiannually.

Under the Taft-Hartley Law it is possible for you to do your first AFTRA job and then work in television or radio for up to thirty days without joining the union. After that, if you continue to work, membership is mandatory.

Screen Actors Guild If you have been a member of either AFTRA or Equity for a year and have worked as a principal at least once in either union, you may apply for membership in SAG. If you have not been a member of the other unions and now have a commitment for a role as a principal in a film, commercial, or filmed television show, you will be accepted for membership. You must bring a letter from a signatory producer or the producer's representative stating that you will be playing a principal part in a specific picture.

SAG's initiation fee is $1008, plus the semi-annual dues payment of $42.50.

Actors Equity Association If you have been a member of either AFTRA or SAG for a year or more and have performed work comparable to Equity principal work, you will be eligible to join Equity.

Since 1978 it has been possible to earn a membership card by means of the Equity Membership Candidacy Program. Under the program, nonprofessional actors are allowed to credit fifty weeks of work in participating Equity theaters toward AEA membership. This work does not have to be at one theater, nor does it have to be consecutive. The program is in effect at dinner theaters, Equity resident theaters, Chicago off-Loop theaters, and in resident and nonresident stock theaters throughout the country. One of the great benefits of the Equity Membership Candidacy Program is that by the time you have earned your union card you have acquired experience and built a resumé: you are qualified to be in the company of professionals. As many as ten weeks of the fifty may be spent doing technical work. Membership candidates at stock companies may also receive credit for weeks as production assistant to a stage manager.

A membership candidate, after securing a position at a participating theater, registers for the Candidacy Program by completing the nonprofessional affidavit (supplied by the theater) and sending it to Equity, along with a registration fee. The fee will be credited to the initiation fee, which is due upon joining the union. Once you've accumulated your fifty weeks of work, you have five years in which to join Equity. During that period if you get a job at an Equity theater, you will be required to join the union.

Equity's initiation fee is $800. Basic dues are $39 semi-annually. Members also pay working dues: 2 percent of gross earnings from Equity employment. If you earn less than $5,000 under Equity jurisdiction in any year, a credit of 25 percent of your working dues will be applied to the following year's basic dues. The maximum amount of earnings subject to the 2 percent working dues is $100,000 per year.

TRANSFERRING AND WITHDRAWING
Performers who join a union in one area may simply apply for a transfer to the branch or local of the city they will reside in. You may be required to pay additional dues to meet the scale of your new local.

If you think that you are not going to be active in a jurisdiction for six months or longer (you may sign to tour with a play for a year or more and therefore be unable to work in TV or films), you may elect to take a temporary withdrawal from AFTRA and/or SAG. At that point you will not be required to pay dues to those unions, but you will, of course, be paying full dues to Equity. If you go on-location for a period to shoot a film, you may temporarily withdraw from Equity.

The important thing to remember is to apply for temporary withdrawal and not let unpaid dues accumulate. An oversight may lead to a fine and may even endanger your membership status. Similarly, once you return to your home base, remember to reinstate yourself as an active member.

For further information about union membership, write to their main offices:

> Actors Equity Association
> 165 West 46th Street
> New York, NY 10036

> American Federation of Television and Radio Artists
> 260 Madison Avenue
> New York, NY 10016

> Screen Actors Guild
> 5757 Wilshire Boulevard
> Los Angeles, CA 90036

AFTRA and SAG have locals or branches throughout the country. You may find them listed in your telephone directory. In many cities, the offices are merged for all practical purposes. If the SAG branch office and the AFTRA local nearest you have the same address, it's likely that the same staff administers the contracts for both unions.

WHEN TO JOIN THE UNIONS
We cannot overemphasize that being a member of Equity, AFTRA, or SAG will not automatically bring you a job. Union membership does not guarantee that you are going to get a job. Your only guarantee is that as a union member you will enjoy the same benefits and protections as all other union members when you work.

A discerning casting person will be able to tell from your resumé whether you have merely purchased that union card or have earned it. If you are really new to The Business, have not had a great deal of experience in any area, and have few contacts among professional people, you should question whether it is essential or even advisable for you to attempt to join any of the unions at this time. As a union member you will be prohibited from working with nonprofessionals. Amateur groups, community theaters, or school groups may be the very places you should be looking to for the experience you need.

> When is the right time to join the union? When you have a job!
> —TONY NICOSIA, *Actors Equity Association*

PROOF OF CITIZENSHIP
The Immigration and Reform Act of 1986 requires that all workers must, at the time they are hired, show proof that they have the right to work in the United States.

While the original intent of this legislation may have been to stem the tide of aliens who slip into this country illegally and get jobs, most frequently doing menial, low-paying work, the result has been to force actors to show proof of their citizenship every time they show up at an audition.

Instructed to bring their passports to every engagement, actors were irate: while proving their citizenship, they were also being made to tell their age. In a business where so much depends upon how old, or rather how *young* you *look*, they knew their livelihoods were in danger if casting directors should discover, for example, that a woman who looked like the ideal young married was really old enough to be the mother of the bride.

The authorities, working with union representatives, have modified their demands. You may bring your choice of documentation to the session. Actors may obey the law and still maintain privacy by showing a Social Security card and a voter's registration card.

Inquiries as to your age and national origin (as well as your marital status and sexual preference) are violations of the law. If anyone asks you, "Confidentially, how old are you, really?" simply answer, "I play from twenty-seven to thirty-five," or, "I'm usually cast as. . . ." Then, quickly, quietly, call your union and let them know what has happened. The union will take appropriate action and protect your anonymity.

FOREIGN ACTORS ON THE AMERICAN STAGE

Performers who are not American citizens will need to show proof that they are permitted to work in the United States. Obtaining the necessary Green Card is a federal matter, customarily handled by the immigration departments and/or consuls of this country and the performer's native country. When a producer really wants to engage a noncitizen for a major role, his legal staff will do its best to offer assistance, but it's nevertheless a matter for the performer to arrange, and the performer must qualify. If you are not a citizen, *do not attempt to lie about your work status.*

Equity endeavors to maintain a healthy attitude toward the use of foreign actors on Broadway, particularly when opportunities for American performers are as limited as they have been over the past several years. There are strict guidelines for the use of British actors (or other nationals) in our theaters. Foreign performers may be employed for work in New York, provided that one or more of the following conditions is met:

1. They are internationally known stars, such as Jeremy Irons, Ian McKellen, Glenda Jackson, Derek Jacobi, or Maggie Smith.

2. Their services are truly unique to the production — the producer has searched through the roster of available performers and has been unable to find an American actor to play the role adequately.

3. The entire company is a unit, such as the Royal Shakespeare Company, the National Theater, and the Abbey Theater. These productions may be engaged for a maximum of twenty weeks, after which American performers are to replace the foreign players.

Exceptions are made also for "Plays of Special Character," which have neither stars nor international recognition, but which deserve attention for their singular quality. An example of this would be *Sarafina!*, which was brought to New York as the result of a special appeal by the Theater Company of Lincoln Center. The cast consisted of youngsters from South Africa, singing the songs of their homeland in a very special way. When they were granted permission to come to America, the entire company gleefully joined Equity.

Equity and British Equity support an exchange of actors or productions. The New York Shakespeare Festival's exchange program with London's Royal Court Theater made it possible for London playgoers to enjoy George C. Wolfe's *The Colored Museum*, a play with a cast of African-American actors, while New Yorkers were able to see Caryl Churchill's *Serious Money*.

Robert Lindsay, a well-regarded British actor who was not then an international star, gained permission to delight American audiences in *Me and My Girl*, for which he won a Tony Award; in exchange for which Ron Holgate, a highly regarded American performer, not yet an international star, was signed for *Lend Me a Tenor* on the West End.

The exchange also works the other way. When the American drama *A Walk in the Woods* opened in London, playing opposite Sir Alec Guinness was the American actor Edward Herrmann, appearing in exchange for a British actor to be named later — when the production, the play, and the role materialize.

The British actress Juliet Stevenson was denied permission to repeat the role she created in *Death and the Maiden* when Mike Nichols mounted his Broadway production of the play. Although she had received rave reviews, Equity took the position that she was neither a star nor a person of extraordinary ability. One man, a lawyer whom she did not know, was so outraged by that decision that he collected letters from numerous outstanding theater authorities and did all the necessary paperwork to acquire a Green Card for her. She recently made her U.S. stage debut at the Mark Taper Forum in Los Angeles, playing opposite Frank Langella in *Scenes from an Execution*.

EQUAL IMMIGRATION EXCHANGE

As a first step, SAG and ACTRA, the Canadian television and radio actors' union, have adopted an equitable exchange agreement, in an effort to equalize the number of performers crossing the border to work in film and TV. Both unions have also agreed to police each other's contracts on productions shooting in either country and to provide help to union members with production problems on location.

THE GLOBAL FUTURE

The industry we work in today would be unrecognizable to many of its founders. In those days when the unions were founded, could anyone have imagined VCRs, videocassettes, laser disks — technology that can put all of *Gone with the Wind* in the palm of your hand?

There are actually more opportunities for performers now than ever before. There will be even more opportunities. But the work is changing. There are fewer

Broadway productions and daytime soaps, but more regional theaters and developments such as the proliferation of cable TV and satellite transmission channels, which may provide new outlets for dramatic programming. Increasingly, the cable television companies are originating films such as *Scarlett*, the sequel to *Gone with the Wind*, shot in London and Charleston, South Carolina, with a stellar cast.

In fact, movies are being made all over the world, by anyone with a script, a camera, and the ability to make a good distribution deal. Foreign investments, co-production deals, multilateral trade agreements, and so on, and so on, contribute to the endless possibilities. *Crocodile Dundee* and *A Room with a View* were among the first of many major successes from independent filmmakers working far from the hills of Hollywood.

In the future, an actor's work may not be in theater, film, or television at all, but on interactive CDs or computer games, or in some new forms that we have not yet glimpsed. With an incredible new process called "morphing" it is now possible to use the images of famous performers such as Humphrey Bogart or Marilyn Monroe, colorize them, and animate them so that these performers of the past appear to be playing in brand new scenes with actors of today!

CHAPTER 8

THE JOBS: WHAT THEY ARE AND WHAT THEY PAY

Never mistake your salary for your income.

—LILLIAN GISH

As you can imagine, the official language of all contracts is extremely detailed. Some codes run to hundreds of pages. This overview aims to indicate what kinds of jobs exist, what they are called, and what you can expect to earn when you land them. In all cases you should check with the union for the fine points.

Equity, AFTRA, and SAG have customarily negotiated three-year agreements. With so many codes needed to cover all areas of employment, the effort has been made to have the contracts expire at different dates. Therefore, some contracts are up for negotiation every year. You should understand that the figures we mention, as well as the working conditions, may be superseded by future negotiations. The unions consistently endeavor to adjust their demands to the needs of the members. For the latest information, always check with the union in whose jurisdiction you will be working.

IF YOU WORK ON THE STAGE

BROADWAY

For a Broadway show, the minimum, or scale, payment for actors, singers, or dancers is $950 per week.

Chorus people who say lines or have a specialty number receive $15 per week additional pay. Dance captains receive an additional $150 per week.

Understudies who are cast members receive $33 per week additional pay for each role understudied, plus one-eighth of a week's salary each time they perform the role. Understudies who are not cast members earn the minimum $950 per week, plus one-eighth the week's salary for each performance they play. Such performers may be signed to understudy as many as three roles without additional payment.

Rehearsal pay is the same as minimum performance pay. This applies to all performers, unless their contracts are negotiated otherwise.

Stage managers on a musical are paid $1,502 per week, and $1,293 on a dramatic show. Assistant stage managers earn $1,190 on musicals, $1,056 on a dramatic show. Scale for second assistant stage manager on a musical is $994.

These days producers are keeping their payrolls down. For example, the cast of the long-running hit musical, *42nd Street* (1980) numbered fifty-six Equity members: four stage managers, twelve principals, and forty chorus singers and dancers who spoke lines or played small parts. By contrast, the company of the 1994 revival of *Damn Yankees* was a tidy twenty-nine.

Dramatic plays may rehearse up to eight weeks. Musicals may rehearse principals nine weeks, chorus ten weeks. If rehearsals last longer, performers then receive whatever performance salary they have negotiated.

Remember, we are giving you *minimum* payments. Actors and stage managers with a long list of credits negotiate higher salaries. Remember, also, that in each instance in which a contract has been negotiated, the producer contributes a portion of the performer's salary to Equity's health and retirement funds; in this contract that amount is 8 percent.

TOURING COMPANIES

Rates are the same for touring companies as they are for Broadway. The producer is responsible for transportation of the company and for the maintenance of sets and costumes. Because performers are required to pay for their own accommodations (and at the same time must maintain their original homes), there is a *per diem* — an additional daily payment to make up for the expense of working outside the metropolitan area — of $83, or $581 per week while on tour.

SPECIAL PRODUCTION CONTRACTS

The special production contract is an arrangement for theaters with 700 seats or less. The lower minimum salary allowed for performances at these theaters may be increased, depending upon the theater's weekly gross. It is possible, therefore, that an actor's salary will vary from one week to the next. Scale is $591 per week on a dramatic play.

THE THEATRICAL ALLIANCE

To stimulate Broadway production and develop a theatergoing audience, labor, management, and the crafts unions have united to create a climate wherein plays can be produced at lower cost. This is an industry-wide effort, with everyone making concessions. Performers' salaries are cut 25 percent, which lowers the scale to $713 per week. The top ticket price is $35.

OFF-BROADWAY

Off-Broadway blossomed over thirty years ago in small theaters away from the immediate Broadway theater district. These theaters were places where a writer of noncommercial or experimental plays, freed from the commercial pressures of Broadway, could enjoy a low-budget production and try to find an audience. At the same time, off-Broadway provided opportunities for new performers — talented people who had no reputation to risk and who didn't mind working for little more than carfare. Jason Robards and the late Geraldine Page are two stars whose lives were changed after they appeared — Robards in *The Iceman Cometh,* Page in *Summer and Smoke* — in productions mounted at a defunct night club in Greenwich Village by a company calling itself Circle in the Square. Not only did those actors go on to important careers, the theatrical company went on to become a respected organization on Broadway as well as off. One of the founders, Paul Libin, is now producing director for Jujamcyn Theaters.

Today, established players are just as anxious as the rest of us to be seen in an off-Broadway play that just might settle in for a run or even make it to a Broadway house. The Roundabout Theater Company's revival of *She Loves Me* won such ecstatic reviews that the show was remounted at Broadway's Brooks Atkinson Theater. The Variety Arts Theater, at 14th Street and Third Avenue, proved an ideal home for *Annie Warbucks* when opening the show on Broadway became too costly and risky. David Mamet's *Oleanna* mesmerized audiences at the small Orpheum Theater on the Lower East Side; that success led to several regional productions, and the show went on to be a sensation in London.

Of course, some productions are content to remain in the house where they first won acclaim. New York's longest-running show, *The Fantasticks,* is still charming audiences In Greenwich Village at the tiny Sullivan Street Theater where it opened almost forty years ago.

The off-Broadway theater contract depends upon the size of the theater and the level of its weekly gross. Minimum salaries off-Broadway range from $591 to $625 per week. Rehearsal pay is the same as minimum salary. A five-week rehearsal period is permitted. Stage managers, as in Broadway shows, earn a bit more.

OFF-OFF-BROADWAY

Off-off-Broadway came into existence in response to the increasing costliness and commercialism of off-Broadway. Productions given in lofts, basements, and hotel function rooms are usually presented for a limited number of performances. Under Equity's Showcase Code, which currently allows for an admission charge of no more than $12, actors are reimbursed for their expenses, which is frequently no more than their carfare. Under the Funded Nonprofit Theater Code, admission of $15 may be charged, and performers may be paid a stipend ranging from $140 to $750, based upon the size of the theater, potential gross, and number of performances. Mini-contract salaries may be negotiated for twenty-four performances in the largest of these spaces. Many of the houses on Theater Row, on 42nd Street west of Ninth Avenue, seat fewer than a hundred people. Salaries range from $207 to $291.

REGIONAL THEATER AND THE LORT CONTRACT

Regional theater now employs the largest number of professional stage actors. As of this writing, more than seventy theaters operate according to the League of Resident Theaters (LORT) contract. Among them are the prestigious Mark Taper Forum in Los Angeles, the Tyrone Guthrie in Minneapolis, Actors Theater of Louisville, Cleveland Playhouse, and Indiana Repertory Theater.

I can only tell you that the regional theaters are the hope of American theater, as far as I'm concerned. We must continue to have the passion and commitment toward producing works which engage our audience on a profound level. My slogan at all times is: "When was the last time you were provoked, engaged, compelled, and challenged . . . and loved every minute of it?"

—LIBBY APPEL, *artistic director, Indiana Rep*

More and more productions originate in these theaters, away from the scrutiny of powerful metropolitan theater critics. After they have ironed out their kinks, regional productions may move to New York. Frequently their regional success inspires a later, sometimes enormous, Broadway success, as was the case with *'night, Mother*, by Marsha Norman, which originated at Actors Theatre of Louisville and captured the 1983 Pulitzer Prize. Sometimes, New York critics fail to comprehend what the rest of the country was raving about. Robert Schenkkan's *The Kentucky Cycle* also won the Pulitzer Prize, in 1992, without playing in New York. When the show arrived on the East Coast, the critics were unimpressed, and audiences stayed away.

We were accustomed to getting standing ovations on tour, and even when we were in previews in New York. But, after the reviews came out, it was as if the audiences had been told that we weren't interesting.

—PATRICK PAGE, *actor in* The Kentucky Cycle

Salaries at LORT theaters are based upon seating capacity and potential gross of the theater. They range from $428 to $547 per week. The theaters provide housing, at no cost to the performer.

Donna Lynne Champlin was hired to do a new musical at the Arkansas Repertory Theater, where she experienced the thrill of being involved in a work-in-progress collaboration:

I have developed a tremendous respect for the Arkansas Rep for taking this chance, footing the bill, and giving us this space. We're getting paid practically nothing, but there's been so much excitement at rehearsal, who needs cable?

STOCK PRODUCTIONS AND THE CORST AND COST CONTRACTS

Summer stock can be the actor's best training ground. Learning and performing eight plays in as many weeks forces you to grow, widens your range, sharpens your skills, and teaches you how to work in front of an audience. There are a number of resident companies employing at least six actors. In their contract — the Council of Resident Stock Theaters (CORST) Code — salaries are based upon theater capacity and potential gross. Minimums range from $450.89 to $538.94 per week. No per diem is paid in these theaters.

There is also a Council of Stock Theaters (COST) Code, for the producers of non-resident summer stock (no fixed troupe of actors for the season). At these theaters they either produce their own packages or book productions, usually starring well-known TV or film personalities in well-known plays; these usually travel to a different theater each week. Scale ranges from $450 to $551.67. Per diem is paid for these jobs. The producer is responsible for transportation and for the maintenance of sets and costumes. The actor is required to pay for hotel accommodations, food, and all other personal expenses.

MUSICAL THEATER
There is an outdoor musical-theater contract for the large theaters in St. Louis, Indianapolis, and Kansas City. Minimum is $520 plus $50 per diem.

OUTDOOR DRAMA
An increasing number of performers are finding employment in this area. The current contract pays $465.75.

DINNER THEATER
Salaries at professional dinner theaters are based upon their restaurant capacity. Minimums range from $261.25 to $412.25.

Many dinner theaters and stock theaters are located in resort areas, where room rates go sky-high during the vacation season. Performers who will be paying for their own accommodations under these contracts are not supposed to spend more than 20 percent of their salary for lodging. Managers must arrange for space the performers can afford or make up the difference between 20 percent and the actual cost. Performers should ascertain what their living expenses will be before they accept such bookings.

CHILDREN'S THEATER
The children's theater code, called Theater for Young Audiences, covers about fifty professional companies. Theaters that run on a weekly basis pay $276 per week. Actors who double as assistant stage managers (a common practice in this area) earn $294. Rehearsal pay is the same as performance pay.

Under this contract, producers have the option to pay on a per-performance basis: Scale for local touring plays is $55 per show; actor/assistant stage managers earn $64.25. Productions using public transportation to reach their audiences pay $41.50. Actor/assistant stage managers are paid $57.

BUSINESS THEATER (INDUSTRIALS)
These are productions paid for by a corporation and performed for an invited, non-paying audience, such as company employees, dealers, or buyers. Many stars, especially those who have become identified with the client's product through TV commercials, perform in industrial shows.

Corporations have lately begun to cut down on such spectaculars in efforts to economize, but industrials remain among the better-paying assignments in live theater. Actors working two weeks or more earn $870 per week. Actors working one week earn $1,088. Those working fewer than seven days are paid at a daily rate, $362 for the first day, $181 for each day after that. Stage managers, as is usual in all contracts, earn a bit more.

Industrial shows frequently travel for four to six weeks. Transportation and housing are provided, as is a per diem of $55.

CABARET THEATER

The success of *Forbidden Broadway*, the uproarious satirical revue originally produced in a restaurant on New York's Upper West Side, inspired a slew of local productions which gave employment to actors in cities across the country. Similar shows, such as *Forever Plaid* and *Tony 'n' Tina's Wedding*, play in similar settings. This work is done under the Cabaret Code. The murder mystery *Sheer Madness* started in a Boston cabaret in 1979 and is still playing across the country! Depending on theater/cabaret size, scale ranges from $295 to $584.

LETTERS OF AGREEMENT

To encourage the development of professional theater, Equity's staff endeavors to work out special agreements to fit the circumstances of each production. Workshops, where director, cast, and writers work in a very fluid relationship, may eventually result in full-scale productions. The most famous of these is the case of Broadway's longest-running musical, *A Chorus Line*, which continues to provide jobs for performers, decades after the original seed work was begun in a downtown loft, under the aegis of the New York Shakespeare Festival.

> It's the union's job to protect the actor and at the same time nurture the area for more jobs. It may take a company a few years to gain a foothold. The Letter of Agreement lets them work with top people, but under modified salary conditions that everyone can live with.
> —ROBERT BRUYR, *executive assistant for communications and development, Actors Equity*

After four years as Carlo Hesser on *One Life to Live*, Emmy-winner Thom Christopher was enthusiastic about the opportunity to play Baron von Trapp in a summer theater production of *The Sound of Music*. As it happened, the Tri-Arts Theater in Pine Plains, New York, was a fledgling theater run by Broadway actor-dancer Ray Roderick and his wife, singer Sarah Combs. A Letter of Agreement made Christopher's participation possible, guaranteeing the high caliber of the show as well as capacity crowds at all performances. And it allowed the actor to broaden his range.

> I have always wanted to play this part. And in a theater like this you have the chance to try things, to learn, to grow. You're unafraid to be lousy! When you see the dedication and commitment of the local people, who really want this theater to succeed and have supported it since its inception just a couple of seasons ago. . . ! It's a great experience for everyone involved, for me, for the kids, and it's doing great things for the community.
> —THOM CHRISTOPHER

Equity invites inquiries about all kinds of arrangements. Special contracts can be designed for other types of live performances. Each production has a life of its own;

things are always in a state of flux. Most of Equity's reps have worked in the industry as actors, stage managers, company managers, box office people, or lawyers. Their experience, therefore, is eminently practical, and their inclination is to do whatever will make a production possible while protecting the performers from exploitation and/or abuse.

> Ours is a global enterprise. *Sunset Boulevard* has opened in London, with Patti LuPone. It's going to California with Glenn Close, and then, finally, it will come to New York.
>
> —ROBERT BRUYR

MATTERS OF SECURITY

With an alarming increase in violence reaching the level of a national scandal, it behooves us all to have our wits about us and our eyes open. That is as true for performers as it is for champion athletes, business executives, or tourists. Some stock contracts now specify that performers will have safe transport provided to rehearsal and performance, for shopping, cleaning, getting their hair done, and so forth. However, as Equity's Robert Bruhr reminds us:

> Actors are so often thinking about something else when it looks like they're out for a stroll. They're thinking about the lines, the costume, the rehearsal, they're going over their business demands. So they're focused on their business and don't pay attention to their surroundings. And they are aliens wherever they are. They don't look like natives. We tell them at least to try to do that. Don't look like the stranger from outer space.

IF YOU WORK IN FILM

THEATRICAL FILMS

Motion picture work is covered by Screen Actors Guild contracts. Actors engaged for a day of shooting on a picture being made for theatrical release are called day players; they are paid a scale rate of $504. If the actor is engaged for the week, scale is $1,752.

Extras earn $99 per eight-hour day. Stand-ins are paid $109. The special-ability category describes an actor engaged to perform work that requires special skill, such as tennis, golf, skating, choreographed dancing, or driving that requires a special license, such as truck or motorcycle driving. These people earn $109 per eight-hour day.

Scale is the same for blockbusters or duds, for extravaganzas or simple stories. The cost of a film does not affect scale payment.

Release of the film to TV means that performers will receive an additional percentage of their salary each time the film is shown. Those percentages will depend upon the cost of the film and the terms of the deal. Likewise, release of the film as a videocassette, for rental and for sale, triggers additional payments to the cast.

Films for TV

Films made for prime-time television, the once-a-week half-hour, hour, or two-hour shows aired between 8 P.M. and 11 P.M., pay the same daily rate as theatrical films.

TV Commercials

Television commercials are covered by both AFTRA (videotape) and SAG (film and some videotape) contracts. For an on-camera principal, a recognizable person who may or may not have lines to speak, scale is $414.25 per day, or per commercial if more than one spot is filmed in one day.

Voice-over performers, those who are heard but not seen, are paid $311.50 per spot.

People who do commercials stand to make more money if the commercials get a great deal of use. Residuals, those payments for additional showings of the performer's work, are computed according to complicated tables that take into account the size of the market (potential audience), number of uses within a thirteen-week period, and whether the commercial is a wild spot (seen during station breaks and the blocks of time between discrete programs) or a program spot (shown within the body of a show).

Extras, persons who are not identifiable, who are used to suggest the environment of a restaurant, an airport, or other setting are paid $139.90 for the session, which includes thirteen weeks' use of the commercial. For use beyond thirteen weeks, the rate is $179.90. Unlimited use, or *buyout*, earns $240.

If, during the shooting day, direction makes you identifiable — you are shown relating or reacting to a product, or to the commercial copy about the product — you are upgraded to the category of principal and will then receive residuals as if you had originally been engaged as a principal. Hand models, whose exquisite fingers are seen using a product, are paid $366.25 on a buy-out, or $243.60 for thirteen weeks' use. Extras and hand models do not receive residuals.

Exclusivity

It should stand to reason that if you are seen or heard extolling the virtues of Salad Dressing A, you cannot work for any of its competitors — Salad Dressings B to Z. To do so is to have a product conflict. Performers may not do competing products in any category. An actor who engages in such conflicting work risks being sued for damages by the first client. If the sponsor — Salad Dressing A — also wishes you not to work for as many as three additional products *not* in the exact same category, the sponsor may purchase additional exclusivity by payment of 50 percent over scale. For total exclusivity, the client will have to pay you double scale, or 100 percent more. These are minimum terms which can be negotiated more favorably for the performer.

Educational Films and Corporate Videos

An increasing amount of work exists in nontheatrical film and television, such as materials used in corporate training, motivational courses, and in point-of-purchase arenas, such as stores, shopping malls and supermarkets. Two wage scales cover this work, depending upon whether the films are for corporate or for audience viewing.

In-house programs pay principals $380 per day, $955 for a three-day player, and $1,333 for a per-week contract. On-camera spokespersons, who essentially play themselves, earn $691 for the first shooting day, $380 thereafter. Voice-over performers are paid $311 for the first hour, $91 for each additional half-hour. Extras earn $99 per day.

Films for use in public places, as described above, pay slightly higher fees. Principals earn $472, three-day players $1,178, actors on a weekly contract $1,651. Spokespersons earn $818 for the first shooting day, and $472 thereafter. Voice-over work is paid at the rate of $346 for the first hour, $91 for each additional half-hour.

In both codes, for performers wearing their own clothes there is a $15 daytime wardrobe fee, $25 for formal wear.

If the material is later broadcast or made available for sale, as in a videocassette, the contracts provide for additional payments to the performer.

As with all union contracts, the employer contributes a percentage of the performer's salary (in this case 12.5 percent) to the SAG's health and retirement funds.

IF YOU WORK IN TELEVISION

Videotaped television shows are usually covered by AFTRA contracts. In some cases, the work may be done at a SAG facility under SAG jurisdiction, but the terms remain the same, for all practical purposes.

DAYTIME SERIALS

Actors on daytime TV serials fall into three categories. Principals, or day players, are recognizable people playing a role, speaking scripted lines. Scale is $435 on a half-hour show; $580 on an hour show. Contract players command substantially more money. Players of nonspecific roles — such as maitre d's, bank tellers, or waitresses — speak fewer than five lines and are called *under-fives* and are paid $206 on half-hour shows, $253 on hour shows.

The most outstanding example of an actor who was upgraded from an under-five is Jacklyn Zeman, of *General Hospital*, who had this to say:

> I was hired to do an under-five on *One Life to Live*. I played a waitress. At the time, Jamison Parker was on the show, playing Brad Vernon. I had a two- or three-line exchange with him in a restaurant, and out of that the producer had me come back two weeks later to do the same part. But this time it was three pages of dialogue, and the contract came after that.

Extras, the people in the restaurant, at the airport, at the party, are paid $99 on a half-hour show, $128 on an hour show.

PRIME-TIME DRAMATIC PROGRAMS

Prime-time dramatic shows (these include comedies) pay the same under AFTRA contract as they do under SAG. Day players earn a minimum of $504. Scale for three-day players is $1,277 on half-hour and hour shows, and $1,503 on ninety-minute and two-hour shows. The weekly rate is $1,753. Actors who speak at all are paid as principals.

Extras earn $99 per day for half-hour programs, $128 on an hour show. Extras who perform special business, that is, action required by the director for the continuity of the show, are paid the under-five rate.

NONDRAMATIC SHOWS

Nondramatic shows using actors, such as *Saturday Night Live*, pay as follows:

Time	Principal	Under-five	Extra
Half-hour	$484	$227	$106
60 minutes	$616	$281	$134
90 minutes	$777	$320	$163
2 hours	$936	$366	$192

Included in all these program fees are a set number of rehearsal hours, to be used within a set number of days. Rates for additional rehearsal are $11 per hour for extras, $17 for all others.

WARDROBE FEES

If you perform in your own clothes, you are paid a wardrobe fee of $10 per garment for daytime clothes, $25 for formal wear. You can see why it's a good idea for men to own a tuxedo and for women to have a long, formal dress.

EDUCATIONAL AND INDUSTRIAL MATERIAL

Rates are the same as those for educational and industrial films.

IF YOU WORK IN RADIO AND RECORDINGS

Work in radio comes under AFTRA's jurisdiction. Anyone who listens to an AM or FM station quickly realizes that opportunities for actors exist in the dramatized radio spots — commercials — which interrupt the music, news, sports, talk shows, and call-in programs.

Actors in radio commercials are paid a session fee of $163.30 per spot. Residuals are based on a formula that takes into account the potential audience and use of the spot.

Nonbroadcast audio is material designed for corporate or educational use. The great body of this work is straight narration by a single person. Scale is the same as for voice-over performance on industrial film or tape.

Job opportunities in radio exist primarily on the local level for announcers, newscasters, disc jockeys, sports reporters, and for specialists — people with expert knowledge of a particular topic or subject. Nevertheless, radio programming is so inexpensive (compared to the other broadcast media), and there are so many small stations, that anyone with the imagination and capacity to create even a one-minute program for which a local station might conceivably find a sponsor should see this as a challenging arena.

A couple of seasons ago, a young woman who had developed a weight-loss system, which taught overeaters how to control their eating habits, was tenacious enough to interest a sponsor in a weekly call-in radio show based upon her method. She called it "Changing Habits."

Think about it. A subject that strongly interests you might also appeal to a great many others. Is there some aspect of it that might be the basis of a continuing program? If so, experiment with a tape recorder. In this business, you never know. . . .

With the current interest in recording material for listening, such as "books on tape" featuring publishers' bestsellers, it is sensible to look at AFTRA's code for the spoken word on records or tape. Scale for actors or comedians is $101 per hour or per side; narrators earn $114.50. A side is defined as five — that's right, *five* — minutes of recorded material.

NEW TECHNOLOGY
AFTRA and SAG have moved to sign contracts with producers of interactive media projects and computer games. Scale for day players has been set at $485.

A new contract covers "infomercials," those half-hour programs in which several people, usually recognizable celebrities, chat about a wonderful new product or service which the audience then has the opportunity to order. Scale for this work is $896 for the first day of work, $448 for an additional day.

LOCAL JOB OPPORTUNITIES
As we pointed out earlier, holding a union card is synonymous with being a professional. A level of experience is assumed. If your own experience is limited, you should be on the lookout for ways to acquire the proficiency you will ultimately need.

> I've been preparing for this career ever since I was fourteen. I went to Performing Arts High School, studied at the Neighborhood Playhouse, played stock, studied voice, studied dance. I didn't seem to belong until my early thirties, when my voice began to match my look, and my career finally started.
>
> —THOM CHRISTOPHER

> I needed to learn more about acting. For thirteen years I worked in different rep companies. The theater was my home. I was in the wings of the Cincinnati Playhouse in the Park, doing Shaw's *Heartbreak House* when I realized I'd had enough of this. I decided to stay in New York, and two months later I had a job on *All My Children*.
>
> —KATHLEEN NOONE, *formerly Ellen on* All My Children

For stage work, investigate local stock companies, community theater groups, acting companies at local theater schools, children's theater, murder-mystery companies, and nearby dinner theaters. Yes, you may be expected to hunt for your own props or wait on tables and play the lead in the play of the week, but if that's the only way you're going to get on a stage, why not chance it, at least once?

> I have been in this business for over forty years, and the moment that really stands out, the high point, was that first summer, when we all chipped in to be at the summer theater in Blauvelt. Herbert Berghof, who was teaching at the New School along with Stella Adler and Erwin

Piscator, had found this abandoned theater (Greenbush was the name of it), and he kept telling all the people in all his classes that they could do it — that it was possible to run a theater by ourselves. He said he would help in the beginning — and for the first play, he did. After that we were sort of on our own.

We all chipped in $150. What a lot of money that was at the time! I don't remember how I ever got it. I know I was working at the Hotel New Yorker as a part-time receptionist, telephone operator, whatever. And we all lived in the barn. It had two halves, and the girls were in one room, the fellas in the other. I learned a lot that summer.

—MAUREEN STAPLETON, *Oscar-,*
Emmy-, and two-time Tony-winner

If there are schools in the area offering courses in film production or communications, students will undoubtedly be required to produce something on film as a class assignment. Working with them will give you an opportunity to learn about camera technique.

It may be possible to work as the spokesperson or narrator for local merchants or businesses, or for the public relations firms serving them. Seeking and landing such jobs in your community lets you gain experience, build a résumé, and be in contact with people as energetic as yourself who also share your dream. That's how you start to build your own network.

My first job, after we came back from Greenbush, was as understudy to Beatrice Straight in *Playboy of the Western World*. One of the actors in that company found out about the opening and said to me, "You've got to call, you're right for it." Well, I was scared to death to go up for anything! He pushed me into a phone booth, and I said I didn't have a nickel. So, he gave me his nickel. And he forced me to make that call and ask for an appointment. Well, somehow, I got it!

—MAUREEN STAPLETON

I was working at Harvard, in the news office. The people around me were all involved in the theater. I asked if anyone could audition. They said yes, and that's how I got my start. I have been passed along from one job to the next. People would see my performance and say they'd want to use me in something. My whole career is about networking.

The best advice was given to me by Gordon Davidson [artistic director] of the Mark Taper Forum, and [casting director] Shirley Rich. They both said, "Whatever you are doing, write and tell me. Tell me where you are. Even if you don't hear from me, let me know what you're doing." And I have taken that to heart, and I do that with everyone I have met.

—PATRICIA ELLIOTT, *Tony-winner, and*
Renee on One Life to Live

CHAPTER 9

PERFORMERS WITH DISABILITIES

*We all have disabilities. Mine just happen
to be in full view.*
                                    —RENE MORENO, *actor*

At the peak of her career, the great French tragedienne, Sarah Bernhardt, lost a leg. Since the idea of using a prosthetic or artificial leg appalled her, she had herself carried onto the stage and "arranged" before the curtain rose.

The British-born movie star, Herbert Marshall, lost a leg due to action in World War I. He disguised the handicap successfully enough to enjoy a lengthy screen career, during which he played urbane, romantic, leading men opposite Katharine Hepburn, Bette Davis, Marlene Dietrich, Greta Garbo, Claudette Colbert, and Joan Crawford. Lionel Barrymore, best known for his portrayal of the sinister bank president in the Frank Capra classic *It's a Wonderful Life*, was forced by crippling illness to play many roles confined to a wheelchair.

Visually impaired performers have included Sammy Davis, Jr., Peter Falk, Ray Charles, George Shearing, Stevie Wonder, José Feliciano, and Trini Lopez.

Mark Medoff's prize-winning drama *Children of a Lesser God* dealt with the relationship between a hearing man and a deaf woman and helped to launch the careers of many well-trained deaf actors. Her performance in the film version earned an Academy Award for the very talented Marlee Matlin.

TO JOIN THE MAINSTREAM

These and other such artists have been able to surmount real physical challenges and carry on with their careers. Today, with the passage of the Americans with Disabilities Act, there seem to be more opportunities for "mainstreaming" than ever before. Advertisers such as K-Mart, Target, and Anheuser-Busch feature principals in wheelchairs in their commercials. Department store catalogs show models with disabilities wearing the latest fashions. Hearing-impaired women have been used to enhance product messages for Scholl's and AT&T.

In recognition of the growing number of performers with disabilities throughout the country, Equity, AFTRA, and SAG have established committees in the major cities to increase the visibility of professional performers with disabilities among casting directors and producers and thereby help create additional opportunities for mainstreaming. There are numerous theaters throughout the nation which produce plays and touring shows that feature performers who are disabled working together with those who are not. Very Special Arts Programs in all the major cities provide creative outlets and networking opportunities for physically challenged artists.

In 1986, the Association for Theatre and Disability (ATD) was established as a not-for-profit corporation whose purpose "is to foster full participation and involvement of individuals with all types of disabilities in drama and theater activities." Membership in ATD is open to all individuals and groups interested in the goals of the organization. These include working with individuals with disabilities in professional, educational, therapeutic, or recreational settings; promoting accessibility for all audience members; furthering training in theater and drama, and advocating appropriate casting and representation of performers with disabilities. The organization publishes a bimonthly news letter and a conference is held each year.

For further information, write: Association for Theatre and Disability, c/o Access Theatre, 527 Garden Street, Santa Barbara, CA 93101.

An Accessible Theater

The multi–award winning Access Theatre was founded in 1979 by Rod Lathim, the company's artistic director. The only totally accessible professional theater organization in the nation, the company creates original work and also trains and employs both disabled and non-disabled, as well as deaf and hearing, actors. Audience members are accommodated with special seating, assistive listening devices, and descriptive visual services. All performances are voiced and signed. Access Theatre believes that making theaters truly accessible enhances creativity. They have designed and created movable, sculpted scenery that communicates in sign language, providing visual clues for deaf actors and technicians. They have also created costumes especially designed to encompass wheelchairs.

According to Rod Lathim (who, by the way, is not a disabled person):

> Access Theatre believes in creating theater with no barriers. We are dedicated to creating theater that entertains, enlightens, and promotes powerful social change."

It has been our privilege to attend a performance of Access Theatre's production of *Storm Reading*, a multimedia entertainment based upon the writings of Neil Marcus, a poet-humorist-actor who has been afflicted with dystonia (a rare muscular disorder) since the age of eight. Working with two fine performers who voiced and signed the narrative, Marcus seemed at times to be soaring above the stage, a creature of boundless creativity and energy. The wit, charm, imagination, and sheer radiance of their work made for an exhilarating evening of great theater.

A Consulting Organization

Access Entertainment Services, a division of Access Theatre, Inc., represents a growing number of Performers with Disabilities (PWD) seeking jobs in theater, film, and television. They provide technical assistance to ensure that actors with disabilities are smoothly integrated into productions. Sign language interpreters are on hand to facilitate total communication on the set, as well as to translate scripts into American Sign Language. Consultants oversee accurate character portrayal, working with writers and directors to guarantee the authenticity of language, situations, and the presentation of deafness or disability in scenes. There are also workshops for actors.

On a recent nationwide talent search to discover PWD outside of New York and Los Angeles, the Access organization provided the casting consultant with names, addresses, and phone numbers of individuals and organizations who could be primary resources in a dozen major cities.

INDIVIDUAL ACTIVISTS

Lyndi Patton, an actress-dancer, is president of HICCUP — Hearing Impaired Consultants Creating Unique Partnerships. Her company arranges for deaf actors to appear in ads. She learned sign language when she played the role of Helen Keller in a regional theater production of *The Miracle Worker*. She acts as an interpreter, facilitating the communication between the casting director, director, producer, and the hearing-impaired actor.

> It all began a few years ago. I was called by a casting director at an ad agency to audition for the role of a hearing-impaired woman, because I was known for my work with the deaf. I felt it was my responsibility not to accept that job, but to help that agency find an actress who was hearing-impaired. That began my company and my consultancy.
>
> From time to time I have overseen the editing process to verify that the sign language used was matching the text. I have helped rewrite the scripts so that they would fit the linguistics of sign language.
>
> Casting directors were comfortable with me, and I could call on the deaf network of actors as well as national resources.

Lyndi has also encouraged her modeling agency in New York to start a division for "models with special needs."

Kitty Lunn started her career as a dancer and performed as a principal soloist with the National Ballet in Washington, D.C. She was preparing for her Broadway debut when she slipped on ice, fell down six steps, and injured her spinal cord. After two and a half years in the hospital, she resumed her career — in a wheelchair. She is the chairperson of the Performers with Disabilities Committee of Actors Equity, is on the Equity Council, and also serves on the national board of AFTRA. A stunning redhead with a delightful smile, sunny disposition, and brilliant mind, Lunn advocates equal access and equal opportunity.

> I am not suggesting that an actor be hired because he is a performer with a disability. I always believe that the best actor should be hired for the role. As far as Performers with Disabilities is concerned, if a role is disabled-specific, very rarely does it enter anyone's head that possibly

Kitty Lunn's résumé carries the universal symbol for disability.

KITTY LUNN

SAG/AFTRA/AEA

Height:	5'3"
Weight:	105 lb.
Hair:	Lt. Red
Eyes:	Hazel
Voice:	Soprano

FILM/TELEVISION

Awakenings	Patient	Columbia Pictures
Eyes of a Stranger	Annette	Warner Brothers
As The World Turns (currently)	Sally Horton	CBS-TV

COMMERCIALS/INDUSTRIAL FILMS
List upon request -- videotape available

REGIONAL THEATRE

Fan's False False Face Society	Mickey	Edinburgh Festival 1990
The Waiting	Katherine	Very Special Arts at Kennedy Center
Sand Dragons	Cam	for Performing Arts
St. Joan	St. Joan	Dramatic Arts Centre of Miami
Dylan	Caitlan	Dramatic Arts Centre of Miami
After the Fall	Maggie	Dramatic Arts Centre of Miami

OFF BROADWAY

All About Me	Susan Maxwell	Nat. Theatre Workshop of the Handicapped
		Douglas Fairbanks Theater
Langtree	Sarah	The Douglas Fairbanks
Hamlet	Ophelia	Neighborhood Playhouse Rep.
Romeo and Juliet	Juliet	Neighborhood Playhouse Rep.
The Importance of Being Earnest	Cecily	Neighborhood Playhouse Rep.

TRAINING
Acting - Graduate - Neighborhood Playhouse, Sanford Meisner, William Esper;
        Gene Frankel Masterclass
Voice - Rose Inghram
Dance - Soloist, National Ballet, Edward Caton; Martha Graham; Matt Mattox; Luigi

ETC, ETC, ETC.
Due to an accident in 1987, I now use a wheelchair.

the performer with the disability could be the best actor! In the audition process, if you are bringing in twenty able-bodied actors for a disabled-specific role, what harm would it do to bring in five good disabled actors for the part?

She cites examples of deaf roles going to hearing actors, when there are well-trained deaf actors who have extensive theater, film, and television credits. She is puzzled by erroneous assumptions that keep PWD out of work, such as that production insurance rates go up when a disabled actor is hired; they don't, because such discrimination is illegal. Or the weird notion that a physically challenged performer is in ill health. She says:

> If I get a cold they think I am dying. If I come to work with no makeup they say I look sick. It is best in this industry if we do not belabor illness. If you are ill, stay home! If you know you are subject to respiratory distress, then you probably shouldn't be out in the rain or snow for long periods of time. Extreme temperature changes have profound effects on people with disabilities. You have to arrange your agenda to avoid the problems. I don't let people in this business see me sick, ever, ever, ever! I take very good care of myself.

The Americans with Disabilities Act, she explains, speaks to "reasonable accommodation." The persons with the disability must inform the prospective employer or casting director what their needs will be — wheelchair access to a building, for example. Perhaps a visually impaired person reads Braille and wants the copy on audiotape, or needs the script in large print. Many actors have dyslexia, a reading disability, and will need the copy ahead of time to be comfortable with the words. There is fear about admitting the problem, but it makes sense to be candid about it, rather than feeling out of control.

Kitty encourages PWD to go to open calls. She feels it is important for them to mainstream, to get out of the mindset that a PWD is special and cannot do what everybody else does. She also wants the person holding the audition to think *actor* and not *disability*. She believes strongly in punctuality, professionalism, and preparation.

> Actors who are really serious, disability notwithstanding, have up-to-date photos, up-to-date résumés, a half-dozen monologues in their hip pocket, a song if they are singers — and are ready to go at any given time!

Mary Verdi-Fletcher, born with spina bifida, founded Dancing Wheels in 1980 as a means for people with disabilities to explore the world of dance. In 1990, after joining with the Cleveland Ballet, she formed a company of dancers with and without disabilities. Dancing Wheels has toured the country.

> Watching Mary Verdi-Fletcher dance is a spiritual experience. It is an expression of the human spirit through dance that you can't experience unless you see this dancer and her troupe. It is real art, real expression, and real human emotion delivering something that is deep inside the individual.
>
> —DENNIS NAHAT, *artistic director of the Cleveland Ballet*

Kitty Lunn, who has appeared as a guest artist with Dancing Wheels, has said:

> What Mary is doing with the Cleveland Ballet is redefining who can dance, what is movement, what is art, and these wheelchair things that we get around in can be used artistically in a non-medical, non-hospital, non-orthopedic connotation. Perhaps young kids with disabilities will begin to have a dance class every day, as I had.

Rene Moreno's near-fatal fall from a fifth-story window ruptured his aorta and damaged his spinal cord. Without the use of his legs, his career as a busy New York actor seemed finished. But two years later, thanks to intensive therapy and the support of a nationwide network of artists, he was on stage once again, as the narrator in the Dallas Theater Center's *A Christmas Carol*. For this role, he was in a wheelchair.

> It was scary going from a reading to a full production. I was the first person the audience saw on stage in *Carol*. What did they see? We live in a society that judges you by the way you look. But I watched them, and by the play's end, people looked at me in a different way.

VISIONS FOR THE FUTURE

Within the next twenty years, Kitty Lunn would like to think, actors with disabilities
will not be seen as extraordinary, but merely as people who happen to be blind, or
deaf, or in a wheelchair. Witness the example of Christy Brown — played by Daniel
Day Lewis in the movie *My Left Foot* — who was profoundly disabled: the physical
condition did not diminish his talent or his genius.

The axiom of Performers with Disabilities is that creative ability cannot be diminished. Whether it is the Cleveland Ballet's Dancing Wheels, the National Theatre of
the Deaf, the Very Special Arts Programs across the nation, union-sponsored showcases for the industry, the efforts of theatres such as Cleveland's Fairmount Theatre
of the Deaf, Atlanta's Shepherd Spinal Center, Access Theatre Company, and Northern Sign in Minneapolis — that opportunity, like a seed under snow and ice, will
become the flower in spring.

SUGGESTED READING

To learn more about what's happening in this area, we suggest:

• *People with Disabilities Explain It All for You: Your Guide to the Public
Accommodations Requirements of the Americans with Disabilities Act,* Mary
Johnson and the editors of "The Disability Rag," The Advocado Press, 1962
Roanoke, Louisville, KY 40205, 1992.

• *Disability Awareness Guide,* Very Special Arts, Education Office, The John F.
Kennedy Center for the Performing Arts, Washington, D.C.

CHAPTER 10

REGIONAL MARKETS

You don't have to go to Hollywood to be an actor. You can act anywhere. I would suggest going somewhere where you are a big fish in a smaller pond.
—MARY JO SLATER, *president, Slater Casting*

There is life — professional, successful, rewarding life — and opportunity to act outside New York and Los Angeles. In addition to Chicago, which is rapidly becoming the third metropolis (thanks to its award-winning theaters, its status as a first-class production center for features and series, and a host of superstar alumni who got their start in the city), there are regional markets where work may possibly be more accessible, union cards more easily earned, and the quality of life more agreeable.

This chapter focuses on the scene in Chicago, Miami, Atlanta, Dallas, Minneapolis, Seattle, Portland, Philadelphia, Washington, D.C., and San Francisco. Each of these cities offers a rich cultural environment, informed by the theatrical climate that exists there.

CHICAGO, THE CITY THAT WORKS

If you are intimidated by the hustle of New York, if you don't have an agent to hustle for you in Los Angeles, you might give serious thought to heading for Chicago. The city that helped to develop the careers of Joe Mantegna, Dennis Franz, John Malkovich, Joan Allen, John Mahoney, Laurie Metcalf, John Cusack, and Shelly Long, to name only a few, is a city of working actors.

> You don't find the marginal performer who thinks, "Oh, someday, maybe I'll get lucky." Here they work at making their own luck.
> —REED FARRELL, *former national president of AFTRA*

Vince Viverito, a character actor in his mid-forties, has worked in the best theaters in Chicago and won the Joseph Jefferson Award (the Jeff) for best supporting actor in a musical. He divides his career between Chicago and New York and says:

> I recommend Chicago to everybody. In Chicago, theater is accessible, everything is available. You can take time off to go to a ball game and sleep late on occasion. It is easier to get an Equity card here than in New York.

Chicago's 5,000 union performers boast higher per capita earnings because "everybody can work!" Outside of New York and Los Angeles, it is probably the busiest market in the country for industrials, voice-overs, and commercials. It is also home to the Second City Company, the birthplace of some of the best improvisational comedians and comedy writers in the country. There are more than 150 theater groups staying alive in Chicago.

It was the Steppenwolf Theater that put the city on the map, so to speak, by premiering new plays and garnering enough critical acclaim to move some of them to Broadway. Recently a forty-seat storefront studio known as the Eclipse Theatre Company won a Jeff. Billing itself as "the world's smallest Equity theater," it has an acting ensemble, most of whom have been trained at the Theater School at De Paul University.

> Chicago theater continues to thrive because it continues to reinvent itself, with young troupes like Eclipse, which do not choose to play it safe.
> —JONATHAN ABARBANEL, *regional critic for* Screen *magazine*

Juan Antonio Ramirez is an actor, writer, director, and the founder of Latino Chicago. He believes in Chicago's rich cultural life and the opportunities which exist for Spanish-speaking actors:

> There is really a conscious effort to hire more ethnic performers here. In my own experience, ten of the sixteen parts I have done in films were not written for Latino actors.

Another Latino actor, Henry Godinez, headed a group of Equity and nonEquity actors who saw a need for better representation of Latino actors and playwrights in the Chicago theater scene. In 1989 he founded Teatro Vista — Theater with a View. Firmly committed to sharing and celebrating the richness of Latino culture with all theater audiences, the group seeks to initiate a youth outreach and training program.

Young actors such as Frederick Schleicher are happy about living in Chicago:

> It is the best place to start out. There is a sense of community. Actors help each other to get a break.

He lives in a good neighborhood, and pays $275 for a one-bedroom apartment. The transportation system is efficient, which saves the expense of owning a car. He thinks it is great that actors in Chicago are beginning to get featured roles that formerly went only to actors in Los Angeles or New York. He does feel that after a couple of years he will have to move on to "the next level."

To Raul Esparza, Chicago is "fantastic." Since his arrival from New York, where he attended NYU and was paying what he calls "a fortune for a two-bedroom rat hole," his career has taken off:

> I don't have to have a second job, I've been able to join two unions, get day parts in TV series, and what I am most grateful for is the opportunity to perform worthwhile roles at an amazing regional theater like the Goodman!

When Nesba Crenshaw moved to Chicago from Minneapolis, where for nine years she had been one of the busiest commercials and industrials performers, she thought the transition would be smoother:

> I was really surprised. Chicago is a much more sophisticated market. I began to feel I didn't have the right wardrobe. Competition is stiffer, and it feels like going from the minors to the majors.

She met people by taking classes. Hoping to broaden her horizons in film and TV work, Crenshaw is relieved she chose Chicago over the coasts:

> Coming here opened my eyes to many areas I knew nothing about, even in terms of style and how to present myself. I think anyone coming here needs at least a three-month cushion, so they don't have to worry about paying the rent.

Performers in Chicago are fortunate in that they can "multilist" with agents, as opposed to signing exclusively with one. According to Marla Cahan, an agent at Suzanne's A+, agents are more open to people just starting out. Agent Lynne Hamilton lists nonunion performers because she feels that if they are good, they will soon be union members. Veteran talent agent Shirley Hamilton, Lynne's mother and colleague, represents 200 actors exclusively and freelances thousands. She is most impressed by an academic background in theater and a great personality. Marla Cahan is turned on by raw talent, that special "it" quality that can't be taught. Agents say there is enough theater in Chicago to keep them going two to three times a week, and they do.

Chicago's SAG/AFTRA office allows actors to pay the initiation fee in installments. The local also publishes a talent directory which is distributed to talent agents in New York and Los Angeles, to music houses, ad agencies, commercial producers, casting directors on both coasts, industrial film houses, and area theaters. Performers, who pay a small fee for the listing, must be members of either union and be based either in Chicago or Milwaukee.

New York casting directors seek talent in Chicago for commercials as well as for soap operas. Casting directors from Los Angeles constantly look for talent for situation comedies, series, and movies of the week. The agents tape their clients and send the tapes to Hollywood every year during pilot season. Since the successful location shooting of the series *The Untouchables* and *Missing Persons*, and features such as John Hughes' *Baby's Day Out, The Fugitive, Losing Isaiah* (with Jessica Lange), and *Richie Rich* (with Macaulay Culkin), everyone expects that there will be more and more job opportunities.

Chicago actors learn about casting opportunities from a union hotline, or by reading the local trade paper, *Perform Ink.*

Acting, Modeling and Dance: Chicagoland's Resource Directory, an annual publication, is a worthwhile investment if you are seriously considering taking up residence in what Reed Farrell calls "the city that works!" For information, write: Don Kaufman, Publisher, 410 S. Michigan Ave., Suite 613, Chicago, IL 60605.

ATLANTA

Atlanta has come a long way in the last fifteen years, and there is still great potential for growth. Because Georgia is a right-to-work state, it is not necessary to join a union to work in the industry. The bulk of the work in this market is radio, non-broadcast industrials, and commercials.

According to Melissa Goodman, executive director of Atlanta's SAG/AFTRA office, the initiation fee is $700 for AFTRA, $970 for SAG, plus $42.50 for the first semi-annual dues period. A payment plan can be arranged to make it easier for new members:

> We work it out with the individual performer on an as-needed basis. I usually ask for at least $250 down. I try to be accommodating and keep my members happy.

Atlanta has proven capable of producing two network series simultaneously and continues to attract West Coast producers for feature shoots as well as movies of the week. Melissa Goodman acknowledges the contribution of casting director Shay Griffin in promoting the industry and the talent pool. She has done the local casting for *I'll Fly Away* and *In the Heat of the Night* and dozens of features, miniseries, and movies of the week.

> Actors can start their careers in nonunion commercials and industrials. With more experience and better training, they can move into feature-film roles. A number of local actors have been cast in ongoing roles in the network series I cast. Plus there is a good deal of professional and nonprofessional theater work.
>
> —SHAY GRIFFIN, *casting director, Atlanta*

She receives calls from casting directors in Los Angeles or New York at least once a month, asking her to do a special search or put out a call for a particular role they want to cast, a clear sign that they acknowledge the talent pool in this market.

The Georgia Film Commission, created in the early 1970s, is one of the most progressive film commissions in the country. The governor's office has supported the desire to attract more films to the state. This department helps film companies get everything they need. Every year, at least ten different films do all or part of their shooting here. *To Dance with Wolves*, starring Hume Cronyn and Jessica Tandy, was even written by a Georgian.

> There is every indication that the wealth of writing and production talent in Georgia will occasion the creation of in-state projects. Actors can cross over into many areas — voice-overs, on-camera roles, theater projects — and make a nice living. It makes me hopeful that careers can be started here, and a lifetime can be spent here, working in the industry. The quality of life in Atlanta can be very comfortable for the actor, adding an incentive to making Atlanta the base of operations.
>
> —SHAY GRIFFIN

MIAMI

Iris Acker, Manhattan-based actress and dancer, realized the potential of Miami in 1972, when she was cast in a play there. Now, after more than twenty years of working in commercials, films, and plays, and serving on the national board of AFTRA, she is the artistic director of Miami's Shores Theatre and hosts her own cable talk show. She has seen the growth of the talent pool and of opportunities for Hispanic actors. She believes being bilingual can open doors to the commercial and soap opera production that is a major part of the income in Miami. With superstars like Arnold Schwarzenegger and Sylvester Stallone investing in property in the area, there is hope that feature-film production there will get a boost.

Peg McKinley, owner of Act One Talent Agency, is vice chairwoman of the newly formed Florida Entertainment Commission, a public and privately funded organization which aims to promote the industry within the state. Tammy Green, co-owner of the Green and Green Agency, believes theatrical activity is expanding.

TheatreWeek magazine recently devoted an entire issue to theater in Florida and concluded:

> Theaters like the Coconut Grove and the Asolo have names that resonate beyond the state of Florida. With greater frequency, New York shows originate here. The Carbonnel Awards, Florida's version of the Helen Hayes Awards, continue to celebrate excellence and promote public awareness of theater. The Theatre League of South Florida has a mailing list of about two hundred theaters and theater professionals from Palm Beach to the keys.

There are numerous small companies surviving, such as the M Ensemble, which has produced African-American plays for more than twenty years; the Promoteo Theatre, a bilingual company; and the Ensemble Theatre, a forty-seat storefront studio which specializes in unusual alternative programming. Since 1979, Teatro Avante has worked to preserve and present the Hispanic cultural heritage in Miami. Under the passionate guidance of its producing artistic director, Mario Ernesto Sanchez, Teatro Avante has become the most actively producing and widely known Hispanic theater in the southeast.

There are a dozen or so excellent talent agents in the Miami area, and a strong union office which is anxious to create opportunities for its approximately 3,000 members.

> I came down here for a long holiday, registered with a few of the agents and, maybe because I was a new face in town, got a call for an audition for a national spot. Then I got a callback, and then — would you believe it? — I got the job. And it was for an ad agency in New York that I could never get into, but they were shooting in Florida!
> —BETH HOLLAND, *actress, former president of AFTRA's New York local*

If you decide to reside in Miami, apartments are more affordable than in New York or Los Angeles, but you will need a car and, probably, a survival strategy.

DALLAS

Dallas is an extremely good market for a young person just getting out of school who needs to build a résumé. The amount of film and television work there would enable newcomers to get their union cards. There are five franchised agents in Dallas, but actors may also list with agencies in Houston, San Antonio, and Austin. The initiation fee for both SAG and AFTRA is $600. There are perhaps 1,500 union members in the whole state.

Sean McGraw, a successful actor-producer and member of the Dallas Industry Council, is an authority on work opportunities throughout the state:

> Governor Ann Richards traveled to Los Angeles to encourage studio heads to use the talent and technical resources here. Producers from the West Coast and stars like Clint Eastwood and Kevin Costner have discovered that Austin is a comfortable place to shoot. If they want a beach look, there is the Gulf coast; mountains, the Big Ben country; deserts, El Paso; and for upscale city looks, Dallas and Houston.

With a state-of-the-art production facility and the success of series such as *Walker, Texas Ranger*, there is a stronger outlook for more pilots, movies of the week, and episodic television.

Don Shook, owner and artistic director of The Actors Company, produces comedies, mysteries, and musicals that employ actors. His "traveling troubadours" entertain at country clubs, hotels, and military bases throughout the southwest. According to Don:

> Actors who live here have to diversify, doing primarily commercials and industrials and voice-overs. There are a handful of full-time professional actors, but there are a lot of people acting who make a living by supplementing their income doing other things.

Theater work in Dallas has diminished. In the Dallas—Fort Worth area, there are fewer professional theater companies, but there are thirty to forty splinter theatrical groups functioning at all times. Actors Equity has instituted an umbrella program on a trial basis: a few non-Equity theaters pooled their resources and now offer contracts to Equity actors on a one-show basis. This has proven very successful for the non-Equity theaters wishing to attract better talent. And it broadens the opportunities for very good professional actors to work on stage.

Equity maintains a hotline, as does S.T.A.G.E., which stands for Society for Theatrical Artists' Guidance and Enhancement. Founded in 1981, this nonprofit service and support organization serves the theatrical and film communities of the north-central Texas region. A clearinghouse of information for a membership that includes actors, directors, playwrights, theaters, production companies, and agents, S.T.A.G.E. is funded by membership dues, grants, donations, and newsletter advertising. *Centerstage*, its monthly newsletter, keeps actors informed about the theater scene as well as developments in TV and film. Membership in S.T.A.G.E. provides access to a library of more than 3,000 scripts, musicals, biographies and textbooks, a low-cost résumé service, and career guidance and counseling. Each month, members who qualify have the opportunity to be seen in Noon Preview, the talent show-case S.T.A.G.E. presents for casting directors and producers.

The Biz Directory: An Actor's Guide has been compiled by Austin-based actress and teacher Mona Lee. A thorough resource, it is available from BIZ Publications, Box 50021, Austin, TX 78763. Available at the SAG/AFTRA office in Dallas is the newly published professional performer's guide, *The Tools of the Trade.*

MINNEAPOLIS

Theater has always been strong in Minneapolis, home of the renowned Tyrone Guthrie Theatre, the Chanhassen, the Old Log, and newer, ethnically diverse the-aters such as Mixed Blood, the Illusion, and The Penumbra.

Nancy Lopez, a talent agent with the Eleanor Moore Agency, attends the theater as often as three times each week to seek new talent:

> Most of the actors in Minneapolis can afford their life-style doing their craft. Theater work, along with commercials, films, and industrials can support the actor and afford a home for his family. Good, working actors don't have to wait on tables.

The Minneapolis Film Board has been actively promoting Minnesota to Los Angeles studios and producers, in spite of the unpredictability of the weather.

> We get calls all the time to put people on tape. In the middle of pilot sea-son, I go crazy trying to keep up with it. Once in a blue moon, somebody here lands something — and we have had several blue moons.
>
> —NANCY LOPEZ

Actor Paul Douglas Law admits he is able to work in Minneapolis. He tasted the New York experience for several years and ultimately decided it was more important to be working than looking for work:

> I do shows back to back. The longest period I was out of work here was two months. It is also much easier to get an agent here. For everything you do in New York, you have to be stronger and present yourself with enormous confidence. People here aren't used to that, so when an actor comes in the door ready to work, they perk up. Per capita, I have heard, there is more theater going on here than anywhere. Playwrights come from all over the country, and there is always new work being produced here.

Minneapolis is a terrific, affordable place to begin. If you want to keep your hand in the theater you can always find a place to work, build your résumé, and then go on to the next bigger market.

SEATTLE

This is a city for actors who love to work onstage. As one actress said, "Seattle in a place for learnin', not earnin'." Yet there is always a chance that theaters such as

Seattle Rep, the Intiman, A Contemporary Theatre, and others will originate productions that can travel to Broadway. Witness the examples of *Conversations with My Father* from Seattle Rep and *The Kentucky Cycle* from the Intiman.

With the success of such TV series as *Northern Exposure*, Miki Mobrand, talent agent at Dramatic Artists, is confident that a sound stage will be built in the near future. Likewise, the Seattle Film Commission wants to make Seattle more hospitable to feature-film production.

There are increasing opportunities in industrials, voice-overs, and commercials for women, older men, and ethnic actors. Seattle has its own Asian-American Theatre, as well as a multicultural Group Theatre. The Seattle Children's Theatre offers extensive training programs.

Before he made his film debut in *Encino Man*, Brendan Frazer honed his craft working in theater in Seattle. The training he received at the Cornish College of the Arts there also helped him make a smooth transition into film. Reiko Aylesworth could not have relocated to New York to create a role on *One Life to Live* had she not been able to develop confidence in her skills through live performance and theatrical training. Talent does not come from any specific region. Talent *is*.

The following resources contain extensive information about how and where to seek work opportunities in this market:

- *The Actor's Handbook: Seattle and the Pacific Northwest*, by Mark Jaroslaw. (Printed annually.) Niche Press, 600 Pine Street, Seattle, WA 98122.

- *The Northwest Film, Video, and Audio Production Index*, Eleventh edition, Media Index Publishing Co., Box 24365, Seattle, WA 98124-0356.

- Barbara Rey's self-published *Talent Resource Guide* contains information about acting schools, résumés, headshot photographers, union and nonunion agents, casting directors, and voice-overs. Write: Barbara Rey, Box 482, Bellevue WA 98009.

PORTLAND

Production opportunities have grown tremendously over the last several years in this city, and there is no end in sight. The Oregon Film and Video Association is actively promoting the area's production crews and talent pool. There is always industrial work and, now, a great deal of voice-overs for CD-ROM, as well as work in the new field of interactive programs. Will Vinton's animation company employs local talent to create character voices.

Chris Cusick has been a talent agent for more than fifteen years. She has 325 exclusive clients in her roster of legitimate actors, voice-over and on-camera talent, and successful print and runway models. She is enthusiastic:

> We are seeing a lot more series pilots, movies of the week, and info-mercials. The state is trying to create a studio for more features and series. I see Portland being a real contender in the movie industry. With the [information] superhighway, we will be doing a lot more CD-video and cable. We are definitely on the cutting edge.

Ms. Sam Downey, owner of Creative Artists Management in Seattle, has been active as a producer and developer of talent for more than fifteen years. One of her clients is a regular on *Northern Exposure*. She also sees production picking up:

> There has been a large influx of actors from L.A. relocating to the Pacific Northwest. That raises the professional level of the market. I think in the nineties the quality of life is more important than necessarily being where all the action is.

Al Strobel, president of the AFTRA local, reports that there are more than 500 union performers and at least another thousand trained nonunion actors:

> A SAG executive from L.A. came up to Portland and exclaimed: "This is going to be the L.A. of the North!" We have everything here, plus a freshness that doesn't exist in the other production centers. Six years ago there wasn't any organization. Voice-over talent was getting twenty bucks a wild spot. Now we are setting up recruiting programs in the AFTRA local, like a conservatory. There is a strong movement to organize Equity with an umbrella contract, similar to the one in Dallas. We are getting SAG to renew their interest. We just might get a jump on the rest of the country on what could be a merged performers' union!

SAN FRANCISCO

This city probably boasts one of the best-organized AFTRA/SAG offices in the country. The executive director oversees an active hotline, so the members are constantly apprised of work opportunities. Theatre Bay Area is another hotline that announces union and nonunion jobs on a daily basis. Talent agents like Janice Erlendsen, at STARS The Agency, are always going to theater to spot fresh talent and videotaping signed clients for casting directors in New York and Los Angeles.

There are mostly non-Equity theaters in the peninsula, Silicon Valley, and East Bay areas. In addition, there are a number of flourishing ethnic theaters, such as the Asian American Theatre Company, which has co-produced new works with Equity theaters and occasionally brings its productions to New York. There are also the African-American Shakespeare Festival, the Theatre of Yugen, Theatre del'Esperanza, and Brava.

San Francisco as a base of operations is only a short flight from Los Angeles, Portland, and Seattle. There's an energy there that is more akin to New York's than Minneapolis' and a theatrical fervor that enables you to grow and stretch and be readier for the bigger ponds down the road.

PHILADELPHIA

Michael Lemon has been casting in the Philadelphia area for more than ten years. A former actor, he clearly admires, respects, and empathizes with talent as they experience the ups and downs of The Business. He worked for Jonathan Demme on casting principal roles for the film *Philadelphia*. Demme was extremely pleased with the quality of the talent pool he found in the city and will probably return at a future date.

Lemon shared his opinions about Philadelphia as an alternative to New York, Chicago, and Los Angeles:

> There are between 2,500 and 3,500 union performers here. Actors who make a living here do a lot of voice-over work, commercials, theater, and industrials. Chemical and pharmaceutical firms in Wilmington, Delaware, and Princeton, New Jersey, employ actors on a regular basis. New York ad agencies have discovered it is cheaper to shoot in the area, so within a year we can cast about twenty national commercials. The train to New York takes about ninety minutes, to do professional head-shots and auditions, and there has been a big surge in theater activity over the last five years. There are union hotlines for actors through SAG and Equity, as well as the Philadelphia Film Office. Actors who base themselves here can also work in New York and D.C. We really have good rapport with the talent pool. With the mayor and the film office so committed to bringing film work to Philadelphia, it has lifted everyone's spirits and their vision.

WASHINGTON, D.C.

More than forty theaters in the Washington region participate in the Helen Hayes Awards. In 1984, when these awards were created to increase awareness of the D.C. theater community and celebrate the excellence of their productions, there were less than half that number. Actors, directors, and designers seek opportunities to work here. According to Abel Lopez, associate producing director of GALA Hispanic Theatre and president of the nontraditional casting project, theater and its artists have contributed to the economic vitality of the metropolitan area and to the enhancement of its quality of life.

The market, which includes Baltimore and parts of Virginia, is actively promoting its locations for film production. Barry Levinson, a Baltimore native, has returned home to shoot the films *Avalon, Diner, Rain Man*, and his gritty TV series, *Homicide*.

Linda Townsend, a leading talent manager in Baltimore, considers the market fairly good for feature-film production. The movie *Major League 2* and films starring Arnold Schwarzenneger and Tom Hanks have used locations for their shoots, as have cable-TV specials. She is also able to book her clients for theatrical projects at Center Stage, Arena Stage, and the Folger Shakespeare Theatre.

The Actors' Center is a membership organization created in 1981 by and for local actors. Their purpose was to help actors improve their skills and to strengthen and support the greater Washington theater community. A twenty-four-hour recorded phone message, updated each week, announces information on auditions, events, and discounts and services available to members. Their bimonthly publication *On Cue!* is another source of news regarding auditions and interviews at out-of-town theaters. The Actors' Center annually sponsors general auditions to showcase the local talent pool for an invited audience of local directors and casting directors. Professional volunteers conduct Saturday-morning workshops on theatrical makeup, musical auditioning, voice-overs, and other skills. The Actors' Center also boasts an extensive script library members may use for reference. Annual membership is currently $45.

For information, write: Membership Coordinator, The Actors' Center, Box 50180, Washington, D.C. 20091.

AND ELSEWHERE

Are these regional markets the only places to be outside New York or Los Angeles? Not at all. They are examples chosen to give you a hint of what's going on in The Business. They indicate some of the possibilities and ways of building a career. We aim to give you an idea of how to make the most of where you are.

FILM COMMISSIONS

As you surely realize by now, feature films, made-for-TV movies, television series, industrial films, and even ten-second commercials are being produced all over the country (and the world). These productions mean a huge influx of dollars to the chosen locations. To alert producers to the scenic and financial advantages of choosing their area as a location for their next shoot, every state government (and many cities and foreign nations) has set up at least one film commission or motion picture development bureau. Would it surprise you to learn that the Association of Film Commissioners International has more than 170 members? Many of their presentation materials are stunningly produced and not only glorify local scenery, but also the available local talent, including performers.

To the actor this can mean that there's an organization of eager government executives working to get job opportunities for you. While the important acting jobs in these projects will usually be filled by name performers, local talent will more than likely be needed for small parts, extra work, and production staff assistance. Your state or city film commission can be a source of leads. The staff may be able to clue you into incoming projects with jobs for local talent. Their directory will list agents, casting directors, production houses, and theater companies. You will discover places to work — as freelance, intern, or volunteer — and people you don't know. Some of the more energetic film commissions invite the local talent to seminars, where sharing ideas can sometimes result in new projects or new work. At the very least, you'll connect with people who are working in The Business, and that's where jobs can begin.

Your telephone directory can tell you whether there's a film commission or motion picture development office listing in your area. Ask for a copy of the bureau's solicitation material or production directory and see where you might find the kind of work you want.

For information about The Association of Film Commissioners International, and a glimpse of what the other places are doing to get movie production business, you may want to write to: Association of Film Commissioners International, c/o Utah Film Commission, 324 South State Street, Suite 500, Salt Lake City, UT 84111.

LOCAL UNION OFFICES

While AFTRA, Equity, and SAG can not pursue work in the same way as film commissions, which are government agencies, the enthusiastic actors in our highlighted regional markets report that the locals do much to help the members perfect their skills and make themselves more competitive in the marketplace. Hotlines, seminars, industry showcases, classes for members taught by members, audio and video equipment for members to practice their camera and mike techniques — these are all possible ways to improve the quality of the work as well as the quality of the performer's life outside the mainstream.

LOCAL NETWORKERS

It is possible to create theaters where none exist. It's possible to do a local TV show and make it the local Emmy winner. And we know it's possible to make a worthy film on a shoestring. All these things have already been done — by others whom we either know or read about.

These successes require an investment of time, hard work, and enthusiasm. But when the performers in an area are working together, developing an ensemble, the effect is exhilarating. Even in a tiny space, such as the Theatre Lab in Houston (a grocery store converted into a sixty-five-seat theater); Eclipse in Chicago and Ensemble in Florida (both storefront studios), the enthusiasm generates a reward: an audience's attention and a community's support.

It *is* possible to start your own regional company. It takes time. But none of the actors we spoke to ever thought it would be easy.

PART TWO

THE BREAKS

CHAPTER 11

INTERVIEW AND FOLLOW-UP

Actors must learn to act the interview. It is part of their job.

—Tex Beha, *partner, Paradigm Agency*

Before you get to work on a stage or in a studio, you will need to succeed at two other kinds of performances: the interview and the audition. Interviews and auditions are the givens of the industry. Or at least they will be until you become so well-known that the mere mention of your name as a possibility for a role triggers an instant "Oh, yes, just the one we were thinking of." And even at that level, you will be invited to "take a meeting" because "Sweetheart, they just want to meet you."

Meetings by any name are interviews, and in Los Angeles they're auditions. The interview is a chance to be seen, at last, by people who can help you. And yet, not everyone sees interviews as opportunities.

> Most actors, when they come into the office, are so damned nervous they can hardly respond. I've had actors read for me, and their hands are shaking. I tell them, "Look, we're not the enemy . . . yet! Just relax."
>
> —Lester Lewis

Why the terror? This is not a screening process. Agents and casting directors do not sit at the entry to the industry, like admissions officers waiting to stamp you "Untalented" and tell you to go away. They want you to be *mahvelous, dahling!*

Of course, how marvelous you appear to your interviewer will depend upon innumerable conditions that you cannot control: the volume of the office's business, whether they are active in the area that offers the most activity for you, whether you look like the agent's brother or mother-in-law (and what those relationships are like), whether the series you might have been exactly right for has just been canceled or put on hold. You cannot possibly know about such things, nor could you change them if you did. Here is how some agents describe the you they want to see:

> The same rules apply when talking to an agent as when talking to any other human being. Be yourself, enjoy the person you are speaking with, and don't push it. Be considerate of the person's time and space. Come

prepared, but be willing to go with the flow. Don't act rushed, but don't overstay your welcome.

—PEGGY HADLEY

I look for a commercial appeal and potential, talent, and the sure feeling that they are good, honest people.

—ROBBIE KASS

I want a prospective client to have common sense, self-awareness, understanding that show business means that this is a business, willingness to learn all aspects of the business and to be prepared for any and all auditions.

—TEX BEHA

I respond to people who have an inner warmth, an appeal that makes me care about them and about how a role filtered through their instrument is different from a role filtered through someone else's.

—RICKI OLSHAN

The interview, then, is a meeting at which both parties can get some idea of whether they like one another and whether there is any possibility of a relationship at this time or in the future.

BEFORE THE MEETING

Do you remember how, as a teenager, you would prepare for a party where you expected to meet Mr. or Miss Wonderful? How you went about getting that paragon to ask you for a first date? Remember the research? Was he interested in football? You learned who Joe Montana was and warned yourself not to call him Joe Mantegna, or vice versa. Did she like classical music? You came up with tickets for a concert. And before the grand occasion, all the time spent planning what to wear, how to look — earrings, matching lipstick and nail polish; aftershave and the right shirt and tie! Remember the excitement, the pent-up energy, the *expectation? The electricity?* Bring that concentration, that fervor and anticipation, to your interview planning.

Find out as much as you can about the person you are going to meet. Your scene partner, your roommates, someone in your circle may be able to give you a clue. Your instructors should surely have some information that can be helpful. Read books written about casting directors and agents, such as Judith Searle's *Getting the Part*, a collection of interviews with casting people on both coasts.

A small warning: Try to latch onto *positive* information. Negative comments, such as "So-and-so is obnoxious" — or demanding, tough, or only likes people who went to Yale — are personal responses from that person's meeting. It may have been a bad day for both people in the interview. Put such data back in your forget-it file. Or try to turn it around for positive use: "I think Yale has produced some superb actors, directors, and writers. I wish I'd had the chance to go there."

Rehearse what you are going to say about yourself that is relevant. We don't suggest that you to launch into a speech about everything you've done since you were in the sixth-grade play, like a machine spewing words until the nickel drops down.

Practice is the only way to attain ease with answers to questions like: "What have you been doing?" "Tell me about yourself." "How did you enjoy working at Such-and-Such Theater?" "What parts have you played?"

THE QUESTIONNAIRE AS A TOOL FOR SELF-KNOWLEDGE

Because you shouldn't trust yourself to think on your feet, we have created a questionnaire to help you to polish your interview technique, so so that you won't freeze when questions are hurled at you by some disembodied voice emanating from the control room, or a stranger standing behind the camera.

PROFILE QUESTIONNAIRE

Name _____

Age range: _____ Height: _____ Hair: _____ Eyes: _____

Training (acting, singing, dancing, etc.): _____

_____

Education: _____

Skills: _____

Sports: _____

Hobbies: _____

Favorite color: _____ Least favorite color: _____

Favorite actor: _____ Favorite actress: _____

Favorite role played: _____

Type of role you would like to play (villain, hero, heroine, bitch, etc.):

_____

A fictional character you identify with on prime-time or daytime television, and why:

_____

_____

What screen role you would wish to play, and why:

_____

_____

After filling out the questionnaire, practice talking it through as if you were delivering a monologue about yourself. Try some humor. Watch the speed of your delivery, and avoid swallowing your words. Ar-tic-u-late. Watch your vocal inflections — for example, don't end sentences with a question mark; make it a period. Avoid fillers, such as "uh," "like," "y'know." Take a breath. Breathing helps you relax.

Be believable, show some passion and commitment. You'll sound wishy-washy if you lard sentences with "I think," or "I guess," or "I'm not sure but. . . ." Look at your face when you mention your least favorite color. That is a real sensory reaction to something you passionately do not like. (Orange, and yellow, and "puke green" are the usual winners in that category.)

Know your age range. You will be asked often enough how old you are, but remember that the unions have strict rules about age discrimination. That is why it is best to know your *range*. Keep it within two to five years of your chronological age.

Don't veer or stray from the subject at hand. Actors have a tendency to share more of their life story than is asked for. Stick to the questions, be brief, concise, and have a definite point of view. Don't feel defensive about your opinions. They are unique to you, so be proud of them. You are an actor and you should have opinions about who thrills you as an actor or actress. You should also be familiar with the medium that you want to work in, and have a feeling for roles you could realistically play.

With all this information about your background on the tip of your tongue, you'll be able to listen and answer intelligently and even show that you have a sense of humor.

Additional Suggestions   Practice shaking hands. It's amazing that this perfunctory gesture can present a problem. Why does this vibrant, healthy person have a handshake like a dying fish? A bone crusher is equally undesirable. If you know your hands tend to be cold, go to the rest room and put them under warm water; if nervousness makes them moist, carry a handkerchief and dry them before you go into the office.

As we explained in Chapter 5, clothing for interviews and auditions should flatter you and be appropriate for The Business. Make sure your outfit is clean and fresh: sew buttons, remove spots, press creases. For men, that means you should wear a jacket, slacks, and shirt; the tie is up to you. Women should wear skirts, dresses, or coordinated pants suits. What you wear also indicates how you see yourself: upscale — which means high-income, more sophisticated (think of Lincoln Town Car commercials); or middle-American (household products and cereals). Pay attention to programs and commercials and learn where you fit in. Apply that awareness to your choices. Remember, the package is you. What you present is what you are selling, and how you want to be remembered.

Plan your day so that you have plenty of time to arrive, relax, comb your hair, check your face, and so forth. All the things you would do if you were visiting another important person in "real life."

If you have several appointments on the same day, make every effort to allow sufficient time between them. Be more than realistic, be generous. On a day that you have your time planned up to the minute, you will more than likely be caught in traffic, have to wait to see your first contact, spend more time than you anticipated in the office of an agent who is on a long-distance phone call, or who asks you to read, or who wants to introduce you to the others in the office. Allow yourself the leeway to deal positively with these things. You cannot concentrate properly on interview number one if a part of your mind is worrying about dashing to appointment number two, and possibly arriving late for appointment number three.

Bring a supply of photos with your résumé attached and your photo postcards. Photo business cards are optional. Ask for the agent's opinion of these. "Oh, that's your picture, eh?" doesn't tell you very much. Bring your tape if you have one, but do not expect the agent to review it at that time. Be prepared to perform your monologue or whatever material you use for a solo audition.

> I like to see a monologue that isn't a big stretch, that is close to who they are, because it is an office situation. It is too difficult to do Shakespeare. We want to see who they are, and, please, some humor.
>
> —TEX BEHA

Be prepared to read copy. Be prepared to show what you can do in the equivalent of an audition. That's part of what the agent is looking to see. Be prepared.

WHEN YOU GET THERE
Look around. Notice the paintings, photographs, posters, collectibles, the color scheme. Get a feel for the atmosphere. Is it musty, dusty, or full of verve? Listen. Are the phones ringing? How are they answered? Do you sense an attitude of respect? Politeness? Would you want these people to represent you? It's a mutual decision, after all.

The agent will conduct you to her (or his) office or desk area, and the two of you will proceed to get to know a little about one another. The agent will explain his areas of activity and where he sees your greatest potential.

WHAT CAN HAPPEN
The very best thing that can happen, and what everyone hopes for, is the equivalent of "love at first sight." Your originality, dynamism, and talent will wow the first agent you meet, who will introduce you to everyone in the office and immediately telephone a casting director who agrees to see you right away. That's *possible*.

It is also possible that the agent will not be able to visualize you in any of the projects he or she is working on. In that case, you will be ushered out with the admonition "Keep in touch."

Between those extremes are lines such as "Let me know when you are doing something, I want to see your work"; "It's been nice meeting you, give my regards to so-and-so [the person who suggested you get in touch]." That adds up to keeping in touch, which is exactly what you must do.

No one will say to you, "Are you out of your mind? Go home, you don't belong in this business!"

You also may get a referral to a friend or colleague at another office, an advertising agency, or a production house, or an opportunity to meet a casting director.

At the end of the day, note down all of this in your record book, and prepare for your next set of appointments.

MEETING A CASTING DIRECTOR

As we explained in Chapter 3, casting directors may be on the staff of an advertising agency, a network, or a production company, or they may be independent consultants who work only on projects going into immediate production. Part of your preparation is to find out who does what.

Ad agency casting departments want performers for the commercials the agency creates for its clients. The Agency Red Book will tell you who these clients are. At the interview, you will be very impressive if you know what accounts the casting director casts for.

Some sponsors use "real people"; some use only beautiful people or models; some employ ethnic actors and character types. If you believe that you are right for a product the agency handles, mention that to the casting director.

Your preparation for the interview will otherwise be the same as for a meeting with a talent agent: photos, résumés, tapes, a conversational attitude plus a lively appearance.

It is doubtful that you will be asked to audition any of your own prepared material, but the casting director may offer you a piece of current commercial copy — especially if you fit the description of a spot they are working on. Take the time to analyze the material (see Chapter 13, which deals with auditions, and the sample audition material in Part 3, which will help you with script analysis), and give it your best.

When you talk to a network casting executive who supervises the casting of principal roles on daytime serials, *know the shows that are on that network*. You should also know the difference between prime-time soaps (which are broadcast once a week, in the evenings) and daytime dramas (five times a week, in the early afternoon).

If you are meeting a soap opera casting director, know what show that person casts, the names of the leading characters, and the names of the actors who portray them. Certainly, you should take the time to watch the program so you understand what is happening and are aware of what the show looks like. If you are unable to do that, purchase *Soap Opera Digest* and read the plot synopses.

Donn Schrader recalls his first interview with a soap opera casting director:

> I was sitting in her office when she got a script and saw that she needed a policeman. She looked at me. "You could play a policeman, couldn't you?" And I certainly agreed. So, getting the job like that was one piece of luck. What was luckier still was that this policeman found the leading man in an alley after he'd been mugged and took him to the hospital. For weeks afterward, while he was recuperating, he kept remembering the policeman who had rescued him. So my one-shot scene was replayed dozens of times!

Meeting the casting director for *any* series requires that you bone up on that show. Can you seriously expect to work in TV if you don't know what's being aired? An interview may lead to an audition.

Casting directors for theater and films are independent consultants. Your interview with them is preliminary to an audition for a role in a specific production, which you must try to find out about through the unions and by reading the trade papers.

The theater interview will usually require you to perform your own prepared material: monologues showing two types of scenes or two types of characters. Some casting directors want to see you do a classic piece and a contemporary selection. You should be preparing these as part of your personal homework. Don't suddenly dash to the bookstore to find a piece you will have to perform the very next day, or memorize the first monologue you find in a book.

Casting directors of films are less interested in what you do with other writers' material; they only want to see what you can do with the script at hand. Writers and directors sometimes try to maintain the secrecy of a project, but you and/or the agent who submits you want to know all you can about the film so that you will behave confidently.

Who are this casting director's steady clients? What has this writer done before? Did you see it? Did you enjoy it? Who was in the cast? Is the director's name familiar?

Screen Credits Get into the habit of paying attention to the opening and final credits of films and dramatic shows. Movies, series, and TV films always credit casting directors, as well as writers and directors. Get to know who those people are. They are all working in a business you want to be part of. Then, when you meet someone like Reuben Cannon, you will be savvy enough to say something about his work, like "I enjoyed *What's Love Got to Do with It?* Angela Bassett was the perfect choice for Tina Turner."

Don't shoot yourself in the foot, like the actor who tried to make an impression on director Alan J. Pakula and went on at length about how much he had enjoyed a film Pakula had directed. Then he added, "I'm so sorry that I was one of the few people who saw it." Mr. Pakula's interest in the actor faded.

HANDLING EMERGENCIES

Despite all your careful preparations, the unexpected can happen. Emergencies occur: your wallet may be lost or stolen; a pipe bursts in your bathroom; you sprain an ankle; you've got strep throat or the flu. You may get a flat tire and find yourself stranded on the highway. Don't panic. You are not missing the opportunity of a lifetime. Do the best you can — call the casting director as soon as you can get to a phone and try to reschedule the appointment. Call your service, or agent, and have them get in touch with everyone you were to see. That is normal behavior.

What is not sensible is to get up from your sick bed and head for the office with your box of tissues or hobble in on crutches. A casting director really cannot tell anything about you, let alone your work, when you're unable to walk, when your eyes are tearing, or when you're sneezing and spraying the office with your germs. A disordered sense of priorities does you no credit.

Emergencies occur on the other side as well. The interviewer's baby may be sick; there may be an office emergency; an actor's sudden illness may have required an immediate casting replacement. Again, it's a disappointment, but life is like that sometimes. You and the casting director will set another time to meet, and all will proceed as if the delay had never occurred.

THE FOLLOW-UP

Between the time of your initial interview and your audition, or your call for a submission by the agent, there is usually a chunk of time, frequently a large one. You fill that in two ways: with personal work — on yourself, on your technique, on relationships, and with the follow-up — the creative pushiness designed to keep you in the minds of the agents and casting people.

Shortly after the first meeting, a brief nice-to-have-met-you note would be in order. Mention whether you've followed any suggestions or advice the agent or casting person may have offered. Thank them for their time and attention and hope to see them again soon.

After that, your most effective means of follow-up is the photo postcard. As we've already mentioned, your face, name, contact, and telephone number should be easy to see. Send your postcard every two weeks or so. Include a brief message: tell what you've been up to, pass on a witty line.

> I keep in touch with casting people the same way everyone else does: cards, and of course a special card whenever I'm working. I have been a freelance actor my entire career. I'm not a household name, or maybe even a recognizable face, but I have been a working actor for decades.
> —DONN SCHRADER

> There are, what, six soaps a week which tape in New York? That means six cards a week you send to casting directors. Is that too much to get a job? I call that being a business person. There are people who work every week.
> —MARY JO SLATER, *casting director*

Remember to keep it simple. An actor we know spent almost all his time creating mini-magazines to advertise himself. He sent them regularly to agents and casting directors. However, expecting busy people to take time to wade through twenty pages of copy was asking too much. He realized he would have been smarter looking for a showcase so that he could tell all those people he was working.

The main thing is to keep in touch, regularly, pleasantly, respectfully, and with the understanding that establishing yourself in anyone's mind is going to require a bit of time.

Be patient. Persevere.

CHAPTER 12

FINDING A VEHICLE TO SHOWCASE YOUR TALENT

I never got a job I didn't create for myself.

—RUTH GORDON

"Call me or send me a postcard when you're in something! I need to see your work!" Every day, actors hear this mandate from agents and casting directors. They also hear, "But please don't invite me to a turkey!"

No matter how wonderful you think you are in a showcase, remember that casting directors and agents are observing the possibly mediocre-to-dreadful performances of your fellow cast members as well. If you stand out because you have no competition, reconsider inviting anyone to see you.

If, in the first days of rehearsal, your instincts tell you this is not going to be a rewarding experience, get out of it. There is no stigma, no blot on your record, no blacklist for trusting yourself and making the right career choice, especially when you're not getting any financial compensation.

The rehearsal period and performances should be an enjoyable process and provide opportunities for paying jobs later. Be sure that the producer and director guarantee advance publicity, and that invitations or flyers are available at least two weeks prior to opening night. The program should contain your brief biography and contact information — your agent or answering service number. If the cast prefers not to have their numbers printed in the program, your management should be sure that casting directors and agents receive a contact sheet with that information. Some showcases offer packets of pictures and résumés to industry VIPs. Some have sign-in books for these guests, so that the cast members can follow up by sending them their pictures.

To discover the better showcase theaters, study the Arts and Entertainment section of your Sunday papers, in *New York* and *Los Angeles* magazines, and in other such publications, because such listings are free. We recommend that you attend performances at theaters whose choice of play strikes a responsive chord. You may be able to open some doors by volunteering to work as an usher, in the office, or behind the scenes. Your hard work and dedication might lead to an audition for a future production.

There are also groups that sponsor staged readings of new plays, which don't have a great deal of rehearsal time and may be performed only once for a specially invited audience — possibly for potential backers. The playwright gets a chance to hear his or her words and discover where revisions are necessary. If the play (or musical) moves from there into production, you may have a chance of reprising your role. It is to your advantage to leave favorable impressions with writers. Debra Monk is a perfect example of someone who did just that, and won a Tony Award: Lanford Wilson's *Redwood Curtain*, which she had originally read for at the off-Broadway Circle Repertory Company, transferred to Broadway with Monk playing the same role she had originated at the reading.

THE ENTREPRENEURS

Actors on both coasts have discovered that if they raise the money to rent a space and finance publicity and refreshments, they can be their own "angels" for a showcase evening of scenes. Having control of the casting process ensures that the players will share a similar level of experience and professionalism. You lessen the possibility of being placed on the program after three boring scenes and losing a segment of that valuable industry audience.

The format of the scene showcase guarantees industry attendance. For approximately ninety minutes, twenty actors can showcase their talent. The time is usually from 6 P.M. to 7:30 P.M., with wine and cheese offered before the show. There is an equal sharing of focus: your acting ability can be evaluated within the context of a ten-minute scene, as opposed to playing a tiny part in a full-length play.

We have attended scene nights where it was obvious that very little attention was paid to packaging and direction. To avoid that, here are some suggestions:

• Be sure you appear confident.

• If an inept director is your curse, reblock the scene yourselves, and enlist the aid of a "third eye" you respect.

• Choose your wardrobe carefully. It should suit the character you are playing.

• Select a scene to which you feel connected. You might even write your own material.

• Don't try to stretch from A to Z in ten minutes. Don't force the emotions.

• Be sure your scene partner is as good as you are.

• If you have an affinity for comedy, do it. We want to be entertained.

• This is not the time to do scenes by Gorky, Chekhov, Strindberg, Ibsen ("Oh, no, not another Hedda Gabler!") or the popular American playwrights whose works have been overexposed.

Actor-produced showcases are of consistently better quality. Some actors discover that the control and the challenge are more creatively fulfilling than the performing and have gone on to become industry producers.

STARTING YOUR OWN THEATER

Upon completion of his theater training program, an actor we know decided that he needed experience. Rather than go to auditions and be rejected, he says:

> I wanted to take the bull by the horns. I wanted to get out there and start my own company. I felt that doing classical theater was the best way to get experience.

He met an actress with terrific marketing skills; they were joined by another actor. They discovered that at the Bruno Walter Auditorium, at the Performing Arts Library in Lincoln Center, they would be able to present plays — no charge for the theater, no charge to the audience. Realizing that only 7 percent of the plays done in the city are classics, and aware that they would not have to pay royalties to those authors, they presented themselves as a company that revives the classics.

To begin an actor-based company that would generate work for everyone, they obtained not-for-profit status through the Cultural Council Foundation, a state-run agency. For a percentage of the company income, the Foundation also acted as financial manager, provided lists of fund-raisers, and assisted with fund-raising events. After a few seasons, during which they acquired respectable resumés, the actors headed for Los Angeles.

What our friend didn't mention, according to Casey Childs, the founding director of Primary Stages, is that 85 percent of your time is spent on the management of the company, which leaves about 15 percent for what he calls artistic fulfillment.

Casey Childs was the casting director of New Dramatists in New York, but found the job unfulfilling because New Dramatists developed plays, but did not produce them. With his own company he produces four plays a season, each of which has a four-week rehearsal period and runs for five weeks, which adds up to a thirty-six-week season. The rest of his time is spent on development, planning, and fund-raising. He calls it a twenty-four-hour-a-day job.

> You will work your way into oblivion if you don't establish that you are in control. The first three years were a real learning experience. Now, I've got it down to a science.
>
> —CASEY CHILDS

THE ONE-PERSON SHOW

Over the years, on stage and on television, we have seen famous players perform one-person shows: Hal Holbrook as Mark Twain, Henry Fonda as Clarence Darrow, James Whitmore as Harry Truman and as Will Rogers, Julie Harris as Emily Dickinson, Pat Carroll as Gertrude Stein, and Robert Morse as Truman Capote. Lynn Redgrave wrote her recent *Shakespeare for My Father* as a tribute to her father, Sir Michael Redgrave, and also to resolve her intricate, often frustrating relationship with the renowned British actor. Originally presented for a limited run at the Helen Hayes Theater, the show garnered ecstatic reviews, played 272 performances, and earned Ms. Redgrave a Tony nomination, a Drama Desk nomination, and the Elliot Norton Award in Boston.

Why do top-level performers venture onto a stage to work alone? For the same reason that we encourage you to do it: They want a vehicle that will exhibit their talent. And for these well-known players the reward is frequently the same one you hope for: They do attract favorable attention to themselves, and the phone starts to ring with great job offers! For Robert Morse, his Tony-winning performance in *Tru* came after he had been away from the stage for a considerable period. The quintessential juvenile of his day, he had starred in the hit musical, *How to Succeed in Business Without Really Trying*. But a generation of casting people who had never seen him perform had no idea of how talented he was. His impersonation of Truman Capote was so inventive and touching that it dynamized new interest in his career — indeed, gave him a new career as a mature character actor, leading to such roles as Captain Andy in Harold Prince's revival of *Showboat* in Toronto.

You may not hope to open on or off Broadway, but there are many outlets for one-person vehicles. Lecture bureaus and agents for concert attractions book lesser-known actors at universities and community theaters with their presentations of the lives, loves, and letters of such figures as Louisa May Alcott, Josephine Baker, Sarah Bernhardt, Edwin Booth, Rita Hayworth, "Shoeless" Joe Jackson, Martin Luther King, Groucho Marx, Ethel Merman, Dorothy Parker, Edith Piaf, Edgar Allan Poe, Damon Runyon, Bernard Shaw, Harriet Tubman, Sophie Tucker, Oscar Wilde, and others.

If you research a life that you want to portray for public approval, you have the wherewithal to do it. Some graduate schools afford degree candidates the opportunity to create a solo vehicle for their diploma.

> The one-person show requires students to make decisions, develop discipline in working alone, and explore a range of characterization and flexibility. The project generates confidence and is similar to the way performers audition for jobs — without play, partner, director, or designer.
> —BILL GRAHAM, *former chairman, Theater Department,*
> *Catholic University of America*

There are scores of subjects in the arts waiting to be given a new life. Getting your production together may take several years, but the effort is worth it if the show pays you enough to survive and allows you creative freedom.

> I have created my own vehicles since 1973. The frustration of being in a to-be-cast situation finally got to me. I decided to create more of a power base for myself, and that was to create a nightclub act, a cabaret act. It has gone through several incarnations and has garnered me more attention from the film and television industry than anything I have done in the theater.
> —MARILYN SOKOL, *Obie-winner*

THREE ACTRESSES' ONE-PERSON SHOWS
For actress Lisa Hayes, creating her one-woman show has been a wonderful, empowering experience:

> It's the first time in my life I feel I have control over my career. I have something I have created and can get up and do on the stage anytime, anywhere.

While doing research on the life of Charlotte Brontë, Lisa realized that the novel *Jane Eyre* was written in the first person, and she felt instinctively that it would make a fine dramatic presentation. It took her a year to complete the adaptation. The actress tells the whole story of *Jane Eyre* in an hour and twenty minutes and performs twenty-five characters, from Jane and Helen to Reverend Brocklehurst and Mr. Rochester.

Lisa believes it's important to find material that really speaks to you, that makes you want to work on it. Trust your instincts in putting it together, then get advice from directors and playwrights to help you shape the piece. If you're having trouble getting it finished, keep yourself from procrastinating by setting a performance date.

> Make yourself do it, even if it's just a staged reading, just to get the feeling of getting it on its feet to see how it works.

Each performance leads to a new engagement, and she is rewarded as a performer:

> To make an audience laugh and make them cry and use every bit of my craft, that is very important to me. It's all shared in this one story. It's been a wonderful experience, and I will be doing it for years to come.

A friend of a friend saw Quinn Lemley working in *Born to Rhumba*. Struck by her resemblance to Rita Hayworth, he suggested she do a show about the dynamic 1940s movie queen. She got together with a writer-director and a musical director. She recalled:

> We read all the books and periodicals about her. We saw all her movies and decided what we wanted to say about her: to keep the fantasy image and yet show the Margarita Cansino side of her.

After six months of research, they started writing *The Heat Is On*. They tested the material as a workshop at Don't Tell Mama, a New York club, and received rave reviews. Their four-week run turned into a six-month engagement.

> I met Anita Ellis, who was the voice of Rita in her movies. When people who knew her said this show had captured her spirit, it was the best gift I could hope to get.
>
> —QUINN LEMLEY

The cost of producing *The Heat Is On* has been $16,000, which Lemley views as an investment in her career. The money was budgeted for the director, the musical director, the arranger, costumer, and publicist. She is now orchestrating the show for five instruments, an additional investment which will enable her to perform on cruise ships and in small theaters.

> One should always be working, always have a project, because as long as you are working and doing what you love to do, I think people will find you.

Quinn Lemley promoted her portrayal of Rita Hayworth with this dazzling photo card. Photo by Roy Blakey.

Leslie Ayvazian created her own show around different pairs of shoes. She would see pink cowboy boots in a store window and create the person she thought would wear them. The show is called *Footlights*, and a review in her brochure states, "In the sequined heels of her prom night, Leslie Ayvazian welcomes the audience to their fifteenth high school reunion. She immediately starts us on a fascinating journey." In sixty minutes she creates eight characters from the feet up, characters who span a wide range of age, experience, and outlook. She is in control. She also speaks to young audiences, encouraging them to use their imaginations.

Having received unanimous praise throughout the country, Leslie recently appeared in New York in a new play at the Manhattan Theater Club.

PRODUCING A SHOWCASE

To mount a play that is not in the public domain — that is, royalty-free — you must find out who holds the copyright to the work, obtain the right to perform it and, usually, pay a royalty fee. Often you can get this information by writing a letter to Samuel French, a major publisher of play scripts. Your request should state the name of the producer, dates of the performance, number of performances, the name of the theater, and the seating capacity. Also include the price of tickets (if any), the nature of the production — Equity, non-Equity, community theater showcase — and how you plan to advertise the production. Give the name and phone number of the person to contact in your company.

This request can be sent to Karen Keri, c/o Samuel French, 45 West 25th Street, New York, NY 10010.

The rate should be a flat amateur per-performance fee. This application takes from two days to two weeks to be approved, as it is passed to the author and the author's agent.

Do *not* attempt to produce a showcase of copyrighted material without obtaining the right to do so. Your show can be shut down, or worse.

Once you have obtained the rights, you may begin the casting process. You must apply to Equity for showcase status. You must also get a copy of the theater's liability insurance policy, with the expiration date, and send that to Equity. The theater must be listed as an Equity-approved theater.

Your budget should definitely include the services of a press agent or publicist. That's the person who knows how to get news about your production into the theatrical news sections, newspaper and magazine columns, local TV and radio news shows. If you want an audience, you have to create interest and tell people where to find you. This publicity is in addition to purchasing space for an ad in the daily theatrical listings directory.

Showcase Protocol and Follow-up Agents and casting directors might not attend showcases that are not in Manhattan or in relatively safe areas; remember, there are a lot of women in The Business, and you might induce them to attend if you offer to see them to a cab after the show. But don't offer expensive gifts or limo rides, which smells of payola and suggests that the showcase may not be great, only well-funded.

In Los Angeles, having to drive long distances to some remote section of the city or to the San Fernando Valley might prevent a good industry turnout. Agents and casting directors work long days and sometimes long nights when there are casting crises. They want their time to be spent productively. If the program is more than two hours long, do not expect them to stay to the end. If you don't appear until the second act, make sure you inform those you invite of when you make your entrance.

If a casting director has made a reservation for a specific performance, the management should inform you of it. There should be some extra courtesy extended — specific seats could be roped off with their names clearly designated. The performance begins *before* the play starts. The welcome, the box office attitude, the ushers, the environment, the proper ventilation, the comfort of the seats — all contribute to the enjoyment of the showcase.

When the run has ended, and been acclaimed, send notes to the casting directors and agents who attended, thanking them and requesting an interview. Response is totally contingent upon their individual needs. You may have been wonderful, but the agent has four like you, or the casting director is not currently working on a part that needs your physical description and type.

Don't give up!

Send postcards periodically, reminding them that they saw your work and should keep you in mind for future projects. And search for the next vehicle to showcase your talent.

CHAPTER 13

AUDITIONS AND SCREEN TESTS

If you don't go, you'll never know. You have to not look at it as a rejection. There are so many reasons you're not picked that you can't even worry about it.

—ROBERT DeNIRO

Auditions are performances. They are your chance to show, in however many minutes you may be allotted, what you can do with a particular piece of material.

I didn't do well at auditions. I had the "clutch" problem. The more I wanted it, the more I got in the way. The voice didn't project, and I didn't know proper comportment. What I learned was: don't walk into an audition as a means to an end to get a job. Leave all that aside. Look at it as an opportunity to perform. I love performing. I played a game: I would say, "This is already my part. It may be for only five minutes, but it's my part."

—ROBIN STRASSER

It is an extraordinary experience. If you walk into a room and see eight people, and they all have something to do with this film, it can be intimidating, difficult for an actor.

—SHIRLEY RICH, *veteran casting director*

I have faced all kinds of audition situations, and I take each one as it comes. I don't expect anything, but I am always prepared. If I have to read with someone who is not an actor, I put myself in the character's place and distance myself from the negativity and obstacles. I leave the audition and forget about it. I don't want to dwell on the experience.

—DEBRA MONK

At RADA (the Royal Academy of Dramatic Art), they instilled in us the awareness that no one can do it the way you can. You are the best you. You have to prove to them that you are the one they should want.

—BOB KALIBAN, *actor-announcer, former president, SAG's New York branch*

The people hiring you need to know that they've made the right decision. Eli [Wallach] and I must have auditioned fourteen times for *The Rose Tattoo* before they decided to let us do it.

—Maureen Stapleton

There were thirteen callbacks over a period of four months. I had an acting coach, a dialect coach. I became extremely focused. I put my heart and soul into it. On the decision day, my family and friends sent me flowers, just so I wouldn't go crazy if I didn't get the part. But I got the part — Eliza Doolittle in *My Fair Lady*.

—Melissa Errico

GENERAL RULES FOR DRAMATIC AUDITIONS

Every audition will have its own peculiar conditions. However, the following dos and don'ts will help you to avoid the most frequently made mistakes.

- *Don't* do heavy, climactic scenes. Moments that are truthful are more effective than screaming scenes.

- *Don't* choose an excerpt from a play or film that has been inextricably linked to a major star, unless you are certain that you can do it much, much better. An example is both the roles of Miss Daisy and Hoke in *Driving Miss Daisy*.

- *Don't* show the audience how hard you are working. This leads to strained neck muscles, tight throat, furrowed forehead, vocal strain, forced laughter, and false emotion. When you are pushing for effect, your timing is off, your partner is forgotten.

- *Don't* choose to do a British character, unless you do a British dialect with integrity and skill. The same is true of any play requiring a dialect: do it well or do something else.

- *Don't* confuse a comedic monologue with a stand-up act. Christopher Durang's *Actor's Nightmare* is a trap piece: we laugh when the man's nightmare is made real. Therefore, pushing for laughs is unnecessary.

- *Don't* choose a scene partner whose performance is weak or dull. Your performance will not look better by comparison. The other actor will only pull you down and ruin your timing.

- *Don't* be general, either physically or emotionally. Unspecific gesturing or a tentative delivery with eyes cast down signifies that you have lost your focus on the scene and will lose your audience's attention.

- *Don't* play MOOD. It is DOOM spelled backwards.

- *Do* realize that we want to know you through your audition. Therefore, the audition begins when you enter, cross, come down, and introduce yourself. How you introduce yourself and your partner is part of the audition process.

- *Do* pay attention to what you wear. How you dress is part of the character you are creating. It is part of the audition. Think about your shoes: jogging soles squeak on floors and rugless surfaces; they do not afford you any grace of movement. Thin spike heels make clicking noises. Any clothing that inhibits your movement or calls attention to itself is inappropriate.

- *Do* choose material that you can connect with — emotionally, physically, and intellectually. Understand your own limitations. We all have favorite musicians, composers, and novelists, and we have playwrights with whom we feel really comfortable.

- *Do* pick a selection that tells who, what, where, when, and why. Not the climax, but the setup. In other words, create a specific sense of time and place. Ask us to imagine with you: who are you? to whom are you relating? who are you supposed to be?

- *Do* make specific choices, physically as well as emotionally. Your body must know what it is doing. Your vocal and interpretative choices must be connected. All parts of you must work together. One terrific physical choice can make the whole monologue or scene come together.

- *Do* know the moment before and the moment after the scene. Be aware of transitions.

- *Do* connect with the material, the audience, the space, your partner, yourself.

- *Do* relate to someone when you perform a solo piece.

- *Do* allow a transitional "beat" between two audition selections. Use a costume accessory: a scarf can become a shawl, a cane a rifle, and so forth. Roll up your sleeves, or take them down. Make use of a belt. Take your shoes off. Think these moments through and unify your performance.

- *Do* choose a scene partner who is a strong performer, whose energy will give you something forceful to react to. You will look better.

- *Do* bring sexual confidence to your performance. Mind and body work together.

- *Do* embrace your nerves. Be in control. Your emotional connectors are the springboards from which everything else flows. Inner truth means that we don't see you working.

- *Do* investigate plays written before 1970! Know the whole play and bring a sense of the whole to the excerpt you are doing. Continually search for ways to keep the scene fresh. You should never get bored with it.

A CAUTION ABOUT SCENE CHOICES

There are some scenes done so often that agents and casting directors would prefer never to see them again. Generally speaking, you should avoid the most current and trendy piece, the choice that is at first glance the hot scene by the playwright of the moment. You should avoid scenes that are repeatedly done because everyone has agreed for years they're exciting. This means you need to research a bit to find out what scenes are too-familiar and overworked. The following plays have been mined for audition material too often in recent years:

Key Exchange	*The Colored Museum*
Beyond Therapy	*Crimes of the Heart*
Loose Ends	*Split*
Lone Star	*Cheaters*
Private Wars	*They're Playing Our Song*
Laundry and Bourbon	*Say Goodnight, Gracie*
California Suite	*Scuba Duba*
Chapter Two	*Lovers and Other Strangers*
Fool for Love	*Bad Habits*
The Rainmaker	*Boy's Life*
Nuts!	*'dentity Crisis*
A, My Name Is Alice	*The Piano Lesson*
Demi-God	*A Lie of the Mind*
Curse of the Starving Class	*Home (Samm-Art Williams)*

Suggested Monologue Sources Here are some plays we think will offer you audition material that represents a fresh choice:

A Social Event by William Inge

Julia by Alvin Sargent

The Man Who Disappeared by Ken Campbell

A Thurber Carnival by James Thurber

Confessions of a Female Disorder by Susan Miller

Geniuses by Jonathan Reynolds

History of World Drama by Ann Hudgins

Watch Over Me by Marie Whittey

Hooters by Ted Talley

In Fireworks Lie Secret Codes by John Guare

Diner (film script) by Barry Levinson

Coup/Clucks by Jane Martin

Chocolate Cake by Mary Gallagher

THEATER AUDITIONS

Casting directors for theater companies planning a number of productions in a season will want to see your prepared audition material — usually a classic monologue and a contemporary selection. Producers of new plays will want to see how you deal with a segment, or "side," of the script at hand.

> We hire actors for one show only, and if we are happy with them after that show we often think of casting them in future performances. But it is a show-by-show contract. We audition in studios as arranged by our casting directors in New York, Chicago, and L.A.
>
> I'm interested in auditions for the specific plays that we're working on, so I expect actors to prepare from "sides". Occasionally we have open calls in Chicago and in Indianapolis, and at that time I'm interested in actors doing a prepared audition of one classical monologue (Shakespeare in verse for the classical) and one contemporary. I don't care if they are serious or comedic, as long as they speak to the actor in a personal kind of way. . . . I try to make actors feel at home in the audition because I want them to succeed just as much as they want to succeed. But sometimes their own fear gets the best of them.
>
> I like it when actors show an interest in the play and some obvious preparation of sides they have been asked to read. However, I'm not interested in long involved stories about the motivation of the character. I like for actors to make strong and interesting choices at the audition, and at that time I usually give an adjustment and see if they can make a change.
> —LIBBY APPEL, *artistic director, Indiana Repertory Theatre*

Your assignment is to be heard and to bring to life the person the writer and director have in mind, or better still, to show them someone they hadn't thought of, but who is perfect for their production!

No matter what you audition for, go with your vision of the role.

COMMERCIAL AUDITIONS

Some actors have for a long time looked down on commercials as a less-than-legitimate way of earning a living. What an unfortunate attitude. Doing a commercial well can be as challenging as making a feature film. Some of today's successful film directors got their start in commercials: Richard Donner, Richard Lester, and Lawrence Kasdan are just a few of the names that come immediately to mind.

As is true of any other material, commercial copy can be brilliantly or poorly written, with most of what we see falling between those two extremes. You may think the copy is poorly executed; the concept may strike you as pure corn. First rule: *Don't judge the material!* You must believe in it 100 percent and never for one second let on that you don't. You must motivate and justify every word you say. If there are no written words, you must make every action and reaction believable. As a trained actor you should be adaptable to sudden changes in direction. Your job is to create a life in thirty or sixty seconds — or ten. There is no time to wait for "inspiration." You are expected to bring that into the audition with you.

Have at least three different approaches to the material. But be selective in these directions. They should never upstage, or interfere with the integrity of, the material. If you are clever and imaginative enough to take a risk, and it pays off for you, bravo! You deserve the job.

Your audition for a commercial usually takes place in the ad agency's recording studio. Your performance will be recorded — on video- or audiotape. These studios are small and usually crowded with the cartons and cue cards from the many projects that the agency is working on concurrently. The demonstration package of your product may not be on hand, and you will have to mime using it. This is where training, concentration, and sense memory become important.

Arrive early. Get your copy of the script. Ask if there is a storyboard — a cartoon-style illustration of the way the action proceeds. Isolate yourself so that you may work privately on your audition. Go to the nearest restroom to practice without interruption. Treat the script you are given as your own property. Mark it, make notes to yourself — whatever helps you to do your best. If the script is more than one page long, remove the staple that holds the pages together, so that you don't waste time or sabotage yourself by losing your concentration turning pages, which is difficult to do.

The audition begins the moment you meet the casting director, who will usually explain what the agency is looking for. If you don't understand, ask questions. When you are ready to begin, you will be instructed to "slate yourself." That means you say your name directly into the camera or microphone. This introductory moment is also part of your audition. It is not invisible time. Use it. No one is interested in seeing you transform yourself from dull to sparkling before their eyes. That's like showing how hard you're working. Just be sparkling from the moment you get your cue. You are meeting the client at that instant.

> In commercials you're basically putting on a play in less than thirty seconds. It's a very expensive play, and you don't have time to build a character. You usually have only a few minutes to look at the copy. Then you go into a strange room with strange people. You have a storyboard, a written cue card. They may have changed the words on you, and they may throw all sorts of adjectives at you as you're looking into the little eye of a camera. You'll usually get two or three tries, if you're lucky.
>
> We see about a hundred people for the average commercial. Approvals come from the art director, the copywriter, producer, creative supervisor; then, on the client side, from the account executives.
> —BARBARA BADYNA, *vice president, casting, Young & Rubicam*

> The writer hears it one way, in his ear. The account exec, the sponsor, each of the people involved in the job hears it in his own ear a certain way. You have to be a good listener. Listen to the writer, the account exec, all those people, the actors you are working with. All this colors your performance, your approach to the words.
> —BOB KALIBAN

Another challenge actors have to contend with at commercial auditions is the Polaroid snapshot. Some clients want to see pictures of all the people who have auditioned for their spots, in addition to seeing them on camera, looking at their photos and résumés, and hearing the audition tapes. Use this as another chance to show yourself at your best. Practice your dazzling smile. You might help yourself by having your roommate take a photo of you, at home, in the outfit you're going to wear to the audition, and bring that with you. You may feel more relaxed and look better. There's no guarantee the casting director will accept your snapshot, but isn't it worth a try?

DAYTIME SOAP OPERA AUDITIONS

Like commercials, daytime dramas have been held in low esteem by many performers. To the thousands of people who work on them, this condescension is inexplicable. Soaps offer actors challenging work at salaries they definitely enjoy.

Nowhere else does an actor have the opportunity to play a wide range of emotions while working with the sharpest professionals in the industry. Soaps avoid the formula plots and predictable resolutions of conventional series; they have shied away from the excessive violence that pervades much of prime-time. Because story lines heighten the kinds of problems and concerns middle-class viewers share — with a dollop of fantasy added — soaps have attracted and maintained large audiences.

Watching a soap for the first time is a lot like walking into a movie theater in the middle of a film: You don't quite know what is happening. Possibly that is why media critics have never caught on to soaps. With repeated viewing — it takes about a month — the relationships are sorted out and the quality of the performances is apparent.

Soaps are for actors who love to work. They are the electronic equivalent of a repertory company. Rather than playing different roles in a series of plays, the actors here stretch by playing the same character thrust into a range of situations.

On soaps, performers may progress from extras to under-fives to day players and to contract roles.

> I've seen actors as extras who then become under-fives and then come in to audition for parts. I know. I sit and watch extras on soaps. If I see an interesting face, or someone does an interesting bit, I make a note to find out who the actor is, and I have a file now. The Business is eating up faces. you're always looking for someone new.
> —GILLIAN SPENCER, *formerly Daisy Cortlandt on* All My Children

Guiding Light's Amelia Marshall began as an under-five, playing a stage manager at Michael Zaslow's TV station. Within weeks she was called back, this time as a day player. Six months after that she was offered a contract.

Day-player auditions usually take place in the casting director's office for the producer. A brief character description is provided by the casting director. Concentrate on the character clues and the meaning of the scene. Remember, the audition starts the moment you enter the room. You are not invisible while you engage in some sort of preparation that the casting director and the actor who will be reading with you are not meant to share. That's the work you should be doing while you are in the reception area.

Relate to the other actor as if he or she were Olivier. Never play to the casting director. Endow the lines with your individuality, your sense of self.

Mary Jo Slater remembers how Brynn Thayer, recently seen as Matlock's daughter, was cast as Jenny Vernon on *One Life to Live:*

> She had been doing commercials and was sent by her commercial agent for a role in the show. She wasn't right for that part, but I put her in the file of actors I might use some other time. When the part of Jenny came up, I remembered her, we tested her, and she got the part. There was something about her that stood out — a beauty, an inner glow. It wasn't great acting. She came so far. She has talent, works seriously. And she has grown. But at the outset, it was her look — classy, sophisticated, urbane — that landed her the part.
>
> Mark LaMura, Mark Dalton on *All My Children*, was tested for another character. He wasn't right for it, but everyone was so impressed with his quality that they created a role for him. Phil Carey originally tested for Palmer Cortlandt, which he was not at all right for, but the producer of *One Life to Live* saw that he could be Asa Buchanan.
>
> —Jo Ann Emmerich, *executive producer,* Loving

Bill Christian, Derek on *All My Children*, was originally a recurring day player:

> I originally auditioned for the role of Jesse's brother. The casting director said I was too young for it, but she would remember me. A couple of years later she brought me in for another role. A couple of years later she called me in to read for a day player, for a cop. I auditioned with two white guys. She offered me the role. It's luck and timing. Angie at the time needed a love interest. I did this day player, the writers saw something in me they liked and put the two of us together.

The casting director and producer will make the decision. There are no callbacks for these roles. If you are selected, you will be called and told when to report to the set or to the costume designer for the show. If you are not selected, keep in touch. If you were submitted by an agent, try to get feedback on your audition.

MAJOR ROLES

Candidates for contract parts go through a lengthier process. Their interview with the casting director is followed by a reading of the audition scene, which they receive a day or two prior to the audition. Success at the first reading will be rewarded by a callback attended by the producer.

No one is required to learn lines for a first reading, but a deep knowledge of the material is essential. While a character description is provided, the actor should try to create a personal history of the character (often called a back story). The more you create a life for the character, the more you will have to play in the scene.

Jacklyn Zeman, Bobbie Jones on *General Hospital*, talks about her audition for her current role:

Uta Hagen, in her book *Respect for Acting* (which I read once a year), has a section in the back of the book about writing a background for every character. I always do that when I am auditioning for something. For this part I think they wanted a horn-rimmed-glasses intellectual. Her name was originally Barbara. Well, that didn't say anything to me. I asked the producer, Gloria Monty, if, for me, the name might be Barbie. She said, "No, no, let's make it Bobbie!" Well, that has a bit of a bounce. I got my whole image of the character from that.

Betty Rea, casting director for *Guiding Light*, remembers how imaginative use of a prop helped an actress win a contract part:

There were six or seven females for the final callback for the part of a recording-studio executive in her early thirties. The actress who got the part gave the most wonderful audition. She entered, dressed in a pants suit, carrying a Walkman and wearing the earphones. She started the audition with her back to us, listening to the music, and she took her time. It was the most wonderful lesson in how to audition.

THE SCREEN TEST

Here is your ultimate chance to convince the producer, the writers, and the network executives that you can do the job better than anyone else. It is also the most difficult time to hold onto the thought that, although they already love you, they want to scrutinize your work under the lights. For this on-camera audition, you will arrive about three hours early, for makeup, hair, and wardrobe. There will be a period of blocking the action of the scene with another actor — usually the one with whom you will be playing on the show. This is the closest approximation to working conditions on the actual show. There will be a run-through, and then lights, camera, action! And your scene is taped. Of course it is difficult to relax under these conditions. Added to the stress is the fact that screen tests are sandwiched between the run-through and dress rehearsal of the day's regular episode or tacked onto the schedule at the end of a long day.

My audition for the role of Ellen (on *All My Children*) occurred on a rainy day. I was supposed to be the mother of a seventeen-year-old daughter. I was thirty-one. I walked into the makeup room. The actress playing the daughter was sitting there, and except for one other woman in my age range, everyone was older. I saw one gal and thought, "Oh, she's so much prettier than I, she'll get it." I told myself all the things that wouldn't get me the role. So I decided to have the best audition and have fun. When I got the role I cried. I just couldn't believe it.

—KATHLEEN NOONE

The prototype for the role of Felicia on *General Hospital* was someone like Linda Darnell or Ava Gardner. The ingenue who actually won the part, Kristina Wagner, is more in the Doris Day tradition. The producer saw in her beauty and freshness the longevity she needed for the show's main story line.

BEING READY FOR THE BREAK

With increasing frequency, actors from all parts of the country and from Canada are brought to New York to audition for major roles in daytime TV. What an opportunity! What a fabulous break — for an actor who is prepared.

One such performer failed to qualify for a second callback, and a sympathetic casting director reviewed the audition with him. Although the script had been sent to him in advance, he had not learned it. Nervousness made his voice flat and uninteresting. He had made no specific choices about the moment before the scene — he hadn't decided whether the character had been having a nap or having his lunch. He didn't know anything about the other people mentioned in the scene, although all were regular characters on the show for which he was auditioning. Nor had he taken the time to watch the show before he flew to New York to read for the part. He had decided that he was not comfortable with the script as written, and so he paraphrased the speeches. It was suddenly clear why this young man had been eliminated from the competition. He had not done his homework. He had wasted his opportunity.

Our definition of luck is *preparation married to opportunity*.

ONE SOAP STAR'S STORY

When Reiko Aylesworth was taking acting classes at the Seattle Children's Theatre, she never dreamed that she would have the opportunity to become a principal player on a network soap opera. New York seemed far beyond her immediate goals. But by the time she was twenty, she had acquired a strong theatrical résumé, and after she had played the role of Wendy in the Intiman Theatre production of *Peter Pan*, her agent in Seattle submitted her for a role on an ABC soap. The casting consultant noticed a special quality at her audition and videotaped her performance. When the tape was reviewed by the East Coast producers, the producer of *One Life to Live* was so impressed with Aylesworth's talent that a role was created for her. She said goodbye to Seattle and set up housekeeping in New York:

> Acting has always been my passion, ever since I set foot onstage. It has been something that hasn't left me. If you're an actor you need to act. The leap from regional theater to a national soap opera was daunting: Initially I was on cloud 9, just so full of myself. That lasted two weeks. Then I got homesick. It is a hard city to acclimate to, and it can be really isolating. I missed the small town feeling of Seattle, of being able to talk to people.

She took acting classes and worked with a coach the show hired to help her understand the medium that was so new to her. Her first glimpse of the TV studio was intimidating. She met all the people she'd seen on TV, whom she never expected would give her the time of day, and found them kind and supportive. She remembers being totally lost at first. She had no idea what the terms meant, and there was no one to teach her. She realized you have to discover your own way, by trial and error. She learned by doing, but adjustments were necessary:

I went in thinking I could put everything I learned in theater into this medium. I found that a performance has to be not so much toned down as focused. You meet the constraints of space. There is no fourth wall, but you have to know you can't go past this line. You have to worry about a lot of technical things that you don't worry about onstage. For the first few months it was like on-the-job training. Getting me ready for the major stuff. They tried me with different people until they knew who they wanted me with, culminating in the story line they developed for me. Theater training helped me, in that I knew how to work in an ensemble situation.

Aylesworth also advises finding a home when you arrive. You need to make your own nest where you can seek solitude. Lastly, she suggested exercising patience, not expecting everything to happen all at once, and using the nonworking time to advantage — reading a great deal, taking in the cultural outlets.

How would she advise young people faced with the same opportunity?

Take it! If they're my age they probably will want to talk to their parents. It would have been very difficult for me without my parents' support. And don't look back. That made me miserable.

Out-of-town actors must experience at least a subconscious nervous reaction when pitted against New York actors. They may believe that they are not part of the mainstream, that they are not yet ready to compete in the major market, not bona fide. But if the out-of-town actor is sufficiently prepared, has a foundation, knows how to analyze a script, is comfortable in any situation — even with a network soap opera producer staring at them during a reading — he or she is ready to assume the awesome responsibility of a principal role in theater, film, or soap opera.

AUDITIONING FOR A TV SERIES

In prime-time, everyone auditions, even for the three-line parts. Callbacks will depend upon the size of the role.

If you have an audition, don't make it the sole part of your day. Be coming from somewhere or be going to some place. Look clean and neat. Don't dress for the part — allow some imagination for the director's process. Don't give them everything. Even if you have memorized it, they don't need to know you've got it down. Use the page. Make them think you're prepared, not finished!

—GENE BLYTHE, *vice president, talent, Disney Studios*

It's important to keep your sense of humor at an audition. I used to say, "Look, I don't want to waste your time or bore you. So, if what I'm doing isn't what you have in mind, please let me know, and I will try something else."

—JUDITH LIGHT

Landing a leading role in a prime-time series entails interviews, auditions, callbacks, screen tests — plus. The "plus" is the unknown factor having little to do with talent that may get you the job.

You have seen series recast parts during a season or between one season and the next. On the award-winning series *Cagney and Lacey*, two actresses played Christine Cagney before the part finally become the property of Sharon Gless; two actors played Mary Beth Lacey's husband Harvey. When *Law and Order* had to replace two male actors, those roles were filled by two women. Jerry Orbach is the third partner to work with Chris Noth, after George Dzundza and Paul Sorvino decided to do other things. Susan Dey was replaced by Annie Potts on *Love and War*. Producer and director participate in these auditions. If the part is important enough, approval of other executives may be necessary. When they all agree that you answer all their separate needs, and they can trust you, you will win.

FILM AUDITIONS

Your film audition will come as the result of your interview with the independent casting director working on the film, or as a result of that person's knowledge of your work.

If the part is small, you may be engaged from that first audition. Actors trying out for pivotal roles will be called back for a screen test.

In a screen test for a film, a prime-time series, a mini-series, or a made-for-TV movie, the casting director will rent studio time. Actors will be made up and have a hair stylist in attendance. Most of the time there will be an off-camera reader. The camera will be on you throughout the scene. Your close-up — how you project the character and yourself — is the test.

Auditioning for a role in a film is decidedly a low-key affair, bearing no relation to the gaudy circus atmosphere generated by motion picture promoters in order to sell tickets. Of course, there is always excitement at the prospect of working, possibly with a director of great reputation or with a star whose talent, or physical presence, makes you giddy.

ON-CAMERA: CHOOSING THE RIGHT CLOTHES

Our interviews with costume designers yielded advice on dressing to advantage for your audition in front of a camera:

- Simplicity is essential. For women that means the skirt, hose, and shoes should be a monotone. If your skirt is beige, so are your shoes and your pantyhose. This is called "playing from the waist up." That's where the color goes.

- It's important and effective to show skin around the neckline or shoulder line. An open collar, pushed-up sleeves — those look very good on camera. Earrings and necklaces are large, often too large to wear in real life, because the camera rarely shows the person's full figure. This is a close-up medium.

- V-necklines are most flattering to round faces.

- The standard sizes for young women are 4 and 6, sometimes 8. Older women can wear size 10 or 12. The camera adds as much as twenty pounds.

- Darker colors elongate the figure.

- Don't overpower the camera with colors that are too bold around your neck. They will affect your skin tone adversely. Choose colors that highlight your face. Make it a rule to avoid loud prints.

- Actresses always want to wear red because the camera picks up red so well; they want to wear black because it makes them look slimmer. But it's important to choose the right red, otherwise the color will leap out of the screen. Black is too hard to wear near your face.

- For women, shoulder pads and belts can help to define the body shape, give a narrow-waisted, slim-hipped look.

- Women should avoid the mid-thigh skirt; it's just not flattering.

- Men look better in double-breasted suits because those jackets give them a triangular shape. Italian suits have the best, most flattering tailoring.

- Many men have been exercising regularly and have built up their leg muscles, and for them pleated pants are preferable. Their calves bulge in narrower pants, and bulges are unattractive on camera.

- Shorter men also look better in the Italian suits.

FACTS OF LIFE

We cannot ignore the fact that some producers and directors are rude, ungracious, and into "power trips." If you are not what they are looking for, on sight, they may ignore you as if you were not there.

Take your place on the stage, and hold your ground. Never let rudeness get you down. You must rise above it and keep your sense of humor!

A Casting Anecdote

This story was told to us by an actress friend of the performer to whom it happened.

The scene is the office of a Los Angeles television production company. An audition is being held for the part of a nurse in a prime-time made-for-TV movie. Seated in the reception area are the casting director and several actresses she has called in to read for the role. Almost all the actresses wear nurse's uniforms which they have rented for the audition. (In New York you would wear a tailored dress or a plain blouse and skirt.)

The door to the producer's office opens and out comes the producer. He is tanned and trim, wearing gorgeously tailored gabardine slacks and a silk shirt that is open to the waist, revealing several gold chains around his neck. He greets the casting director and surveys the assembly of women, who are looking at him, smiling.

He seems to recognize one of the actresses. He snaps his fingers, pointing at her, and says, "I know you! You're . . . you're. . . ."

She tells him her name.

"Yes, that's it. And I used to see you on . . . on. . . ."

She tells him the name of the show.
"Yes, that's right. And you were a . . . played a. . . ."
She tells him she played the role of a doctor.
"Yes, that's it! You were a doctor!"
He wheels upon the casting director.
"What kind of casting is this?" he asks. "How can a doctor play a nurse?"

Dissolve to black!

CHAPTER 14

CONGRATULATIONS! YOU'VE GOT A JOB!

With Woody I just got so lucky that he said,
"Oh, yeah, let's pick her."
—DIANE KEATON

"Dear, they want you to do it."

Seven one-syllable words, and it's hallelujah time. You are going to be a working actor. You've got a job!

If this glorious message means that you've been selected for a part in a stage play, you will be signing an individual contract, which we discuss in Chapter 16. This chapter is about work in TV and films, which is a bit different.

Actors whom the casting director has called directly — usually the extras and under-fives — will generally confirm with the assistant the date, time, and place of the call (the industry term for day of employment). If you've been submitted by an agent, the agent's office will give you your call and will then confirm your acceptance of the call with the casting director.

In either case, you will be asked to pick up a script at the production office (or the studio), and you'll be given the name of the wardrobe person to talk to about what you'll wear on camera.

WHAT ABOUT MY CONTRACT?

The standard contract will be presented to you after your arrival on the set on the day of shooting. At some time during the day the production assistant will collect the signed forms, and your copy will be mailed to you or given to you at the end of the shoot. Simple.

WORKING WARDROBE

Costumes are created or rented for special events — historical series or fantasy or sci-fi sequences. But for the normal life depicted in commercials, soap operas, and most nighttime shows, designers are happy when a performer's wardrobe is suitable for the scene; that saves the production shopping time and rental expense. You will be asked to describe your clothing to the wardrobe person, who will tell you to bring the best-sounding outfits to the studio at the time of your call. The actor gains a wardrobe fee for each garment used, plus the comfort and confidence of wearing something that fits well.

Before she became an Emmy-winning costume designer for *All My Children*, Carol Luiken had designed costumes for opera companies all over the world. As a favor to a friend, she did the costumes for a short-lived play, which was seen by the producer of a daytime serial who asked if she would consider dressing the actors on *Love of Life*. Carol Luiken's advice to actors, in regard to wardrobe, is:

> Actors should be aware that they will most likely work in commercials, and for those they have to think of middle America. The clothes to wear are those for a housewife or husband, a young, attractive, middle-of-the-road, classic look. Not expensive.
>
> It's easiest for women to do with a skirt and blouse — a simple shirt look. For men it's slacks and a shirt, with or without a tie, depending upon the product, of course. This look is hard to find in New York and Los Angeles stores, which are all trying to be upscale and trendy. Brooks Brothers exemplifies the look, and, in catalogs, it is L.L. Bean.
>
> When you bring clothes, bring choices! For the ladies, a number of blouses, so you can have variations on the housewife look. Definitely a dark skirt so that you can play a waitress. Everyone on a soap is always going to the local restaurant. An evening dress, because there are several party scenes on soaps each year, and they need extras. It should be pretty, but not glittery, since that can catch the light and shine way out of all proportion. And the fabric should not rustle — like taffeta — because that makes noise when you move.

Men, she says, need a tuxedo, a navy blazer, and gray slacks. A business suit is being used now, too. Shirts should be in pale tints — blue or pink, but not white.

Women shouldn't wear white either; it leaps out at the camera and makes for difficult contrasts. Nowadays a woman should also have a jacket for the young executive look. And, Luiken points out, actors should hang onto their quirky, "period" stuff. "We had to do a farm scene, and the gals who came in with their country things were just great!"

She added that actors should be on time and be polite. If the designer says "wear this," they are supposed to do it. Color choices are made for a reason. And, she said, "It's most important to develop as a person. Enrich yourself, and that enriches your work."

YOUR PREPARATION FOR THE DAY

If you have words to say, *learn them*.

If you interact with any of the running characters on the soap, watch the show so you will recognize the actor you will be talking to. If you have any questions about the character, the scene, or the words that were not answered at the audition, make notes to yourself to ask the director during rehearsal of your scene. Wait until the director tells you what he (or she) wants; the director may have anticipated your query.

The day before, make sure everything is clean and in wearable condition. Pack the garments in a lightweight suitcase or wardrobe carryall. Do not plan to do all this in the morning; it will inevitably take longer than you expect, and you will risk being late for your call. Pack everything that you will need — personal items, shoes, mirror, comb, brush, or whatever you use to do your hair. Prepare your healthful food to get you through the day. Yes, there is a lunch break, but you may need nourishment before that time.

Check the weather report. Try to anticipate any emergency, and set your alarm early enough to go about your morning tasks without insanity.

If you feel a cold or a sore throat coming on, take care of yourself! Nothing prevents a professional actor from appearing at a job. If this were your senior prom, would you even dream of staying home? Bring your vitamins, cold remedies, tissues, and nose drops with you, and be as unstressed as possible.

On the morning of your call, or the night before, wash and set or blow-dry your hair so that it can be shiny and healthy-looking. Yes, there is a hair stylist on the set, but the stylist's first responsibility is to the principal players. Every project has one or more makeup artists, but be ready to do your own face in case they are very busy.

Ask your service to give you a wake-up call; alarm clocks have been known to fail. Get a good night's sleep.

We'll see you on the set.

CHAPTER 15

YOUR FIRST DAY
ON THE SET

*There are these three cameras. Technicians waving hands
and being busy. Lights come on. You have to be really
focused in on what you are doing.*

—BILL CHRISTIAN

BEHIND THE SCENES AT ABC'S *LOVING*

Loving is produced at the West 66th Street Broadcast Center, in New York City.
Ordinarily fans — who have figured out when rehearsals begin — cluster around the
entrance. But shortly after 9 A.M. on this frigid January morning, the entire area is
blanketed with snow, and an arctic wind gusts across the ice-blocked Hudson River.
No one is out strolling on this winter's day. We duck inside to watch the making of
this prominent daytime serial.

DRY REHEARSAL

Work on *Loving* has already begun. In the rehearsal room, Director Bob Scinto has
had the cast blocking scenes since 8 A.M. The boundaries of each playing area are
marked on the floor with tape, while gray metal folding chairs are placed to serve as
sofas, desks, and tables as well as chairs. The actors read their lines and, following
his directions, move from place to place, marking the action in their scripts. After
this preliminary stop-and-go blocking, they have time to go over the scene again, to
establish the flow of movement and words.

Today's cast consists of twelve regulars, including three children who, according
to union contract regulations, will arrive later (the stage manager takes their place
in these blocking rehearsals), plus one under-five, an actor playing a hotel
concierge. Despite the stops and starts, the associate director takes a rough timing
of each page.

As their scenes are blocked and rehearsed, the actors are released to go to make
up and wardrobe.

MAKEUP AND HAIR

Lights are on and the mirrors gleam on both long walls in the large makeup room.
Loving employs two full-time hair stylists and two makeup artists. The show is

unique in that these stylists are responsible for the actors' personal as well as their professional hair care. "We do cuts, colors, pieces, and perms, so their hair is always perfect on camera," Russell Latham explains, rinsing the conditioner out of Catherine Hickland's (Tess) long blonde hair. Then he turns to combing Linda Cook's (Egypt) "car wreck" wig, which he made. Wigs are Russell's specialty.

"And they don't suddenly come in with a new hair style in the middle of a story line," adds his partner, Joyce Carolla. "The actors sometimes forget they're playing a character who doesn't always look the way they like to in real life. Sometimes, when they're home, they look in the mirror and decide they need a big change. Well, you can't do that when your character has another look. That's what you're playing. It's your job."

Getting the last touches of her makeup, Nada Rowand (Kate) is already in costume, a habit learned from years of theater. She has very little to do today, but her scenes are crowded, and she has a succession of props to handle. Timing her lines and her crosses with the other characters' moves is complicated, crucial.

Catherine Hickland, on the phone, worries that her special lunch may not be delivered in time because of the snowstorm. "Isn't it weird? We have this great facility and no commissary! We always have to order our food, or bring in packages that we can heat in the microwave. I have a lady who cooks and delivers special meals. It's important for me to be able to eat early, so I have time to rest before taping."

RUN-THROUGH

"Cast of *Loving*, Item 1. Cast on set, please." The loudspeaker can be heard throughout the building. Cavernous Studio 24 comes slowly to life.

"Cameras 1 and 4," calls a voice over the "talkback." "We're here," answer the camera operators.

Director Scinto takes his place at the movable lectern. It is equipped with a monitor and intercom, so he can view the shots and talk to the technical staff in the control room as well as to the cast and crew in the studio. "Camera 1, you're outside, on the porch."

"Oh, you want me *there!*" One cameraman had anticipated shooting through the doorway, from inside the house.

"Yes. And the boom has to be on the other side."

The boom operator climbs down from her platform, calling "Re-po, re-po." Crew members kick cables and reposition the microphone. But there's still a noticeable boom shadow, and Camera 1 is blocked. Finally, Scinto has the back wall of the set angled so Camera 1 can move in to get the shot he wants. While these changes are made, the actors wait, holding their positions.

"We're really ready now. No kidding," Scinto says.

"Quiet down, folks," barks the stage manager.

"Lisa, you were by the door. What's your first line?" the director asks Lisa Peluso, who plays Ava. As the actors' dialogue continues, he talks softly, via his headset, to the camera operators, to the technical director, calling shots, complimenting work, watching the action. "This is a two-shot. Now, shot 7, then we go directly inside to you ladies."

The scene moves into Kate's living room. "Cue her in with the tray. Cue Sandy down the stairs." The stage manager stands in for the child. "Camera 2, you can't be that far right. That's better. And this is shot 17, 18, 19 — mark her position, please." A crew man tapes an X where the actress's toe was pointed.

"Catherine, sit back a little. Thank you."

From inside the control room, the technical director speaks: "Bob, I can't avoid a boom shadow."

Scinto answers, "Can't we have a fan out there to blow the leaves?" The problem appears to be solved. "And we're on page 25. Item 3, ladies and gentlemen. Let's go on. Camera 3, start left and go right."

This episode of *Loving* calls for six sets. All the scenes played in each set are shot as one continuing scene. They are the "items" everyone refers to. Thus, today's episode consists of six items. Later, these six items will be edited into the eleven scenes of Prologue and Acts One, Two, and Three that the audience sees each weekday. It's a system that saves the actors waiting time, and it's also easier on the crew; that way, cables, cameras, and booms don't have to be trekked back and forth from one end of the studio to the other.

"Five minutes, everyone," comes the voice from the control room. They've been on *fax* — which in a TV studio means "facilities" — for an hour. It's time for a break.

This technical rehearsal is the camera crew's first chance to see the day's action. They receive lists of shots, as preplanned by the director. But in rehearsal things frequently change — the unexpected shadow, the wall that has to be moved, and so on. The camera operator must be as attentive and ready to improvise as the actors. During this break the crew tries to solve the boom shadow problem, while the prop department sets fresh flowers in the various rooms.

"Will this affect your shot, Hutch?" asks the set decorator as he hangs a potted plant in a living room window. "We'll have to wait and see," the cameraman answers.

"We're in the penthouse, ladies and gentlemen," the stage manager calls. The break is over.

In this spacious Art Deco set, the director discovers a better shot than the one he had originally planned. "Camera 3, as she walks to the sofa, you can catch her in the mirror! See it? Let's do it again." Scinto signals Randolph Mantooth, who plays Alex: "Randy, you're emptying your pockets downstage of the bench. And, go ahead, please. Good. Do you need a mark, Lisa?"

"No, I can find it."

"Fine. And . . . we go to Egypt's bedroom, Item 6."

Egypt notices that the scissors — an important plot clue — are not the same as those she used in the previous episode. The prop department is dispatched to find the right pair. The concierge's entrance is late. The door sticks. A carpenter is paged.

The child actor, Geoff Wigdon, who plays J.J., walks into the living room set. While rehearsal continues in the other sets, he and Lauren Marie Taylor (Stacey) run their scene quietly.

With the door fixed, Item 6 runs smoothly, and the camera rehearsal ends just in time for the lunch break. Before the crew is released, a voice comes over the loudspeaker, "George from Technical called. Does anyone need accommodations because of the snow? Let him know."

And the studio is deserted once again. The next time the actors are on the set, they will be in full costume and makeup for dress rehearsal.

BEFORE THE DRESS REHEARSAL

Back in the makeup room — which serves as a sort of social hall — actors are ordering food, running lines, doing what they do to get ready. Asked about the lack of true rehearsal time, Lauren Marie Taylor (Stacey) says:

> They rely on you to rehearse by yourself — you and your partner. You go back up to the rehearsal room, or wherever you can find a place, and you run the lines, you work on the scene.

The show has four directors, who undoubtedly have different ways of dealing with actors. And, she observes:

> Sometimes we get a new director. You have to learn each other's personality. Some directors, especially at first, want a performance at 8 A.M. Well, my job is to give it on air. The director has to trust me, that I'm going to do it — to be serious, sad, nervous, whatever. Respect and trust, that's what you have to have with four different ways of working. And it's there. Anyone on a soap knows there's no time to do anything else.

She began as a teenager on *Ryan's Hope*.

> My first days on that show, I felt like an outsider. No one tells you anything! You don't know! And you don't want to step on toes. You have to ask. And you don't even know what to ask! I feel so for people who come in to do a day on a show like this. They're so grateful if you tell them, "Move a step to your right and people will be able to see you." Everyone has to take care of himself. Pay attention.

Except for Catherine Hickland, the cast carried scripts during the run-through. "I try to be off book right away," she says. "That gives me more time to build the performance. It frees me." While she has impressive credits in prime-time and films, she prefers working in daytime television. "It's different every day. You're always trying something new. And you see it right away. It's instant gratification. And it allows you to have a life."

Philip Brown (Buck) joined the cast fairly recently, after a busy career in Los Angeles; he offered a different perspective on this life:

> This is absolutely the hardest work I have ever done. Ten times harder. We do a show a day! This is instant family. It has to be. I was on *The Colbys* and *Knots Landing*. Well, that's a show a week. And sitcoms rehearse for five days, then do it in front of an audience. I have been in this business for thirty years. I played Doris Day's son on her TV show when I

was a kid. I have been very lucky. But this is hard. You have no life here. After this I can do anything.

Relaxing in the community room, with a grand view of the snowstorm, is Geoff Wigdon, who has played J.J. since May. He's done a movie and loads of commercials, but *Loving* is his first soap. "My first week I wasn't so comfortable, but now, I feel like I have a home here. I love the soap the best." How does a twelve-year-old get to be such an experienced show business hand?

> My mom put me in an acting class when I was a kid, and I really liked it. I got lucky. The teacher, Nancy Hillman, had showcases for her students every six months. Someone saw me and liked what I did. Then I worked with James Moody, who had us do monologues. We just do those for a few people, not a big audience. But my mom and dad help me with my lines for this show. It's great.

Is acting what he wants to do when he grows up? " Well," he thinks for a moment, "I would really like to be a basketball player — and an actor!"

DRESS REHEARSAL

"*Loving* cast and crew on the set for dress rehearsal, please!" In the crowded control room, the director, associate director (A.D.), and the production assistant (P.A.) are seated facing the wall of monitors — forty screens — showing what's on the other networks and the local stations, the episode of *Loving* being aired that day, and the possible shots on the four cameras in the studio. On a raised tier behind them, executive producer, Jo Ann Emmerich, watches her personal monitor. With her are the costume and lighting designers, the line producer, and the associate producer. The A.D. starts the count, "5, 4, 3 . . ." which is picked up by the stage manager in the studio, "3, 2, 1," and the dress rehearsal begins.

"The flashback needs to cut out sooner," says director Scinto, "let's try it again."

"Her makeup looks different," says Jo Ann Emmerich, "what is it? Application?"

"Everything is the same," answers the makeup artist. "We'll check it later."

"There's still a lighting problem on the porch." The lighting director whispers into his mike.

"Let's go again. 5, 4, 3, 2, 1."

"Tess has to be coiled like a spring," says Emmerich. "This means she's out on the street if they find out." The P.A. takes notes.

"What's that light in the window? Where did that come from?"

"We'll take care of it, Bob."

"Cooper's line is, 'I wish I'd never taken them off.' It's better than what he's saying."

The new plant hanging in Stacey's living room happens to rest right in front of her face. She pantomimes eating the leaves as she tries to look out the window. The lighting director wants to remove it. "May I?" he asks the director.

"You can put it wherever you want!"

"Her slippers are noisy," notes Emmerich. The costume designer replies, "Do you want her barefoot?"

"Aren't there any ballet slippers?"

"That robe she is wearing is beautiful. The color is perfect," adds the technical director.

"Egypt's hair is too neat. And her face is too clean. She's playing for sympathy, remember," says Emmerich to the hair and makeup artists. She turns to the costume designer. "Doesn't she have a sequined jacket? Something definitely Egypt's? We should use that in the closet shot."

"The concierge is good, but he's reacting to the clothes in the closet, which he can't see. Her dirty face, that's what he needs to see. But he's O.K."

Notes Before Taping

Within an hour, as scheduled, the dress rehearsal is over. Cast and director head for the makeup room. One by one the players sit at the table with Scinto to get their notes. He wants the child playing Sandy to face the camera: "Y'know how, when you look through your Daddy's glasses, you have to hold them away from you, up to the light?" The little boy nods. "Well, you do that, O.K.?" "Yeah." Scinto pats him, and the child skips out to the hall, where Buck and J.J. are shadow-boxing.

After he's given all the notes, Nada asks, "Bob, how about if I come in and walk straight over to the sofa?" "Yes, excellent," he replies, "I should have thought of that!" She walks away, and he turns to the others. "She's amazing. She's been worrying about that moment ever since we got on the set."

He leaves to confer with the technical director. The actors go off in pairs to rehearse their scenes. In half an hour, taping will begin.

A Chat with an Actor

Linda Cook, who plays Egypt, has dirt applied, artfully, to her face. She then crosses to the hair-dressing side of the room to have Russell Latham properly muss her wig. She talks about how she got the part of Egypt.

> I auditioned for Mark Teschner. He said the character was sort of low-class. I read. I got called back for a test. And my agent said, "They've changed the idea of the character. She's really a tramp. Can you do that?"
>
> Well, I figured I had to dress the part. But that's not exactly what I had in my wardrobe. I figured everyone would be coming in in a black miniskirt — that was the style then. And I thought she should be more fun, colorful. So I wore a bright turquoise tube top as the skirt. And a hot pink cotton sweater that buttoned in front, open, but tied at the midriff. And I had my hair all fluffed out, with a colorful bandanna tied around my hair. In the makeup room the stylist started to neaten my hair. But I'd heard all the other girls playing the scene so bitchy, and I said, "No, that's not how I want her." He tried to insist — those were his instructions, after all. But I said, "Look I'm the one who's gonna get the job or lose it, so let me do it my way."
>
> They loved it! And I got another callback for a screen test. Only this time Mark Teschner told my agent, "Can she tone it down a little?" I

decided to leave off the bandanna. We were in the middle of the scene, on camera, when over the talkback they said, "Do you still have that scarf you wore the first time?" I put it on. I got the job!

I played Egypt for three years, with four different producers. You see, the way I saw the character, it was like she'd just won the lottery; she was going to get all this money, from blackmailing her husband. And it was just going to be a whole lot of fun! Then the character got into a lot of dramatic stuff, and she got more and more serious, and they couldn't get me back to being fun.

Now Linda appears on a guest basis, because the executive producer wanted the character back on the show. She finds it hard to do soaps all the time and likes to do live theater to "rev her motor."

She slips on Egypt's messy wig, shakes her head to fluff up the hair, and hurries to the taping.

THE HOUR SHOW: A VISIT TO *ALL MY CHILDREN*

Due to the siege of record-breaking cold weather, the dry rehearsal of *All My Children*, Episode #6433, is proceeding irregularly. As usual, they've been working since 7 A.M., but this is not a usual morning. Every few minutes the P.A. takes a call from one actor or another whose train is delayed, whose car is stuck on the road. This time it's Julia Barr (Brooke). "She's stuck on the parkway, snow and ice. But she'll be here as soon as the traffic moves."

Director Chris Goutman nods, and marks his script. He had already released her scene partner, veteran actress Elizabeth Wilson, to wait in her dressing room until Julia's arrival. He proceeds with the cast on hand: Dixie and Adam.

David Canary (Adam) is still trying to warm his legs, after running down Broadway from the Upper West Side. "It was the fastest way to get here. I thought it would be like skiing, but I'm not really dressed for it. The front of my legs is like ice." Then, feigning shock, he adds, "Chris, my right eye is frozen! I can't see the script!"

While he responds easily to the playful antics of the cast, Goutman nevertheless works very briskly. He gets the actors into position for preplanned camera shots and also manages to pay attention to performance at this early stage of rehearsal, telling one actor, "You don't have to hit that line. You say it again in the next scene." Later in the scene he tells the actress, "Cut the rest of that speech. Just convey it.

"On page 50, let's do the phone call."

Michael E. Knight (Tad), Bill Christian (Derek), and Richard Shoberg (Tom) join the group, just as Julia Barr arrives, breathless. Goutman has the P.A. page Elizabeth Wilson, who appears almost immediately. He introduces her to the other actors, then has them take their places for the next series of scenes.

With five actors in the scene, there are frequent stops and starts, to place them for close-ups and two-shots, then cuts to include the entire group. Lines are changed. They proceed very slowly, to learn the sequence of words and moves. Then they run the exchange again, more rapidly, to see if it really works.

"Page 69, people." Knight asks for a cut. "The line doesn't feel right, can't I just play it?" Goutman watches the scene. "No, Michael, she needs you to say that line. She needs to hear the words."

"Oh, all right. If she needs it, I guess I'll have to say it." They all laugh.

"That's it, folks," the director says, gathering up his pages. "See you in the studio for blocking."

Just as the cast leaves the rehearsal room, the technical director (T.D.) enters, in a hurry. "Chris, you may not have cameras at 10 o'clock. There's no power at Penn Station. Some of the guys are stuck. And there's no extra personnel." Goutman looks unruffled: "We'll just have to do whatever we can."

DRY REHEARSAL

At 10 A.M. the T.D.'s voice booms over the talkback: "Good morning, *All My Children*, it is time to block. We begin with Boom B, and Cameras 3 and 4 in Dixie's living room." Stage manager Tamara Grady speaks softly into her headset, "David Canary, on set, please. This is Item 17, page 4." Then Grady scrunches down on her knees to stand in for Junior, Dixie's child.

Goutman uses no lectern, but works almost within the set with his actors, watching the action in front of him and checking the overhead monitors in each playing area. He calls shots, repositions cameras, working quickly. Following almost stealthily behind, the lighting director whispers instructions into her walkie-talkie, and a trio of stagehands moves in to refocus lights, change gels, and eliminate shadows.

"O.K., let's mark the position of the closet door. We do the farm kitchen next."

The control-room voice announces, "Item 23, Cameras 3, 4, and 5." The stage manager shouts "Quiet on the set!" then talks softly into her hand-held mike, signaling the next team of actors.

As the run-through progresses to playing areas at the far end of the huge studio, a second stage manager, Minnie Bergman, takes over. Goutman shouts: We're on page 24. I need Cameras 3, 4, 5, and 7. Is there anyone to operate Camera 7?" From the far end of the studio a voice answers, "Bobby's here!" Goutman calls, "Give him a headset, somebody." As the cameraman prepares, Goutman gives the T.D. some changes: "Make shot 72 on 5, please, then make 73 a four-shot."

He turns to the actress. "Elizabeth, as soon as they go out the door you move to the window. Push the curtains. Exactly. Now, where's the mailbox? We need it."

"Mailbox, mailbox, please. Take five, everybody!"

During the break, Goutman tells us, "Shooting in sequence is a thing of the past. There's such a need to be more creative, more fluid. It would be impossible to do an hour show any other way. My A.D. will edit this tape tomorrow, and I'll be able to direct another show. But, no matter what, it's still the actors. If they don't do it, I can't show it."

"Places, places, please, for the next act," Tamara Grady calls the cast on set.

This episode calls for one day-player, a jewelry saleswoman, and two extras as the customers in her shop. After the run-through of their scene they are released for wardrobe and makeup. One of the extras has done the show before; for the other it's a first. The newcomer is Lisa Spears, a Californian who decided that New York was the place for her to do serious work on her career:

> You can take better classes here. You can do everything here. No one cares if you do an extra, or a lead. In California I got to do a lot of production jobs; then that was all they could see me doing. I just feel that things are possible here. I've been sending postcards since I met the casting director, and see, I got a call. I've been doing movies since I got here. And I've had callbacks on commercials. I feel really good about the way things are going.

Her partner in the scene, Lydia Schmitt, has concentrated on commercials and print for several years:

> I came into this business almost by accident. I was working in an office, and they asked me to be in the photos for the company brochure. I discovered I really loved the work. I thought that I might be in brochures for other companies, and I found I was able to get jobs. I was too short to be a high-fashion model, but I managed to do quite well in this end of the business. I have always looked like the typical suburban wife. Then I took classes, so that I could compete for commercials. I stuck to what I thought I could do. And it has continued.
>
> Of course, there is a certain skill to it. When you're cast as background, that doesn't mean you're supposed to hide. It means you have to be in the background where the audience can see you. You have to learn to find the light on the camera — without looking for it. Pay attention to what's going on in the scene. And, that way, I have been upgraded on many commercials.
>
> You have to come with the right clothing. Today I brought two things, with a choice of color. It's important to get yourself into a niche — a lot has to do with how you look. I am in this up-scale matron category. I have a good wardrobe, with a selection of long gowns, dressy clothes, so they'll think of me for those scenes.
>
> I never felt that I was aggressive enough to compete for the acting jobs. Or, maybe I could compete, but I wouldn't get them. You have to be realistic.

LUNCH BREAK

Elizabeth Wilson welcomes the chance to talk before the dress rehearsal. She admits she's both weary and excited. Weary because yesterday was a very long day. "I find it's hard to work past 9 o'clock and then come in here again early in the morning." The excitement comes from the realization that her career is going better than ever. She's flying soon to London, where *Scarlett*, the big-budget TV sequel to *Gone with the Wind*, has been in rehearsals.

She has been a working actor for fifty years, starting out in Syracuse, New York, working for $10 a show. She came to New York in 1944 to attend the Neighborhood Playhouse, where she studied as a scholarship student under the renowned Sanford Meisner. A big star recognized her potential:

Helen Hayes wrote letters to people, telling them she thought I was talented. She told me I was not a leading lady, that I was a young character woman. And she was absolutely right! That's what I am today, a character woman.

You might say my big break came in the 1960s, when I appeared in *Big Fish, Little Fish*. John Gielgud was the director. Mike Nichols saw me in that, he liked my work, and he used me. I have done seven productions with him.

Working on the stage was always most satisfying, but she finds that the Broadway theater has changed.

You can't really make a living at it the way you could before. The audiences aren't there any more. I was just in the tour of the A.R. Gurney play, *The Cocktail Hour*. Well, once we got through New York, Boston, and the first week in Chicago, I felt the audience didn't know what we were talking about!

I think, too, you need such stamina for the stage. Eight performances a week! But if you have the strength and can do it, then regional theater is really the most exciting nowadays.

And what has brought her to *All My Children*?

I was in London, rehearsing *Scarlett*, and my agent's office called, wanting to know if I was available just for two days, and I said yes! There was something exciting about working back-to-back like that. There was no script. They sent me a rough version of what I'd have to say.

She echoes what the newcomers say about doing a soap:

No one tells you anything. You don't know where to go or who to talk to. You're really on your own. Of course, now that I'm here the second day, and I'm starting to know my way around, I must say that what these people do is amazing. But I don't know that I could keep it up for very long; I think it would wear me out.

"In fact," and she stretches out on the chaise, "I think I'll take a little rest before going up for the dress rehearsal."

DRESS REHEARSAL

Not all forty monitors are functioning in the control room. The feed from Los Angeles is delayed. "*General Hospital*'s studio was damaged by the quake," reports the P.A.

Goutman, trying to set up for the first item, wants to know why the actress in a fantasy scene is fully clothed. "Can't she be in a slip? Something that looks like she has nothing on? Otherwise the fantasy makes no sense." Designer Carol Luiken tells him there's a slip in Wardrobe that looks right. But the decision is not theirs to make.

Executive producer Felicia Behr takes her seat on the upper tier and, after listening to Goutman, okays the costume change. Her attention then goes to the scene on her monitor. "Wasn't that big poster hanging in another bedroom?" It was, and it's taken down.

The actress returns wearing the slip, and the countdown begins in the control room and in the studio. The camera moves in and. . . .

"Relax a minute, people. We're having problems with the tape."

Neither the tape-playing machinery nor the recording equipment are working. The cameraman on 5 can hear, but he cannot talk into his mouthpiece.

"Take five, *All My Children.* We have technical problems."

THE WARDROBE ROOM

In the second-floor hallway, outside Wardrobe, a clothes rack is being loaded with outfits. Wardrobe mistress Marilyn Putnam has arranged them by character. "These are being prepped for tomorrow's show," she says, smiling. "Come in."

We enter a huge room, almost entirely filled with clothing. "This room is the closet for the principal players. There is another room downstairs for the supporting cast. And there's still another, a warehouse for the clothes that are out of season. This show requires four assistants. We are like maintenance; we take care of everything. Hems up or down. Seams released, or ripped, or just checked."

Her assistant, Margo LaZaro, leads us on a tour. "Those seven racks are Erica's new wardrobe, day wear and negligees. That bookcase is for her jewelry, all sorted and labeled, and here are the shoes, boots, purses. Everyone has a rack. Over here we have the belts, they're all color-coded; here's the general jewelry. And the men's things are on the other side. David Canary has a double wardrobe. He plays two roles, and this is the wardrobe for his double, the actor who plays in the scene when David is talking to his twin self."

In one corner, a washing machine is chugging away. "When things get soiled, we take care of them here. We get the scripts in advance, we look to see whether the same clothes are used; if so, will they need care? If a new person is coming in, will there be fittings? Everything has to be ready. And ready for changes."

All the while, Putnam has been glancing at a monitor hung near her desk. "That slip will have to be steamed. The creases are showing on camera."

THE MAKEUP ROOM

The contract players have left the makeup room, and Jane Gabbert, who's debuting on *All My Children* as the jewelry store owner, is getting Norman Brytt's full attention. A good makeup artist does more than make the performers look terrific; he or she makes them feel confident that they look terrific. When we note how beautifully Brytt has made up Gabbert's eyes, he says, "She has great eyes to work with." She studies her face in the hand mirror, uses the eyelash curler, then he carefully applies her mascara.

Like the wardrobe people, Brytt glances regularly at the color monitor, noticing how his actors faces appear under lights, in costume, on screen. Then he checks his cast list. "We're going to be here late today. Some actors won't get on camera until after 3 P.M." He tells Gabbert, "You look great. Get into costume now. Whatever we need to do we can fix after the dress rehearsal."

DEBUT ON A SOAP

We will not see the actual taping. Before we go, we chat with Jane Gabbert in one of the dressing rooms. In New York for eleven years, Jane is proud that for the past seven years she has been able to support herself as an actress:

> In the beginning I was spending a lot of time as a word processor. But I started doing regional theater, then some commercials, an industrial, and a couple of infomercials, and now I'm not working at the law office any more. It's all from networking. I was doing a play at Cornell University, and one of the actors did a lot of work at ABC. He introduced me to the casting department. I auditioned. Then, while they didn't call me for a part, I did work as a reader when they were auditioning actors for other roles. That is such marvelous experience. Dozens of people all reading the same script, yet each one is completely different. What good practice that is — you learn to change what you do, because the other person in the scene is different. Well, the people at ABC got to know me and trust my work. So when this part came up, I was called to read for it. I felt very much at ease. I don't know how many other people read for this, but I got it!

All dressing rooms have a loudspeaker. The volume in this room is quite low. "Did you hear what she called? Item 8? Oh, that's me!" Jane Gabbert grabs her purse and script and hurries out the door to the studio.

TAPING TIME

A veteran filmmaker asked the director of a daytime soap: "How much do you shoot each day?"

"How much do you see?" the soap director answered.

"Well, that show of yours is an hour," the veteran said.

"That's how much I shoot."

"But that's not possible," said the film director.

"I know, but we do it just the same."

Thom Christopher, who went from the *All My Children* cast to a role on *Loving*, longs for what he calls the relaxation of the hour show:

> In the half-hour, it's rush, rush, rush. As soon as you finish one run-through, you're due on the set again. With the hour show, you have the time to develop your performance over the day. You have the length of the show to do your work. It may sound strange, but I love doing an hour show.

THIRTY MINUTES OF PRIME-TIME

Judith Light, two-time Emmy-winner for her work as Karen Wolek on *One Life to Live*, moved from the pressure of a one-hour daytime show to the relative ease of a half-hour weekly prime-time show, *Who's the Boss?* She described that routine for us:

> We get a new script on Sunday. On Monday morning at eleven there is a "table read." That is over at noon, after which we discuss costumes

for the show, and directions. The following day I have a costume fitting, at 9 A.M., then there is a blocking rehearsal at 10. We do the entire show. Late in the afternoon, 3 to 5, we do a run-through for the network, writers, producers, and pertinent personnel. Afterward there are notes.

The next day, Wednesday, we rework the sections that need it. We have another run-through between 4:30 and 5.

On Thursday we report at 10 A.M. and spend the entire day on camera blocking, till 3:30, 4 or 5. There is a run-through, followed by notes. Usually this is a late day.

Friday is makeup and hair at 11 A.M. At noon we have a run-through till 2:45. We have forty-five minutes for touch-ups. Then we perform for a live audience at 3:30 and another live audience at 6. We are usually finished by 8 P.M.

We are constantly cutting, changing jokes, shifting something. There is an amount of flexibility, and you have to do it immediately. There is no time to have an ego. There are people with titles, who are important because of those titles, but when we sit in production meetings, titles don't exist. Everybody has input. The director is from the theater. The writers and producers want creative participation; they want to discuss problems. We work like an ensemble. We do this for three weeks, then have a hiatus on the fourth week. Our season ends at the end of February. We are off during March, April, May, and June. We begin again in July.

These people on sitcoms work banker's hours, compared to the rest of us.
—JERRY ORBACH, *of the hourlong* Law and Order

A FILMED SERIES

Dan Lauria, who starred as Fred Savage's father in the award-winning series *The Wonder Years*, discussed working on a half-hour filmed series:

Our rehearsal for *The Wonder Years* was Tuesday through Saturday, with Sunday and Monday off. We got the script the previous Thursday or Friday. Tuesday was first rehearsal day. It was a one-camera filmed series, and you had to come in on Tuesday with your lines learned. The director took you up to the set for blocking and read-through. Then you went to makeup and costume while they did the lighting. There was a camera and boom rehearsal, followed by the final shot.

Since children have to be released by 6:30 P.M., Fred Savage's close-ups were shot first. After he left they did my closeup — I would really be talking to an empty chair. Every time you see me or Fred's mother in a single shot, we were not talking to anybody.

Ninety percent of the show was filmed on the set. The school scenes and the exteriors were shot in Culver City. We could only use the school on Saturday, so on Saturdays we worked late.

In a filmed show there can be six- to eight-hour waits between scenes. And you don't leave the set because there could be an accident or a change in the schedule. If you have some real emotional scenes you'd better be able to cry on cue. It's a discipline. You have to be able to match what you've just done, get the emotion at the same pitch. My advice to actors is to have a very solid character and your lines set before you go in. They'll think you are Laurence Olivier. Don't ever expect a lot of help. Be the best actor you can be. If they only give you a minute to prepare, then be the best actor who only has a minute to prepare.

FILMING COMMERCIALS AND MOVIES

To actors accustomed to completing an hour show in one day, the idea of spending an entire day of shooting to achieve one perfect minute of film is, well, kind of like sleepwalking. How can it take a whole day to do a minute? they ask. It can, and does, primarily because the motion-picture camera sees and magnifies everything. On one-camera film shoots, every detail must be flawless. With time and reshooting, technical perfection becomes an attainable goal. In the shooting of a commercial, the product is the star and it *must* look perfect. A full day's shooting is not uncommon. Actors called for 8 or 9 A.M. know that they may not be called to the set until after lunchtime. Technical matters will hold up their work. Yet, they must be ready.

> As Orson Welles once said, "They must pay us for the waiting because we would gladly do the acting for free."
>
> —JERRY ORBACH

At a commercial shoot, the number of people and the noise will equal that of a soap opera set. Everyone moves with careful speed: spraying down the shine on a doorknob, masking the light behind a window. The director decides to put a table on blocks, so then the lights must be repositioned.

Even on a thirty-second commercial, the director will break the script down into short shots. Each of these moments will be filmed again and again, from different angles, and at different distances. For each change the lights will need adjusting. These changes may, in turn, reveal other details that require attention. If the cake frosting melts under the hot lights we will need another take. If the camera wobbles on the dolly, we will need another take. If an actor sneezes or sweats visibly. . . .

Now the shot will be perfect! But a light blows. Take it again.

Technical problems. Human error. On location, the sun disappears behind a cloud; a passing plane ruins the soundtrack; someone forgets the bug spray. Saying the lines is the easy part. Synchronizing words, picture, and product can take a whole day. And it does.

ON LOCATION WITH JOE MANTEGNA

The scene is the Armory building in Chicago, where the final night of shooting a John Hughes farce, *Baby's Day Out*, is about to begin. The call is for 7 P.M., and "wrap" time (completion) won't be until 4 A.M. at the earliest. The script has called for a lot of physical stunts, and star Joe Mantegna has had to do many of them without a stunt double. He, his co-stars, and the crew are all anxious for the film to be finished. Before he goes to makeup and hair, Mantegna describes a typical day on a movie set:

> Even typical days can be untypical because film is a director-driven medium. A typical day on the set with Woody Allen is going to be different from a typical day with Francis Ford Coppola or David Mamet. Each director sets his own parameters, depending upon how he works. A typical day on a Woody Allen set will have less communication between actor and director, because he felt you were the right person for the role, so there really isn't much to talk about. His whole process is based on camera angles. He shoots "in master" a lot — no rehearsals. You go out, he'll say "Roll 'em" and you do it. It is like life, and that is the way he is.
>
> Mamet may want to sit down and spend the first couple of days just reading the script. It will be two weeks before you even get to the set. He will listen and maybe make some changes and then put some of it on its feet.
>
> I have found that rehearsing for film is a whole different ball game from rehearsing for theater. Its benefits are not as great as one would imagine; there is a limit to its value. What you find out in film is that, nine times out of ten, when you are ultimately shooting a scene it is going to be in an environment that is totally alien to the way you rehearsed it, because you are going to be adding a million other elements. For example, let us say the scene is going to be outside on a bridge, and it is going to be 30 degrees, and then there are the cameras and the lights, and you have to deal with all those conditions. So the rehearsal hall system doesn't apply any more. If you rehearse too much, then it is difficult to be flexible.
>
> Some directors love to shoot sequentially, but it proves to be very costly. Mamet tried in *House of Games*. There is a reason to shoot out of sequence: logistics. If the writer wrote it that way, then you can do it. But let's say you have a scene that takes place in a house three different times in the movie. You shouldn't have to break down the set three times. You shoot them all at once.
>
> What is really difficult is when you shoot the last scene of the movie on the first day. You might be a victim of the location or the weather. The movie might span a three-month period. It is supposed to end in the dead of winter and start sometime in the early fall. Your shooting schedule might start in late February, and then you will have to shoot the end first because of the snow on the ground. If you are fairly new at this game, and you have come primarily from the theater, you might panic at the thought of shooting the last scene first. You are not sure what the character has been through — where he has been, what he has done — all the motivation questions. You start to realize that unless you want to make yourself crazy, you have to trust that what you shoot on Monday

is going to match up with what you shoot on Tuesday, which might be the *first* scene of the movie. I would certainly know the whole script and the structure. What works for me is that you take each day's scene, or work, as a film unto itself. You give each day a beginning, a middle, and an end, and play it for the reality of that scene. If it has been written correctly, you don't have to worry about it. You play the reality of that scene. You do every scene that way and then it is the editor's problem to put it all together, and it will mesh.

From the first moment they say *Action!* you have to make your choice. You have to be whoever you are going to be, and that is disconcerting, especially the first couple of days. You are making a commitment with little or no rehearsal time and no history of relating to the other characters or actors. Most actors would say, after two weeks of shooting, "Great, now I feel comfortable, so let's throw this film away and start over." Woody Allen can and will do that. Few directors will, because after the film is put together, no one in the audience is going to know what scene was shot on the first day.

When they say "Roll 'em," it doesn't matter where you are. I learned that in the theater. When I was opening on Broadway [in *Glengarry Glen Ross*] the anticipation was awesome. The first moment you step out you realize it is just people in seats, and it is no different than when you did it in high school. It is the same thing filming at different locations. Shooting in Moscow was an amazing, unbelievable experience. But when you are in the scene you are not thinking,"Oh, I am in Moscow!" but rather, "I have to walk across this street in character and say this dialogue," and so on.

There is not a lot of difference between directors, outside of their personalities. There is no magic one way of doing things. The bottom line is, they all have to say "Roll camera," and you have to act, and they have to say "Cut."

I have been lucky because some of the great directors I have worked with also write — Coppola, Mamet, Allen, Barry Levinson, Steven Zallien. The advantage is that the director is more in tune with the creative process. Coppola is very big, very expansive in his descriptions. He paints pictures with everything at his disposal.

There has to be trust between the director and the actors. Onstage, when the play starts, the actor is steering the car. It is like when the gun goes off for the race: I have to run it now — there is no stopping until the finish line. In a film, there are a million finish lines. The director can totally orchestrate how you run to that finish line. If he doesn't like it, he can stop it and say, "No, run this way." So there has to be tremendous trust. Because even if you run it ten different times, and you think number nine was the one, it may not be the one he liked. You are at the mercy of the director's talent and decisions. Mamet is terrific with actors. He is patient, knowledgeable, and smart. But no director will give the final editing approval to any actor.

ON THE STAGE

We are assuming that our readers have some familiarity with theatrical production — the relatively long rehearsal period and the hoped-for long run of performances. In this medium the challenge is to keep the performance fresh, to retain the illusion of the first-time. You may be doing the show for the hundredth time, but the audience has never seen it before.

There is a classic story about the great actor Alfred Lunt, who always grew in performance. In 1948, the tour of *O Mistress Mine* was closing. The matinee before the final performance, Mr. Lunt told Dick Van Patten, who was playing his son, to come to his dressing room before the show. Lunt said, "I think if you say this line at this particular point, we can get another laugh." Van Patten did, and got it. This was after two years of performing!

That's what actors should never forget.

CHAPTER 16

THEY WANT YOU TO SIGN A CONTRACT

I am proud to have been in a business that gives pleasure, creates beauty, and awakens our conscience, arouses compassion and . . . gives millions a respite from our so violent world.

—AUDREY HEPBURN

You are going to sign a personal contract. You are going to create a definable character on a stage, on a soap, or in a movie. It is a great feeling. You will be paid a salary every week, for as long as the project, or your story line, lasts.

Your agent will do the negotiating for you. If you have managed to win your role without an agent, this may be a smart time to get an agent or theatrical attorney to represent you. Many performers view this as giving away 10 percent of their salary. Try to see it as an investment: the agent will try to get as much for you as you are worth — actors are not as knowledgable as they can be about the subtle business aspects of their jobs. Moreover, the agent may start seeking additional work for you, work that does not conflict with your new job. Think about it.

Once you're working steadily, it invariably follows that other people will want to hire you. Be sure you understand the terms of your contract. Are you precluded from doing commercials or any other jobs? If you happen to be presented with a better opportunity, what are your options? For example, on soaps, actors generally need to give six weeks' notice for four weeks out, after their first six months on the show. These things are negotiated before you sign.

A word-of-mouth agreement isn't worth the paper it's written on.

—SAMUEL GOLDWYN

JOINING THE FAMILY

One thing to understand deep in your soul is that once you sign with any company — stage, film, or TV — you are part of a business family. Respect it. Avoid the childish temptation to test their love for you by behaving sloppily — forgetting to learn your lines, losing your script, failing to set the alarm and being late, or not showing up at all. You are considered too grownup for that. Remember how hard you have worked for this reward. Put kid stuff behind you. Love your business, and love your-self. And have fun with it!

Too Much, Too Soon?

It seems strange to us that, after working so hard and so long, anyone would flee from success. Yet that is precisely what one young woman chose to do.

She had a contract role in a highly rated daytime soap. It was, she said, a dream come true. But as her story line progressed she began to dislike the work. Doing the show two, three, or four times a week was too tough. She didn't like her story line. She hadn't made any new friends. She wanted to be with her boyfriend. She missed her family. She even "kinda missed" her schoolteachers, too.

And so, without consulting anyone — her agent, her producer, or her union, all of whom had helped in some way to ensure her respectable status in her chosen career — she announced, "I don't want to be here." And she quit the show.

There was no way that she could be persuaded to stay until the end of the story line, or until a replacement could be found. She refused to consider the actors whose careers were linked to hers. She just wanted out. Her story line was accelerated, and out is what she was.

She has since tried the job scene in Los Angeles. She wasn't happy there, either. She is back in New York — seeking auditions. She feels she has gained maturity, and is now able to handle her career as a business. Would she consider doing anoth-er soap opera? Oh, yes indeed!

We tell this story not to be smug or to point fingers, but to alert you to the natur-al anxieties that can suddenly overtake you when everything seems to be going almost too well. When, or if, you start to wonder, "What's it all about, what am I doing here?" turn to the people whose job it is to help you — your agent, your producer, your union, your therapist, your family. Talk it out. Calm down.

Give yourself, and the people you work with, a chance.

CHAPTER 17

COPING WITH SUCCESS

You have to have focus, dedication, commitment, and passion to put yourself through the physical, intellectual, and emotional agony it takes to achieve your goal.

—RITA GAM

Let us assume that you are working and have become highly successful and very visible. Your television and film exposure have enabled you to move into a bigger house or buy a condominium, to expand your wardrobe. You get invited to "in-crowd" parties and are ushered to the best tables at posh restaurants. In California you drive a Mercedes to the studio lot; the parking space has your name on it.

You have had to hire a business manager to take charge of your finances, a publicist to handle requests for interviews, and a secretary who handles your fan mail and related correspondence. A personal manager has become indispensable for making decisions about properly advantageous career moves. You have a fashion consultant, tailor, hairstylist, masseuse, personal trainer, a housekeeper, and, most important, a bodyguard. You've got what you've always dreamed about.

But what is missing? Where's the support system you relied upon as you were climbing up the ladder? Those trustworthy friends and family members? What happened to the agent who got you your first big breaks?

What sacrifices you have made! And for what? To lose your privacy? To succumb to a reliance upon alcohol or drugs? When you look in the mirror, who is that drawn, anorexic, burnt-out, unhappy actor? The dream has become a nightmare.

The short scenario we have just outlined is not an exaggeration. You frequently read about a celebrity's cocaine habit, drunk-driving arrest, barroom drawl, or overdose, and the predictable visits to clinics, detoxification centers, and courtrooms.

After all the hard work, the dues-paying, and rejections, it is essential that you maintain your sense of self. Judith Light offers excellent advice:

No career is more important than the way you are as a human being. That philosophy has enabled me to go through just about everything. Nobody stays a star. A long-range goal or a series of goals is important for a long-term career. You have to have a foundation, be a person of integrity.

Find the right support system — people you trust: agent, manager, teacher, psychologist, friends, spouse. It is important to put everything in the proper perspective. If you know where you are coming from, all things are possible.

When I came to L.A., I didn't know how to drive a car. I had to learn and was terrified. But I made the adjustment. You work very hard. You have to get up very early. You can't be out all hours of the night partying. You have to be at your best on the set, in rehearsal, and in performance. These are the requirements of your career, and you must be prepared to meet them . . . because you love it and you want to be there.

I was very lucky to have wise agents who told me to work well with my money. I hired a business manager. I still allowed myself to live well. There is this old myth about the "struggling actor who lives in a cold-water garret and starves for his art"! When you can move yourself up from the poverty level, move up.

Coping with the pressures of staying on top must be very difficult for those who have been catapulted to stardom without training and experience, for they have not paid their dues. Actors who have extensive stage credits and have studied for years with such teachers as Uta Hagen, Robert Lewis, Alice Spivack, Flo Greenberg, or Aaron Frankel are ready to accept the applause of an adoring public without going off the deep end. But the very young — whether exceptionally beautiful, magnetic, or off-beat types — who have been lucky enough to be selected, say, from an open call and relocated to New York or Los Angeles to assume contract roles in soaps or features, have the most difficulty maintaining their perspective. They are ripe for the temptations of "living it up," listening to the wrong people, and believing their publicity. They lack a solid support system, the family, teacher, mentor, close friend, or sweetheart who can exert a positive moral influence or give them a reality check.

Actors can become commodities associated with dollar signs — that loathsome word "bankability." They must remember that their art lies within themselves. They have the option to continue to grow in their craft or to stagnate and become lazy. Respected and successful industry professionals have shared with us the following valuable insights:

What kept me going was the relationship with my wife and the internal belief that I knew it was going to happen. And every time I came back to it, I came back bigger, and clearer.

—THOM CHRISTOPHER

Some young actors who become matinee idols are coddled instead of being reprimanded. They don't know what it's like to get out there and be in a play that's a flop, to make an absolute idiot of themselves. At sixteen or seventeen, when have they ever had to risk anything?

—KATHLEEN NOONE

Christian Slater began his career as a child actor on the stage and gained critical acclaim in *The Name of the Rose,* playing opposite Sean Connery. His performances in *Heathers* and *Pump up the Volume* made him a teen idol. He became impossible. Christian admits:

> I definitely went through an extremely irresponsible stage, where I was just doing what I wanted to do. I thought, "Ah, the career will take care of itself." All the clubs and things that I was trying to get into before, people were letting me in! I'm getting free booze! I'm getting a really cool booth for me and my friends to hang out in at all of these lovely establishments!

His mother, casting director Mary Jo Slater, agonized over his behavior:

> It's hard enough to be a parent, much less the parent of a movie star. When you love someone so much and see that he's falling, you're trying to stop it. But you know he has to fall, because it's part of life's experience.

His repeated failure to appear on the set led to rumors that he suffered from narcolepsy. Then, fortunately, he took a good look at himself.

> I wasn't the type of guy who would have a beer while watching a football game. I was the type of guy who would have a bottle of tequila and just hang out. So, it was pretty clear to me how unhealthy that was.

Christian sought help at Alcoholics Anonymous. The death of his friend River Phoenix occurred shortly afterward, giving him a sense of relief that he cleaned up his own act just in time.

> The worst thing that an actor can do is think that he's indispensable. No one is indispensable. I remember another producer told me what she did when certain people's contracts were coming up for renewal and they had let it be known they had "demands" to make: she'd have the reception room in front of her office filled with actors who all looked as if they'd been called in to audition for the same part! At the sight of all the competition those temperamental stars got the message — how easily they could be replaced.
>
> —ERWIN NICHOLSON, *producer*

Let us offer some suggestions to help you realize your worth as a successful human being and artist.

1. Keep in touch with who you were before success came along. This is your "reality base." This connection is easy if you have a family. Your kids don't treat you like a star, but just as a parent.

2. Live well, but not beyond your means. Do not attempt to create an image or a lifestyle for yourself that is exaggerated and dishonest.

3. Invest in yourself. Continue going to classes, rehearsing plays, reading, participating in creative projects such as writing or producing. Gain a sense of control over your own life.

4. Love yourself. Value your psychological and physical well-being. Do nothing to harm your body or alter your consciousness. Otherwise it will show, not only on camera but in life, and will continuously jeopardize your personal life.

> I went through a personal and emotional crisis in the mid-1970s, when I was living here in Los Angeles. I sort of reached my wit's end. I saw that my life was running downhill. So I started a whole series of new habits. When I made that conscious decision to change direction, it was like that hand of fate came down and said, "O.K., you want to change direction, we'll help you." It was a peculiar change of destiny. I can't describe it exactly, but ever since that day my life has taken on a whole new color and hue of brightness. My life has been blessed ever since.
>
> —ANTHONY HOPKINS

Keep your sense of humor, and continue to enjoy the process.

CHAPTER 18

THE LITTLE STARS

Dear Someone: I am a twelve-year-old boy that would give anything to be an actor!

It is a well-known fact that adult stars of the vaudeville circuits refused to appear on the same bill with children and animals because they were constantly upstaged by them. W.C. Fields always sneered at Baby Leroy in his films, and while his sarcasm was hilarious, there was true fury behind it.

In movies of the 1930s and '40s, appealing moppets like Shirley Temple, Freddie Bartholomew, Natalie Wood, or a wide-eyed, sweet-voiced Margaret O'Brien could steal the focus from any adult in the picture. Can anyone forget O'Brien's Tootie in *Meet Me in St. Louis*? And then there were the irresistible musical comedy talents of such teen stars as Judy Garland, Mickey Rooney, and Deanna Durbin.

Behind every young film star or stage child there seemed to be a very strong, aggressive parent. The "pushy stage mother" has been immortalized on stage and screen in *Gypsy*, the saga of Mama Rose and her daughters June (Havoc) and Louise (Gypsy Rose Lee), whom she pushed, dragged, and forced into show business.

Stage musicals, such as *Oliver!, The Music Man, Annie, The King and I,* and *The Sound of Music* have employed many children who were eager to get out there and give their all singing, dancing, and acting. When Kathryn Zaremba studied dance and learned songs at a theater school in Broken Arrow, Oklahoma, she never imagined that a production of *Annie* in Oklahoma City would lead to an audition for Martin Charnin in Houston for the lead in *Annie Warbucks* in New York. A year after that she landed the role. Co-star Donna McKechnie observed: "Watching Kathryn was like watching a little flower, a little star, emerge."

Today's gifted children have more opportunities than ever before to work in commercials, soap operas, films, and theater. Commercials probably use more children than any other medium. However, in recent years there has been a noticeable increase in young people getting leads in films. Ever since *wunderkind* Macaulay Culkin reaped millions for the makers of *Home Alone*, there has been a constant search to find the next blockbuster child star, and in the wings are talented youngsters such as Elijah Wood (*The Adventures of Huck Finn, The Good Son*); Joe Mazzello

(*Jurassic Park, Shadowlands*); Corey Carrier (*Young Indiana Jones, Men Don't Leave*); Noah Fleiss (*Josh and Sam*); Mason Gamble (*Dennis the Menace*); and Max Pomeranc (*Searching for Bobby Fischer*).

By definition, TV's family shows require several children in every family. Shows like *Home Improvements, Full House,* and *Roseanne* have filled their sets with various kids, toddlers to teens. Soap operas feature roles for babies, preschoolers, grade-school children, and, of course, teens of age fifteen to nineteen for the more sophisticated story lines.

Kids enter The Business by various routes. Sometimes a mother will read in the local paper about a beauty pageant that features a talent competition. Judges at these events might be casting directors, agents, or managers who specialize in young talent. Elijah Wood was discovered by a manager at a modeling competition. School plays, choir and instrumental recitals, and dance festivals afford opportunities to perform in front of an audience and acquire a sense of discipline. Participation in the high school drama club, in speech contests or forensic events such as debating, original oratory, humorous, dramatic, or oral interpretation are all invaluable for developing good speech, projection, poise, timing and appearance, as well as acting and writing skills.

Competing for awards is excellent preparation for a career. Parent and child will be able to tell whether the desire is real.

INITIAL CONCERNS

Both parent and child need to know the right ways to seek stardom or simply good, honest work opportunities for a child. The important rule of thumb is: *the child must want to do it!* We think it is appalling when a parent forces a young person into a life of commercial auditions and tap, singing, and acting classes when the child would prefer to be playing with the neighbors' children. It is dangerous to attempt to live vicariously through children. Let the choice be theirs!

Mary Jo Slater, mother of Christian Slater and never a "typical" stage mother, reflected on her son's beginnings:

> I didn't want my child to go into the business. Commercials were some-thing else. He was adorable and had this typical American face they were looking for, and it was easy. But when I saw him in Reno where the show [a revival of *The Music Man*] opened, there was this wonderful little person! You had to admit he had something special. And Christian loved it, he wanted it!

Letters from eager parents seeking breaks for their beautiful babies, talented dancers, or child prodigies pour into the offices of casting directors and agents. Unfortunately, bogus talent scouts prey on such people. They may lurk around elementary schools ready to charge unwitting parents a fee to get their little Drew Barrymore or Leonardo DiCaprio on television or into the movies. These con artists take advantage of the parent who envisions the monetary rewards of having a successful child in show business. Greed as much as parental ambition should never be the motivation for thrusting a child into the limelight.

MAKING THE CHOICE

On the other hand, there are examples of children who do make that choice. These letters from aspiring children came to a network casting director:

> To whom it may concern,
> My drama teacher told me to spread the word that I am available. I'm not beautiful, but I try.
>
> P.S. I'm very responsible and reliable.

> Dear network,
> I am twelve years old. I want to become an actress. My mother says she is up to taking a chance for her only child to become an actress. But if there is any kind of papers I have to sign I would like them to be mailed to me.

A ten-year-old wrote:

> I had four years of drama, and I write my own plays for school subjects. My parents say I have the talent. I get lots of compliments.

We wonder if the following letter was actually written by a twelve-year-old:

> Dear sirs,
> I realize that positions have not been offered, but I would really like to join your network of actors on one of your fine television shows. I have acted in school plays since first grade, and I am almost twelve years old now. Per your request I am willing to fly to New York or Los Angeles for an interview to get a television part as a main role or a guest star.

An eleven-year-old actress shared this confidence:

> I do not want the part for a bunch of money but just to be in front of the cameras. If you think that I want the part because I am rich and want to get richer, don't think that. Last year in fourth grade, my teacher gave me the part in a play. I asked my teacher why I always get good parts and she said, "You get the good parts because you can remember and say things the best."

And finally:

> I'm a fifteen-year-old girl who wants to be a famous movie star. So will you please help me to reach my goal, my dream, if it's not asking too much.

A number of illustrious performers of stage and screen, established working actors, have talked about when they decided to pursue acting as a career. Some stumbled into it. When she was eight years old, the late Geraldine Page (Oscar winner, *The Trip to Bountiful*) decided to emote at her church's theater. The audience responded positively. She alternated her stage-sweeping chores with acting.

When I was nine, my father took me to a live performance of *Me and My Girl*. We sat in the second balcony. It cost one pound apiece, and the people were very tiny. I watched those little people, and I said to my father, "That's what I want to do." He said, "Well, then, I think you should learn to move." And I started taking lessons — all kinds of lessons, in dance, ballet, tap.

—JIM DALE, *Tony winner*

When I was little, about three years old, I started to memorize poetry. I enjoyed performing for people. I had a revelation that I would be doing this, and I would be successful. It hit me in the gut, rather than my head.

—JUDITH LIGHT, *star,* Phenom, Who's the Boss?

I turned to acting to escape from being myself. I looked to my toys and my little space as a fantasy retreat. Early photos indicate my makeshift sets and props for my performance. Between four and five I was taken to see *Peter Pan*. That cinched it. It was the only thing I wanted to do with the rest of my life.

—ROBIN STRASSER, *Emmy winner,* One Life to Live

My family was in the theater, so it was a natural. I grew up in that atmosphere. I saw a book of Helen Hayes's life and saw pictures of her acting and I thought," Oh, you could put everything that is fantasized in your head outside of yourself." And that is when I became interested in acting.

—GILLIAN SPENCER, *actress and writer*

I was lonely and unhappy as a child, a loner. I didn't really relate to the people around me, but I did have a rich fantasy life.

—JESSICA TANDY, *Oscar winner,* Driving Miss Daisy

KNOWING THE REALITIES

The Business offers a life of intense competition, not necessarily relieved by the insensitivity of directors and producers. Children are frequently treated as adults. They may lose touch with their schoolmates who, out of envy, sometimes ostracize them. Much too soon, they feel like part of the adult world.

Jean Fox has been managing young careers in New York and Los Angeles for more than a dozen years. She represents young stars who do feature work, and she regrets that some film directors do not relate well to kids:

Young stars are left to their own devices, or seek help from the more experienced actors on the set.

It is not uncommon to hear children at commercial auditions comparing their residuals and product conflicts. We see them reading the trade papers! If they become mini-adults, or if they start to behave like automatons who cry on cue without real motivation, it is time to end the career and get them back to the real, as opposed to the reel, world.

Young people are extremely impressionable and, like adults, sensitive to rejection. They can become hard, as well. They need constant encouragement and a solid base of support at home. Parents who disagree about the wisdom of a show business career for their child often become so combative over the subject that their marriage is jeopardized. We hope such cases are rare.

OPPORTUNITIES FOR YOUNGSTERS

How does a family living far from the production centers help and support the talented child? You can begin by inquiring about children's theaters, community theaters, and university theaters in your area. In many cities there are productions that need children, such as annual presentations of *A Christmas Carol*. Regional outdoor plays produced every summer may require children.

No one doubts that, with their continuous production, New York, Chicago, and Los Angeles offer the greatest number of opportunities for child actors. They have the best photographers, the largest reservoir of teachers and coaches who specialize in working with young people. There are talent agents who handle children exclusively — in New York alone there are approximately forty-five talent agencies and forty managers who represent kids. The agents are listed in *Ross Reports;* managers are listed in *USA Ross Reports.*

REGIONAL POSSIBILITES

Across the country there are more than 500 AFTRA/SAG—franchised talent agencies who submit children and teens for features, series, and commercials. The local AFTRA/SAG office will give you a list of their names and addresses, or you may find them in the Yellow Pages. Agents or casting services in cities throughout the country know about the film, television, and theater jobs. They are frequently contacted by East and West Coast casting directors who ask them to screen-test clients and submit their tapes for consideration.

> I really believe that casting directors from Los Angeles and New York come to Chicago to see children. The children in the Midwest aren't jaded. they are fresh. They lead normal lives.
>
> —MARLA CAHAN, *Suzanne's A+*

Talent Searches   Patti Kalles, casting director in Seattle, held open calls for children to play Danny DeVito's son in *Jack the Bear.* In Portland, Oregon, 1,500 children showed up; in Seattle, 800 came to the call. For Jessica Lange's son in *Men Don't Leave,* Maureen Brookman, director of Stewart Talent Management Corporation, in Chicago, recalls:

> Chris O'Donnell was the only actor I presented to the casting director. He blew off the audition three times! I finally called his mom and told her to promise him a car, just get him there. The rest, as they say, is history.

Entertainment Tonight announced to the nation's parents that videotapes of five-to-seven-year-olds to be considered for the title role in the film *Dennis the Menace* should be sent to the Warner Brothers casting office. The casting director was deluged with more than 20,000 tapes.

Laura Sisk was working in her dad's gas station in Maryland when her manager, Linda Townsend, got the call from an ABC casting director to put together a tape of girls for the part of Ally on *Loving* and send it to New York. She was flown to New York to screen-test, got the part, and has grown as an actress on the job, while continuing her studies.

Linda, a former teacher and performer, has managed young professionals in the Washington and Baltimore area for more than a dozen years. Her clients have appeared in prime-time series, feature films, and more than a score of Broadway shows. She tells parents with talented offspring to send a recent snapshot and brief biographical information:

> I'm not necessarily looking for the most beautiful child. I'm looking for real kids with charisma who like other people. There's usually a special little something. I think it's born in them.

She tries to keep picture and résumé costs to a minimum. Parents need not invest in an expensive portfolio. As far as photos are concerned, snapshots will do for babies and for children up to about four years old. Children change so quickly that it is foolish to invest in professional headshots before the child is at least five.

> If they have no work or experience, that's fine, because everyone has to start somewhere. I make it clear to them to put nothing on the résumé that is false. If you say you can do karate, you better be able to show me a karate kick.
>
> For parents the moment of truth is when you have to spend money in order to make money. Parents in it for the quick buck find it is not as easy as they thought. Because of the area we are in, they have to spend money to get to most of the auditions.
>
> Most of the children who are able to make money and save it are in the national touring companies. Both parents and children receive per diems, and usually they can live on it while putting most of the salary into their kids' educations.
>
> —LINDA TOWNSEND

Townsend's procedure regarding the audition makes use of her teaching and performing skills. When the scripts are faxed, she works with the children one-on-one, so they can get a good feel for what the character is about.

Summer Theater Camps   A summer theater camp is another possibility. For instance, Stagedoor Manor, in Loch Sheldrake, New York, caters to children interested in the performing arts. For more than twenty summers, Carl and Elsie Samuelson have provided a nurturing environment, in the scenic Catskill Mountains, to teach acting, dance, singing, comedy, TV, and modeling for grade-schoolers and teens who simply love theater. There are classes for beginners, intermediate, and advanced students. High school students can get college credits from the local community college. (In addition to the performance classes, there are the typical camp activities, such as swimming, tennis, and roller-skating parties.) Every summer, alumni who have made it in The Business — directors, agents, and managers — stop by to see the children perform. Jennifer Jason Leigh, Helen Slater, Robert Downey, Jr., and Josh Charles are among Stagedoor Manor's famous graduates.

There are five theaters on the premises, plus a number of resort-hotel theaters in the area. The camp motto is: *Every Stagedoor camper is in a show at all times.*

SPEAKING AND READING ABILITY

Children who grow up in the metropolitan New York area may have the advantage of plentiful theater and television job possibilities, but they are frequently disqualified from major roles because they talk with a regional accent. Their intonation and pronunciation are peculiar to Brooklyn, the Bronx, and Queens, and New Jersey, Long Island, and Yonkers.

Any regional dialect is limiting, be it Southern, Midwestern, New England, or Texan. Children whose speech shows signs of becoming so accented should go to authorized speech teachers who specialize in standard American speech. The earlier they start speech lessons, the easier it will be to develop good speech habits and a good ear, so that they will be able to assume whatever dialect a role demands.

Reading ability is also important. It is shocking nowadays to discover that a great many high school graduates cannot read properly. Reading skill, vital to every audition, should be developed as early as possible. All children should be encouraged to read aloud. Parents are advised to set aside the time to listen to poetry, a story, or an essay, perhaps even one that the child has written.

Too often a parent will coach a child with commercial copy or with a scripted scene. The child ends up sounding just like an adult and may, out of terror, forget memorized words. Unable to read phonetically (dividing the words), such a child may become very frustrated and tense and lose jobs as a result.

Proper training and study habits will give the young actor a better chance at winning the part, without the parent's well-meaning interference.

> This is a craft. A ballerina has to study and study before she can perform a solo. Some people are lucky enough to have that magic and that instinct right away.
>
> —JEAN FOX

CLOTHING

Some mothers have been known to dress their daughters to look like dolls in a toy store instead of real people. The child should be permitted to wear something comfortable, and should have a choice in the outfit. A casting director, director, or producer may be completely won over by the individuality and personality expressed by the clothing. Boys tend to wear certain caps, T-shirts, or jerseys. That is appropriate.

If the casting director wants to see a specific wardrobe for the audition, the parent will be told in advance.

AT AN OPEN CALL

The open call is perhaps the fastest way for a casting director and producer to see a great number of children for a leading role. In January of 1994, the producers of *Annie Warbucks* held an open call for children to appear in the touring company of the show, which was about to end its New York run. The notice had gone out to casting directors and talent agents, and had been sent to the theater sections of the area's newspapers.

The call was scheduled for 4 P.M. By 3:15 there were ninety would-be orphans on line outside New York's Variety Arts Theater, on Third Avenue and 14th Street. Altogether more than 200 six- to eight-year-old kids — of all races and backgrounds — showed up, with parents or grandparents, carrying their photos and résumés. Most had already had years of singing and dancing lessons. Many of them already had long résumés. Several had auditioned for director Martin Charnin before. And he seemed to remember who they were.

When asked what he was looking for, he explained that the criteria went beyond sheer talent. "They have to be able to concentrate, they have to do all the things that the grown-ups do."

As Charnin noted, there are some naturally incredibly, talented children. As a warm-up, he asked everybody to sing Annie's song "Tomorrow." They all knew it! Then he divided them into groups of six, and they worked with the choreographer. Then each group took center stage, and one at a time the kids were told to step forward and sing a few lines.

One child froze. Charnin walked over to her and asked quietly, "Do you want to be here?" She shook her head fiercely, no!

"Did your mommy make you come?" She nodded, yes!

"Would you sing for me?" She shook her head again. He smiled. "Well, that's O.K."

Another sang well enough, but suddenly stopped in her tracks when she had to dance. His solution was to have the next child dance with her. Somehow, both opened up and had an exciting moment.

There was one child, possibly one of very few, who had no previous experience at all. Her mother had read the call notice, and was curious enough to take a chance, join the crush, see what it was all about. Asked what the experience was like, the seven-year-old said, "Oh, it was the best thing I did in my whole life! I was on Annie's stage! I want to be an actress!"

YOUNG PROFESSIONALS

It is important to remember that all the children Charnin saw also went to school. Those who work frequently go to Professional Children's School, in New York, or they have tutors. In theater, they work at night and do their school work during the day. Children who do commercials may have a day or two of shooting, but nevertheless keep up with their school assignments.

Before Macaulay Culkin became a megastar, he had been featured in smaller roles in *See You in the Morning,* with Jeff Bridges, and *Rocket Gibraltar,* with Burt Lancaster. He had starred in an episode of *The Equalizer* and performed in marathons of new plays at the Ensemble Studio Theatre. All this job experience had been accumulated by the time he was seven years old!

Christian Slater began at the age of nine. He accompanied his mother to a local talk show and ended up singing "Zip-A-Dee Doo-Dah." Director Michael Kidd happened to be watching the show, tracked him down, and cast Christian as Winthrop in a production of *The Music Man*, starring Dick Van Dyke. He spent nine months on a national tour, prior to opening on Broadway. Christian remembers:

> I was terrible. They almost fired me. I had no discipline, no technique. I didn't know what I was doing. I couldn't do the same thing twice. I would wave at the audience as if it were a school show. Mom helped me. They kept me on. When we came back to New York I went to Professional Children's School and kept on auditioning.

It is extremely important that the pursuit of a career should not upstage education. They should grow, hand in hand. Studies in science, languages, social sciences, history, geography, and English literature expand the mind, open the doors to the imagination, provide comparisons, and increase comprehension of the peoples and religions of the world. This awareness will produce better actors and more enlightened, articulate adults. The professional standards of the future are formed during these years.

GROWING UP

When kids reach puberty, their bodies are changing and they become so aware of themselves that their performance can become inhibited. Girls frequently wear too much makeup and elaborate hairstyles, and clothing so sophisticated that their genuine appeal is hidden. This, too, is sometimes engineered by a pushy parent who thinks the thirteen-year-old will have more job opportunities if she looks eighteen. The teen years are so important in the development of self that to deprive anyone of them is truly unforgivable.

Unfortunately, the teens who get cast in soaps and features are sometimes expected to behave as if they have the emotional experience and sexual confidence of their older siblings. If they lack the strong support of healthy parents or a strong spiritual foundation, they may experience traumas that will take years to resolve.

There are some teens whom we will call the "old souls," They come into the world with a history. Adults marvel at their poise, maturity, sensuality, concentration, and artistic instincts. They are the ones who clearly know what they want to do and how to go about it.

A NETWORK OF PERFORMING ARTS SCHOOLS

Fame, the popular movie and television series, brought national recognition to New York's LaGuardia High School of the Performing Arts. Certainly, the school's alumni comprise a who's who of the worlds of music and art. However, the broader-based Network of Performing Arts High Schools, which has been in existence for more than ten years, shows that there are accredited secondary schools of the arts in almost every state of the nation.

Most of the schools require an audition and a degree of academic excellence as entrance criteria. Others may not be as stringent or sophisticated. It is exciting to know that the states have responded to the need for specialized training centers for artistically motivated teenagers. We hope that the network, which now numbers more than 100 schools, continues to expand.

For information about a school near you, write: Executive Director, International Network of Performing and Visual Arts Schools, 35th and S Streets, N.W., Washington, D.C. 20007

THE NFAA ARTS® PROGRAM

If you are a young artist, or the parent of a gifted teen, you should know about some innovative programs concerned with the future of America's new generation of artists. The Miami-based National Foundation for Advancement in the Arts (NFAA) is a nonprofit philanthropic and educational institution that assists young artists at various stages of their development. Its Arts Recognition and Talent Search, or ARTS, program has had enormous impact on young artists in every state and major city, embracing teenage hopefuls of every artistic discipline.

Approximately 6,000 high school seniors participate in ARTS each year. They have an opportunity to share in scholarship aid worth $3 million, and cash awards of $300,000. Each year about 300 national ARTS awardees are named in dance, music, theater, musical theater, visual arts, and writing. Awardees are recruited extensively by major universities and professional schools, such as the Juilliard School, New York University, and the University of Michigan. ARTS is the exclusive vehicle through which the White House Commission on Presidential Scholars annually selects twenty Presidential Scholars in the Arts.

ARTS has its own affirmative action program, designed to ensure widespread participation by all who are eligible, regardless of race, creed, color, geographical location, economic disadvantage, physical disability, language, or sex. Through information networks and telephone consultations, minority and disabled youths are assisted in participating in the program.

Since 1980, theater awardees have enjoyed careers as working actors on and off Broadway in shows such as *Miss Saigon, Cats*, and, more recently, the revival of *Grease*, to name only a few. They've appeared in major films and television shows too numerous to list.

The formal ARTS prospectus is distributed to every public and private high school and to various arts and education associations. All high school seniors or other youths aged seventeen to eighteen who are U.S. citizens or permanent residents are eligible.

Applications are evaluated by screening panels of experts. Portfolios are then reviewed by ARTS adjudicators who select a maximum of twenty applicants in each art form. During this final phase, applicants in dance, music and theater are brought to Miami, at NFAA expense, for live auditions and related activities. They may participate in observed master classes and exercises to assess their talents.

One hundred major universities and arts institutions subscribe to the NFAA Scholarship List Service. These subscribers receive the names of ARTS registrants and awardees. The Foundation supports young people in the arts in their formative years of growth by informing them about special scholarship opportunities that are available.

Registration for ARTS begins each spring. For information about specific eligibility requirement and registration materials, write: National Foundation for Advancement in the Arts, 800 Brickell Ave., Suite 500, Miami, Florida 33131.

THE WALDEN THEATRE

Another very special organization, in Louisville, Kentucky, is the Walden Theatre, founded in 1976 by its producing director Nancy Niles Sexton. This theatre trains young people from grades four through twelve in acting and writing. Its Theatre in the Making program, instituted as a showcase for young talent within the company, produces new works by young playwrights and classics adapted by the students. The Folk Heritage program produces dramatic plays based upon Kentucky's rich historical heritage. The professional theater training program offers afternoon, evening, and Saturday classes in movement, voice, improvisation, vocal music, playwriting, and auditioning. Graduating seniors of the Walden Theatre do well in the college selection process.

Performing is part of an actor's training. The Walden Theatre mounts four productions during the regular season; a summer academy performs in July. Advanced students get the chance to perform in the annual Humana Festival of New Plays at the prestigious Actors Theatre of Louisville. They also audition for roles in major motion pictures and television.

The Walden Theatre's Young Playwrights Program has been in existence since 1981. During that time the theatre has had six scripts published. According to founder Nancy Sexton:

> We began the program because our company was maturing and wanted
> to prepare for university auditions. Youthful material was in short supply
> for the necessary, contemporary monologues. The obvious answer was
> to write our own!

More than forty of the young playwrights have been receiving royalties. The theatre has been filmed by Public Broadcasting Service and won numerous awards. (Samples of original audition pieces written by the Walden Theatre's promising young playwrights appear in Chapter 19.)

Walden Theatre is supported in part by grants from the Kentucky Arts Council and the Community Arts Council of the Greater Louisville Fund for the Arts, as well as various other corporations and individuals. A caring unit designed to provide the opportunity for young people to gain a solid foundation in the performing arts, the Walden Theatre will, we hope, inspire similar programs in cities throughout the country.

RITA LITTON'S ACTEEN®

Acting academies across the country specialize in classes for children and teens. In New York, a marvelous curriculum of courses has been developed by Rita Litton, founder of ACTeen. Originally the "Acting for Teens" division of the renowned

Weist-Barron School of Television, which was established in 1956, ACTeen is now a separate and vital acting academy, offering five semesters through the year. Since 1976, ACTeen has been in the business of training young adults aged thirteen to twenty for careers in film, television, and theater.

Rita Litton, whose career began at UCLA and San Francisco's American Conservatory Theatre, has appeared in more than a hundred roles in theaters in New York and across the country. She has extensive television credits and has taught improvisation classes and advanced commercial workshops. She has staffed the school with other working actors and qualified teachers who understand the demands of The Business and who respect young actors. Classes are small, so that students can receive individual attention. Students' work is videotaped and reviewed in class. Courses include commercial audition technique, film/soap opera acting technique, speech, musical theater audition, and theater. Rita says:

> I feel responsible for giving my students a professional attitude about their work. . . . It should be fun, but there are requirements — homework, preparation, taking responsibility for the work.

Graduates of the ACTeen program have been seen in scores of commercials, on prime-time series, and in feature films.

SAFEGUARDS

If you are in doubt about a teacher's qualifications, if you find that certain schools are interested only in financial profits, or if they make false promises, report them to the local attorney general's office, department of consumer affairs, or local union office. There are a lot of get-rich-quick entrepreneurs who prey on naive parents. Some have been wanted in six states!

There are state laws to protect working children. The Children's Committee of Screen Actors Guild has assembled an information packet that states:

> The rules about obtaining work permits in the entertainment industry for children from birth to 18 years of age are quite explicit and in many cases difficult. The work permit application must be signed by a qualified employer before the Labor Board will accept it. The application must also have the signature of a doctor who has examined the child within the six weeks prior to applying for the permit. The application must also be signed by the principal or teacher at the school your child attends.

Many times, in addition to this, the labor board will require you to produce the child's latest report card or progress report. The first time a child applies for a permit, he or she must appear in person at the labor board office. There is no charge for this permit, but it must be kept up to date, because the child cannot work without it. Remember, if your child's grades slip below a C average, the work permit will not be renewed.

The SAG packet contains other rules about schooling, plus advice on getting homework from the child's school for the on-the-set teacher, and having three hours of homework for your child to do.

There are important safety rules concerning stunts or any potential health hazard. You are advised to have an authorized guardian if you cannot accompany your child. Dos and Don'ts for behavior on the set and rules about unemployment are also part of the packet. Additional sections thoroughly describe the industry — they make impressive reading, even for an adult.

While the basic rules will remain the same, laws keep changing. For the most recent information, write to Screen Actors Guild, 5757 Wilshire Boulevard, Los Angeles, CA 90036-3600.

A SENSE OF PURPOSE

Several years ago, a young man from a small town wrote a most passionate letter to a network casting director. His desire, humor, honesty, and fearlessness represent the kind of energy it takes to make it in The Business. Here is an excerpt:

> I know that I should wait to go to college before looking for work, but that seems so far away (1½ whole years!) I can't wait that long. Acting is in my blood, my veins, my arteries, my soul, my being. . . . If you could just tell me where an audition is, I'll walk on my hands to be there! (Although I may not look my best when I get there!) I'll sing, dance, trapeze, eat fire, whatever it takes to become a part of the acting family.

Those young actors and actresses who have become part of the acting family on soap operas have not always been prepared for the pressure that accompanies rigorous production schedules, long hours, sudden attention from hordes of fans, public scrutiny, and lack of job security. It is difficult not to let fame go to your head and believe your publicity. But a supportive family and discipline based upon the work ethic, can keep you firmly grounded.

Parents whose children have become successful in any or all phases of the entertainment industry know the hard road it took to get there: the hours spent driving the child to classes, the waits, the auditions that seemed interminable, babysitter fees, meals out, clothing expenses, class costs, photos and résumés, the personal sacrifices just so these efforts could be made. The rewards are obvious: a trust fund for college, working with celebrities from the stage and screen, first-class treatment, travel to a variety of locations, help with the family finances, and most gratifying, the pride in talent being recognized.

PART THREE

SCRIPT ANALYSIS

CHAPTER 19

THE THEATER AUDITION

Let anyone go upon the stage before an audience and say the same things and act the same deeds which occur in everyday life, and he will appear wholly stupid and uninteresting.

—*A dramatic coach on the art of acting, August, 1891*

In this and the next three chapters we offer you the chance to work on new material — the same kind of copy you will be called upon to read or perform at an audition for a play, a repertory company, a commercial, a soap opera, a prime-time series, or a film. These pieces of copy are, in a sense, waiting for you to bring them to life. They are not snippets from standard, classic plays or contemporary hit shows; no one's previous stellar performance has been stamped on any of these selections. They are all as new as your next thought.

You are free to make whatever choices you can think of, go wherever your imagination takes you, to illuminate the text.

GETTING READY

Before you audition for any kind of material, try to relax, so that you can prepare for the moment leading up to the scene. One suggestion is to play some very soothing, not distracting, music and focus on the character's experiences, behavior, choices, the relationship with the other character in the scene, and motivations for the decisions that lead to discovery. When you can go into the waiting room, sit if you can and avoid feeling "stressed out" by the competition. Then you will be more in control and have a better audition experience.

If you can, wear part of the wardrobe from the character's closet. It can be a ring, pendant, brooch, belt buckle, favorite shirt, tie, lucky charm — any object which helps to define the character or gives you an immediate key to a personal choice. Sometimes all it takes is one visual clue to create a whole life.

In Chapter 15, Linda Cook recalled that for her audition for *Loving* she decided not to wear a predictable black mini-skirt. She chose a turquoise tube as her skirt, a bright pink sweater, and a bandanna. She used what all actors should possess, like the essentials in their makeup kits: imagination. Unfortunately, that cannot be taught. But it can be developed.

THE SOLO PIECE

In her acclaimed book, *Respect for Acting*, the brilliant actress and teacher Uta Hagen defines the monologue as "an actor talking to himself out loud, or to absent characters, or to objects surrounding him at a given time in a given place for a specific reason at a moment of crisis." (Example: Macbeth's "Is this a dagger that I see before me?") Even though the words must be heard in the last row of the balcony, the monologue "will always be words that represent the character's thoughts or a part of his thoughts," when talking alone. In Shakespeare's day this was called a *soliloquy*.

When someone else is in the same setting and can respond with a look, a snort, a yawn, by turning away, by smiling, by giving you a rapt look of attention, that is actually a dialogue. For example, Strindberg's one-act play *The Stronger*, a dialogue, consists of one actress's long speech, punctuated by the reactions of the person she is talking to, who speaks no words. In a dialogue you are pouring your heart out to, sharing a personal experience with, confronting head-on with an ultimatum, or confessing a secret to another human being, and it demands a response.

According to Ms. Hagen's definitions, when the audience becomes your partner, you have delivered a duologue. There is no one specific person you wish to impress. You are taking on the whole assembly. Lynn Redgrave, in her brilliant duoloque about life with her celebrated actor–father (*Shakespeare for My Father*), embraced all of us with her spectrum of experiences.

Whoever the subject of your address happens to be, the quality that will impress the audience most is the *truth* you bring to the experience shared.

This chapter focuses on examples of the monologue, the dialogue, and the duologue. Several of the pieces we have chosen represent the artistic skills of teenagers who have been a part of the young Playwrights Program at the Walden Theatre in Louisville, Kentucky (mentioned in Chapter 18).

The three short pieces that follow are extracted from two full evenings of theater, *Glimpses* and *Rites*. The full texts can be obtained from the publisher and may be performed upon payment of a royalty. For texts and/or permission to use these works, write to: The Dramatic Publishing Company, P.O. Box 129, Woodstock, IL 60098.

"HUT, HUT," A MONOLOGUE BY CHARLES SEXTON

Charles Sexton was seventeen when he wrote "Hut, Hut" as part of the Young Playwrights Program. Since then he has received a degree in theater at SMU in Dallas. He is currently associate director of the Walden Theatre.

CHARLIE (RUNNING IN)

Hut, hut, hut .... (He takes a football stance.) Down, set, hut, hut, hut. (He mimes the action.) Charlie takes the ball from Center ... Drops ... He's going to pass, ladies and gentlemen! No, folks, he's going to run with it! (He mimes more action and moves to C on the sidewalk.) Oh, my gosh ... he plows over the whole defensive line for the T.D.! (He mimes "spiking" the ball.) Oh, yes! Thank you, thank you. They mob him and carry him on their shoulders.

(He mimes the action ... then slowly removes his football helmet and takes a solemn pose.) The mayor presents him with the key to the city. (He mimes receiving the key.) Oh, thank you, Mister Mayor ... and thank you, beautiful people ... but now ... (He dons the helmet again). He must play defense. The fans return to their seats. A hush falls over the stadium as we kick off. (He mimes the action.) Touchback! First play at scrimmage ... Charlie at linebacker ... every eye riveted on the "rumbling wrecking machine" ... the opposing quarterback calls the cadence. Down ... set ... Charlie is poised, ladies and gentlemen ... hut, hut. The play. A thirty-yard drive up the middle! Charlie plunges the hole and slams into the fullback, popping the ball loose like a kidney stone, picks it up and rumbles for the T.D.! Oh, ladies and gentlemen! The induction committee for the Pro Football Hall of Fame has just announced that the Louisville kid, Charlie, will be inducted today. What a day for Charlie! Thank you. Thank you.

ANALYSIS OF "HUT, HUT"

Character: male, teen.

Charlie's dream is to be inducted into the Pro Football Hall of Fame. He is not addressing the audience or another person. He is in his own world, a world he has created of football heroes, pivotal passes, crowd worship, keys to the city, the strategy that leads to the winning touchdown, and his acceptance speech. We watch all the moves; we hear his dream, but for Charlie, we don't exist. This is his secret world, like that of James Thurber's Walter Mitty.

The actor who uses this monologue should connect with the sport. Only if you fully understand the game will the language and the actions be believable. There is a specific rhythm and timing to the "Hut, hut, hut." The attack at the start is bursting with energy, and that must be present to carry you through to the final thirty-yard drive up the middle to the touchdown. There should be a breath following that line before the speech to the imaginary crowd. You could use your own name and town in this audition piece to make it your own. Use it as the humorous selection.

If you were to write your own monologue, this is a prototype for a range of sports events: a swimming competition, a tennis match, any athletic feat that you enjoy or do well.

"HAPPY BIRTHDAY," A DUOLOGUE BY CAROLINE WHITE

Caroline White was fifteen when she wrote "Happy Birthday." She is a graduate of Princeton University and is an editor for a magazine in New York City.

The curtain is up. The stage is dark. Light comes by way of a match lit in the darkness of a full-stage blackout.

We see the face of a young girl in the light. She lights birthday candles. As the area spot slowly rises, we hear:

                    GIRL (SINGING)
Happy Birthday to Claire ...
Happy Birthday to Claire ...
Happy Birthday to Claire ...
Happy Birthday to me ...
     (Lights up full in spot. The girl holds one
     birthday candle in her hand and she blows it out
     at the end of her song. Beside her are a litter
     of pictures, some birthday candles and a
     scrapbook. She sits on the floor.)
Sixteen ... sixteen candles ... I'm the only person my age
in the world who's never been out on a date.
     (She drops the candle and lights another and
     begins to sing again.)
Happy Birthday to me ... (spoken) well ... not on a real
date ...
     (She blows out second candle.)
I mean, like, I go to parties and movies with my friends,
but no guy has ever called me up and asked me out ....
     (She shuffles through her pictures. She finds a
     newspaper clipping of a high school athlete from the
     Sports page. She practically faints at the sight of
     the picture as she begins gushing about him.)
Oh, God, he's so gorgeous ....
     (She shows the picture to the audience.)
His name's Ben, and he's got blond hair and bright blue
eyes that make me melt every time I see him ...
     (She gazes at the picture.)
And one time I was standing in back of him in the lunch
line ...
     (She raises the picture slowly to her nose and
     inhales deeply)
and I could smell his after-shave, even above the lasagna
... It smelled ... just like he should smell.
     (She places the clipping in her scrapbook.)
Anyway, Ben called me one Thursday night a few months
ago. I was so excited! My stomach ... my stomach did four
flips. He asked me for the math homework ... 'cause he had
slept through class ... and ... I knew it was just a way of
starting the conversation. Well ... it wasn't. He just
said, "Thanks a lot. 'Bye."
     (She embraces a Pizza Hut menu from her scrapbook.)

Well ... I have gone on a sort of a date. It was set up ...
by my friend ... My friend Jan. She got this boy she knows
to come pick me up and take me to a movie and then to
Pizza Hut. He was okay-looking ... medium-tall ... brown
hair ... brown eyes ... Nothing special, but okay-looking.
We didn't talk on the way to the movie or all through it.
What can you say to someone you don't know? He didn't
smell of anything, like ... well ... after-shave ... No ... a
... bright blue eyes ... When we got to Pizza Hut we had a
deep dish pizza with pepperoni and mushrooms and sausage
... and even anchovies ... disgusting ... But he wanted them
... so we had them. And onions ... on the first date ...
onions ... God! We ordered, or rather he ordered ... and
then ... well, silence. God! What to say! Well, something
had to be said ... so I asked him what classes he was
taking, and he said ...
     (She takes a piece of paper from her collection
     and reads from it.)
English, French, pre-calculus, physics ...
     (She flings the paper aside.)
Or something incredible like that. And I said, "Oh." He
didn't ask me anything. He just answered my questions ...
like he didn't even care about me. What a DUD! I was bored
to death! Why? Tell me why Jan would set me up with that
STUD! er, I mean dud, dud ... She must think I'm really
desperate or something! I don't want her feeling sorry for
me! It's not like I'm a social outcast or anything!
     (She hums a few bars of "Happy Birthday" while
     rummaging through her scrap book.)
I go out with my friends, for God's sake ... (She stops
short.) But not with guys. I mean on dates ... I ... guess
... well, maybe ... maybe they just don't like me ... I'm
not ... desirable ... I guess I'll just go through high
school ... without a ... date.
     (She lights another birthday candle.)
Maybe college, too ... I just wait every day for THAT
phone call ... Everyone else gets them.
     (The lights go down slowly.)
Why not me?
     (She blows out the candle as we BLACKOUT.)

ANALYSIS OF "HAPPY BIRTHDAY"
Character: female, sixteen.
The problem Claire experiences in this piece is universal. What "sweet sixteen"
doesn't think about dates, popularity, the blond, blue-eyed jock who smells of sexy

after-shave? At this age, the greatest fear is the thought of sitting home waiting for the phone to ring. Claire is obsessed with Ben. Anyone else, like her blind date, is just "okay-looking." She realizes Ben has used her crush on him to get her math homework. That leaves her vulnerable to her friend Jan's matchmaking. She describes the date in great detail: the pizza with the anchovies ("disgusting") and onions ("on the first date . . . God!"); the horrible silence. She was forced to keep the conversation going when it was apparent that he had no interest in her. The result was boredom, and her questioning why her friend would set her up with such a dud. She doesn't want pity, but she feels undesirable and unliked and considers her situation to be hopeless.

This is an excellent example of character revelation. You can substitute your own name and experience and your scrapbook memorabilia . . . to remind you of dates and dinners or Pizza Huts, blind dates, phone calls, the first kiss, junior prom, and so forth. Create a real mood, place, situation.

This duologue has several major transitions in thought and feeling. The first one occurs after she says "but no guy has ever called me up and asked me out." Ben's picture causes a change. She shares her feelings with the audience. Use sense memory for the smells of after-shave and lasagna. Picture the cafeteria lunch line. The mood change is caused by placing the clipping in the scrapbook. "Anyway, Ben called me one Thursday." Another change on "Well . . . it wasn't." Then there is the change cued by the Pizza Hut menu. "Well . . . I have gone on a sort of date." This detailed description of the date should be animated and believable. You are sharing the moments with us. Next change: "Why? Tell me why Jan would set me up with that STUD! er, I mean dud, dud." Here she shows her sense of humor. Humor is the element that will keep Claire from complete despair. If she can get through high school, she'll probably blossom in college. She is bright and witty. Someone will connect with her personality down the road.

Try not to give in to self-pity in this role. There is a drop in energy in the last section. The character goes from "I go out with my friends for God's sake . . . But not with guys." to "Why not me?" There is a sense of low-key frustration. Rehearse this part in the mirror. Believe it!

"ANGIE'S SONG," A DUOLOGUE BY RUTH JACOBSON

Ruth Jacobson was fifteen when she wrote "Angie's Song." She has since graduated from Southern Methodist University, Dallas, with a theater degree and is living and writing in Chicago.

GIRL

I guess I've always been of "dubious reputation," as my minister puts it. I never thought much about the rights or wrongs of it all when I was panting in the back seat of someone's car. It wasn't that I especially enjoyed it. If you want to know the truth, it was more like mild distaste. I never heard any bells. I don't know why I did it. I just didn't mind it. I got lots of friends that way, I guess.

I always was really careful — I was on the "pill" since
eighth grade. I never missed it. But then — I don't know
what happened. My dad started giving me a bunch of
garbage about my life. He always does that, but it was
really starting to bother me. It wasn't much — he'd slap
me around a little and then tell me to go away ... and I
would. I'd go right to Steve's or Phil's or Mike's and
just go to it.

Well, around that time I kind of stopped taking the
"pill." I kept forgetting, and finally I ran out and
didn't refill my prescription. I thought I could last a
little while without it. Well, I sure didn't. When I
found out I was pregnant I didn't cry. I don't know how I
felt — kind of relieved. I didn't feel any of that
"miracle of life" bull that you're supposed to. I just
felt kind of relieved, like I'd finally done something
right. I don't know. That's kinda dumb, I guess.

Well, my dad wanted me to get an abortion. I couldn't.
I said I wouldn't and he got mad again. I racked him, and
I mean HARD, and I ran out of the house blubbering like a
jerk. Later that night I called from a pay phone and Mom
kept askin' me to come home. I had to. I didn't have a
job or anything.

Everything went fine. Then I was getting really big,
about six months along. My dad got mad. The toothpaste
was missing. He got so mad he pushed me down the stairs
— by accident. I screamed. It hurt so much — like
someone taking a knife and scraping out your insides. I
just kept screaming and screaming. I think I was
bleeding. My mom called an ambulance, and I think I kept
screaming until they clapped that mask over my face and
whisked me away ....

I had a fracture in my elbow. Angie wasn't so lucky.
She was so far along, they could see her face and
everything. I didn't see it but I know she was very
pretty. I know she was smart, too. When we were alone I
would talk with her. She would bump around and I would
talk to her and everything ... she was a good kid, I know
....

Now, I just kinda walk around. Above it all. Nobody
bothers me. Nobody touches me. I still talk with my
Angie. I don't know what I'll do. I don't know if I care.
I don't know.

    (Lights slowly out ....)

ANALYSIS OF "ANGIE'S SONG."

Character: female, fifteen to seventeen.

This confession could be shared with an audience or with one person. The girl could be talking to an old friend. It is important not to play it to elicit sympathy. She has accepted what has happened to her until that final acknowledgment when she says, "Now I just kinda walk around." We realize she hasn't let the baby die. It is here we realize how alone she is.

She is very direct about her promiscuity. The pill started in eighth grade. Her dad has been berating her, and his abuse would send her to the "back seats." Her ignorance about the pill helped get her into trouble. We must understand her when she says, "I'd finally done something right." She stood up to her father on the abortion issue. She ran away, but she had to return because she had no place to go. There is a great deal of pain, emotional as well as physical in her life. Yet when she describes her father's violence and beating, she is not judgmental. This was the way it happened. Her suffering was intense; the screams were real. Yet it was her mother who called the ambulance. Where was her father?

She will never be the same after the death of Angie. The poignancy of her story and the depth of her feelings are truly realized if the actress chooses not to bring attention to it by commenting on emotional choices or becoming too self-indulgent. Let it happen. Let it unfold. Don't play results.

Imagine what it would be like to live in a loveless home. Imagine not having a childhood. Do you have a close friend or relative who has had a similar experience? As a sense-memory exercise, put a cushion under your dress. Observe in the mirror how pregnancy would alter your shape; practice sitting, rising, lying down. Take the cushion away abruptly. Project the loneliness by simply being quiet and reflective. Think about an ambulance, an emergency room, anesthesia, bright lights, strangers in white, the cold of an operating room. Visit a hospital; sit in a waiting room. Get a sense of place.

Write a duologue describing in detail an accident you witnessed, a fight you observed in your neighborhood, a schoolroom brawl, a verbal tirade you overheard, a scolding you received from your parents — any conflict you can relate to. Make us see it and hear it with you. You will increase your understanding of how to give truth and meaning to "Angie's Song."

"HE TOLD ME . . . #1," A DUOLOGUE OR DIALOGUE BY JESSICA JORY

Jessica Jory is a theater major at the University of Colorado, Boulder. She has been a member of the Walden Theatre's acting and playwriting program for many years.

                                    GIRL

He told me once that he thought it was sexy when I put on my lipstick. He liked the little sound that I made when I, ever so delicately, smoothed my lips together to blend in the color.

Well, needless to say, I went through at least three tubes of lipstick that week.

Usually I wouldn't try that hard to please him. It's just that he so rarely tells me that he thinks I'm sexy or pretty or even remotely good-looking. In fact, I think one of the only compliments he ever gave me was a remark about how much I reminded him of his Aunt Eunice.

Now don't get me wrong. He loved his Aunt Eunice, but I was hoping for more of a "You really remind me of the teacher I was totally infatuated with in middle school."

Or maybe, "You remind me of my best friend's older sister that we used to spy on getting dressed." Or how about, "You remind me of Cindy Crawford."

I just think that guys don't understand how important it is to us to feel like we are attractive. My God, we spend a lot of our lives and most of our money trying to make ourselves look good. It seems like it would be a hint.

But, I know my little honey really does think I'm attractive, at least I have to keep telling myself that, because if I don't I'll find myself getting really mad at him and he won't understand why, and I'll be too embarrassed to tell him, and it will be just this huge mess that I could have prevented in the first place.

So, I just need to tell myself, would he really be dating me if he thought I looked like some kind of mutant aardvark?

Well, what I'm trying to say is that I need to think that I'm beautiful regardless of what he thinks, right? Right.

ANALYSIS OF "HE TOLD ME . . . #1"

Character: female, seventeen to nineteen.

A pivotal line in the character's lament about her boyfriend is: "I just think that guys don't understand how important it is to us to feel like we are attractive." Obviously, there are all sorts of hormones raging and self-discoveries and insecurity in her. This accounting of the need to be complimented is a rather universal problem, not confined to the teen years. All of us experience the desire to feel beautiful and special. She approaches the subject, however, from a rather lighthearted, insightful, open point of view. Comparisons are evocative — Aunt Eunice (imagine a rather pleasant and unexciting, plump, sweet-voiced character), the teacher image, the fantasy of the best friend's older sister, and finally the ultimate coup — model Cindy Crawford. Ultimately she rationalizes the whole inner dialogue with the conclusion that he wouldn't still be with her if she looked like a "mutant aardvark."

If you put "Sis:" in front of the speech, it takes on the aspect of a dialogue to one special person whom you want to include in the conversation. If you put "Dear Diary:" before you begin, then it becomes just you, in the room alone with your thoughts, placing them on paper.

Or maybe you are discussing the beau with a group of girlfriends at a slumber party. You can put this speech into a variety of places or situations. In the opening you might want to be putting on lipstick, and that motivates the memory of how he reacted to your application — "He liked the little sound that I made. . . ."

Color the phrase "mutant aardvark." If you are not sure what that is, look it up.

"HE TOLD ME . . . #2," A DUOLOGUE OR DIALOGUE BY MEGHAN LOVE

Meghan Love, a member of the Walden Theatre Young Playwrights Program, is a theater major at Florida State University, Tallahassee.

> GIRL

He told me that his top priorities were his skateboard and his Bruce Lee video collection. I'm still wondering which of those categories I fit into.

I mean, I would love to think that I was a priority of his. And, the fact that I fall behind a piece of wood with four wheels and a man whose only talent, as far as I'm concerned, is mouthing the wrong words and breaking wood with his foot really disturbs me.

Basically, it looks as if my main man is into wood. Maybe if I disguised myself as a big 4 by 4 he'd come running.

I understand that he needs time for his "guy" things. What female does not have to live with that? Is it too much to ask to see him, oh, I don't know, twice a week? For a while I considered taking up skating. I know. I'm insane. The fact that I almost took up a sport that would probably endanger my physical health greatly, and also make me look like a total fool, just to spend time with a guy that is probably too skinny for me anyway, scares the shit out of me.

Maybe I should just give him a call, let him know how I feel. Don't you think? (doesn't wait for a response).

Of course I probably wouldn't be able to get a hold of him until Tuesday, since today and tomorrow are his days to skate. And then when I call him on Tuesday, he'll have to call back on Thursday because he has his Bruce Lee Fan Club. And then I'm not home on Thursdays, so I guess next Friday I'll be able to tell him exactly how I feel.

Analysis of "He Told Me . . . #2"

Character: female, fifteen.

As an interpreter of life's difficulty, again centering on a high school girl's choice of boyfriend, this young writer talks with such affection and humor that you almost want to see her on the phone chatting away a mile a minute to her best friend (whom she talks to in the downstairs closet every night — their teen ritual). What would life be without complaining? It can't be perfect. She wants her boyfriend around, not at the Bruce Lee Club, not skateboarding, but where he should be — on her agenda — holding hands, watching a video of her choosing, and snuggling every now and then. And, of course, the rationalization again — I can't call him on this day because of this reason, I can't call him then because of that reason, and before you know it that imagined confrontation never happens. The phone call with the best friend will continue as long as it is necessary to get through the daily events in that relationship. There is that delicious and very telling instruction, "doesn't wait for a response." Of course she doesn't, for she could be talking to herself or to the wall. But without the idea of the other person, there'd be no heightening to the moment.

Both these young writers capture the wit and humor that all of us need to overcome small crises in life, the ones we master to be prepared for the bigger ones down the road.

These selections depict the genuine feelings that define life's experience either through humor or sadness. You, the actor, are encouraged to create a piece using your distinctive inner voice. Observe the situations around you, those mentors, parents, friends, camp counselors, celebrities who inspire you, or recall encounters with family members during the holidays — any event in your first sixteen or so years which changed your life forever. Write poetry, short stories, essays, one-act plays. Share your insights. They are valuable.

"EMOTIONAL RECALL," A DUOLOGUE BY JOHN PIELMEIER

The gifted playwright John Pielmeier is best known for *Agnes of God*, the Broadway hit play which was later made into a film. A prolific writer of solo plays, like *Willi* (about Unsoeld, who climbed Mt. Everest) and *Courage* (about playwright J.M. Barrie), over the years he has conducted workshops for the Young Playwrights Program at the Walden Theatre.

ACTRESS
Let me tell you about my father's death.
  I was only five.
  It was in a field, on our farm, and I'd been playing in
a tree when it started to rain. My father came to bring
me home, first calling me from across the field, and I
didn't come, and the rain fell heavier and harder, and he
walked to the middle of the field, calling, and I didn't
come, even though I heard him I didn't come, and he came
closer, three-quarters of the way through the wheat,
calling me, "Please, (actress' name), come home," and I
didn't come, and I didn't come, and then
    there was brightness
    incredible light
    and my father was a torch
    screaming

and I called to him
"Daddy! Daddy!"
and he didn't come
and he didn't come.
    (She is crying. She stops, recovers.)
Let me tell you about my father's death.
I was three-and-a-half.
It was in a field, on our farm, and I'd been playing in
a tree when it started to snow. My father came to bring
me home, and I didn't come, and the snow fell, and he
walked to the middle of the field, and I didn't come, and
he walked slower and slower, and I wouldn't come, and he
froze, all blue, solid ice, and ....
    (She is crying. She stops, recovers.)
Let me tell you about my father's death.
My mother was eight months pregnant, and they were in a
field, a big, wide field, and it was night, and suddenly
there was this huge light, falling from the heavens, it
was a space ship, and it fell on my father, and it
squashed him ... flat ... like a pancake ... and my mother ...
who always liked pancakes ....
    (She can't go on. She is crying. She stops.)
A wild elephant came racing across the ice. My father,
fishing, didn't see him, and ....
    (She is crying.)
An invisible force drew him to the house, where the
ghost of his fiancée, hungry for blood, was ....
    (She is sobbing.)
A wild Chinaman, an escapee from Devil's Island ....
    (She has lost control.)
I'm sorry. I'm sorry.
    (She regains control, composes herself.)
Let me tell you about my father's death.
He was an acting teacher. Mad for emotional honesty.
He drove his students to the edge.
Over, if necessary.
They loved him for that.
It has to be real, he said. Even the silliest, most
impossible situation, you have to believe it. Dig into your
heart. If you don't have a dead parent, use a dead pet.
He was a pusher for honesty. Honesty was his drug.
I suppose he pushed Ellen too far.
Tell us about your father's death, he said one day in
class.
No, she said.

Do you remember?
No.
Were you there?
No.
You're lying. Tell us, Ellen! You wanted him dead, didn't you?! You wished him dead, didn't you?!
I don't know what you're talking about, she said.
New day, he took a new approach.
Did he do something bad to you?
No, she said.
Don't be ashamed, Ellen. Don't be afraid.
I'm not.
You are! Face the facts about him! Face the ugly, dirty, smelly, disgusting truth! You'll never be an actress if you can't face the truth! Did he hate you?! Hit you?! Worse?!!!
I don't know what you're talking about, she said. I wish you'd leave me alone.
Next day he took a new approach.
So did she.
I'm your father, he said. Did you love me?
No answer.
Did you hate me?
No answer.
Did you feel anything?! Only dead things don't feel. Are you dead, Ellen?! ARE YOU DEAD?!!!
No, you are, she said, and shot him.
Turns out she never even knew her father. She just didn't like people shouting.
And the amazing thing is that I saw it all.
The gun, the pop, the blood.
Dad screaming.
It was pretty awful.
I don't like to think about it.
Let me tell you about my puppy's death.
He was just this little thing, and this ... this witch, from the gingerbread cottage down the road ....
    (She is sobbing. She stops, recovers.)
Let me try that again.
    (Blackout)

ANALYSIS OF "EMOTIONAL RECALL"
This is not an easy selection to use for audition purposes. It needs to be part of an actual production. However, as a practice piece for sense memory and sharpening transitions and emotional facility, it is excellent.

The actress is allowed to use her own name, which makes it more deeply personal. She is trying to project the reality of losing a parent and the resultant sorrow, making the recall more powerful. Every story she recreates is about her father's death. And the memory of images is helpful in telling the story. So, in the first instance, there is a field, hard rain, lightning, and her father becoming a torch. There was nothing she could do, because she was five and in a tree watching it. Then she becomes younger in the second example. There is still the field, but now there is snow and the father freezes. Your dissolve into tears would not build as much as in the instance, when she was five. In the third instance, she is in her mother's womb, again in the field. With the arrival of the space ship, that squashes the father "like a pancake," and in the fourth and fifth instances, her imagination has taken over and she has lost control.

The previous instances must build to her frenzy. The author gives her a chance to regain control and compose herself.

Now it begins to feel like what really happened: recalling the acting teacher–father who was "mad for emotional honesty." He pushed a student over the edge trying to dredge up the past childhood memories about her own father so that she could realize sensory truth in recounting his death. Now the whole direction of this piece shifts to what can happen in the acting class when method can become madness. The constant drilling, obsessive questioning, harassing tone he takes with her motivates the final instant: student shoots teacher.

With dark humor, the storyteller rationalizes that it turned out she never even knew her father, "She just didn't like people shouting." But this instance doesn't lead to the uncontrollable sobbing the actress has shown before. There is something rather antiseptic and distancing about the narrative. However, when the next instance concerns her puppy's death, she stops, recovers, and opts for a second take on it.

Any of us who have taken an acting class with a teacher like the one in this duologue can recognize the pseudo-Freudian *schtick* and empathize with the students. So, with a wicked wink and an attempt to avenge us all against the mind-game gurus, we can claim justifiable homicide for Ellen. Again we see a similarity to "The Secret Life of Walter Mitty," when Thurber's hero fantasizes about acts of derring-do which he cannot perform in real life.

The playwright's interesting take on the episode is that when the actress refers to the puppy's death, she is truly moved; the connection becomes more immediate. Maybe because at last the life-experience behind it is real, as opposed to forced.

TWO DIALOGUES

Each of the following selections is excerpted from a complete play. Each character is talking to someone who might yawn, smile, cry, turn away, giggle, start to interrupt, or even leave the room.

In this audition you have to focus on an object or an empty chair for an imagined physical presence. Don't, as a rule, look at the people you are auditioning for. You must concentrate on whom you are trying to reach.

Alice Spivak, one of New York's finest acting coaches, suggests three ways to achieve this concentration:

1. Pretend you are rehearsing the speech to tell the person on your next encounter.

2. Imagine that the person you are talking to is in an adjoining room or behind a screen.

3. Put yourself at a mirror where the person you are addressing is behind you and you are talking to the mirror image.

In your mind the person must be fully pictured and specific.

William Hathaway, the author of the dialogues in this section, received an M.F.A. from the Catholic University of America in Washington, D.C., in 1981. He has won the Joseph Kesselring Playwriting Award twice, for his plays *Bless Me, Father* and *That One Talent*. This dialogue is a good exercise for storytelling, sense memory, and variety:

BLESS ME, FATHER BY WILLIAM HATHAWAY

FATHER O'BRIEN

If you haven't been around the stockyards, you haven't been to Chicago. Meat stinks, Father. Worse than any of your automobile factories. Of course, growing up next door to the meat plants, you don't really think about it. It's a smell and that's it. Besides, those yards gave my brother and me something to do. Every Saturday morning we'd walk over to where they unloaded the cows. And we'd do what kids do when they see cows.

(O'Brien lows.)

Moooooooo. Moooooooo. But this one Saturday on our way to greet the cattle, I said something that my brother didn't like and he squared off and punched me in the mouth. Son of a bitch. Of course, Thomas being older and bigger, I wisely turned around and roared home — bleeding, crying, and accusing. Mother immediately took charge. She slapped me a good one to stop my crying and then she ordered Thomas inside and gave him a good whack. Then she got a cold, clean, wet cloth and stood directly over him while he cleaned my lip. And she made him apologize. Which he did. And she made me forgive him. Which I did. Then she sent us into her room. That usually meant the brush, followed by two rosaries, on our knees and out loud. But not that day. She sat on the edge of her bed and pulled me up and to her left and put Thomas on her right. Well, my mother wasn't much for words. Dad influenced that. God love him. She simply said, "Thomas do you want to be the doctor or the priest?" He didn't even blink. "Doctor," he said. Son of a bitch. Then she turned to me and said, "James, you'll be the priest. Now go on, both of you, get out."

(O'Brien pours himself another drink.)
And no, I'm not saying it's in the stars. When I took my
vows, it was my decision. But I am saying, Father Mosley,
that he called on me and you, long before we made any
decision to call on him. So believe me, man, you're
already spoken for. If you really love this girl, you
tell her to go away.

ANALYSIS OF FATHER O'BRIEN

Character: male (character actor), fifty to sixty.
The play deals with a young, rebellious priest, Father Mosley, who has fallen in love
with a young woman. He is struggling with the decision whether or not to remain a
priest. Father O'Brien, his pastor, has just found out about the affair. In this speech,
O'Brien confronts Mosley. The pastor is an alcoholic. Although he is drunk during
this dialogue, he is still coherent.

It is important that the actor practice degrees of inebriation. Start with extreme
lack of control and work backward, slowly, to trying not to let anyone know you are
out of control. Work on this exercise, physically and vocally.

An alcoholic will never admit that he has a problem; he is a "moderate drinker,"
not a lush.

Father O'Brien is frustrated, bitter, and self-pitying. Although he loved his family, his childhood was difficult because of a domineering father, a strong mother, and
an older brother with a temper. He tells the story of his brother's attack and his
mother's decision to give him the vocation in order to make a point with the
lovestruck priest. He implores him to put his personal feelings aside, to remember
that he was called by God to serve, and to give up the young woman.

O'Brien is a human being underneath the priestly robes. He is from a poor neighborhood of Chicago. He would say "son of a bitch," and when under the influence,
say it more than once. We have here a flesh-and-blood, imperfect man — and he is
colorful.

A CROOKED FLOWER BY WILLIAM HATHAWAY

MO

Mom, after I told you and Daddy what you could do with
your expectations of me, I came down here and I thought I
had it made. I was where it was at, right at the bottom.
This is where I'd make the difference. I got a job tending
bar, and for a while I'd paint furiously during the day
and work and play just as furiously at night. But it seems
I forgot about sleep and pretty soon it caught up with me.
I stopped painting. Just sleep, work, party and sleep ...
then I met Scott. Talk about a rush. Can't be anything
better than the first few weeks of being in love. Can't be.
He was beautiful. Brown eyes to hypnotize and the

smoothest skin, so black it was blue. But, color aside, he
was my spittin' image. From money, best schools, sky's the
limit potential, all that crap. Princeton, 1963. And three
years later he had a room above a liquor store and was
writing poetry about junkies and whores and magazines like
The New Yorker were lapping it up. He was perfect. A match
made in heaven, as you'd say, Mom. He got me to cool out
my night life and got so damn excited about my art, it
scared me. I'd anguish over every painting wondering
whether or not he'd give it his seal of approval. He was
the one who put me in touch with the gallery in New York
that still gurgles over anything I churn out. Mom, what he
was doing with his poetry I want to do with my art. Reach
out and shake up all of you that we'd left behind. "Hey,
we're down here and we're making it!" I saw the future
perfectly. My painting and his poetry and from out of the
ashes of Detroit, beauty and truth.

    (Mo laughs softly.)

It was September. Almost two years? Hot and humid and I
couldn't work. So I walked over to Scott's. Up the stairs
that had more steps missing than steps. I had to kick
open the door. He never locked it. Just the heat made it
stick. He was there. Sitting on the floor. He never sat on
the furniture. I don't knosw if he heard me come in or
not, it didn't seem to matter. He was only interested in
finding a vein. I watched. He'd put the needle in, pull it
out, put it in, pull it out. When he finally hit one, he
let out a sigh of relief and looked up at me and
shrugged. I turned around and closed the door, jumped
over the missing steps and walked fast through the
streets. And back here, I threw up. Just threw up. It
turns out everybody on the street knew, except me. Talk
about your little girl in pigtails. Mom, I thought he had
a handle on this place, but all the time it had him. and
if it could get him, it could certainly get me.

ANALYSIS OF MO

Character: female, twenty to twenty-five.

Mo resides in a crime and drug-infested area of Detroit. The year is 1969, and she's
been living there for three years. Coming from a well-protected environment, her
ignorance about certain people and situations comes slowly to light. Her first affair
was one of her first lessons. In this dialogue she tells her mother about it.

    This young woman has had an awakening. Her idealism has been shattered by a
lover's use of narcotics. Yet she has learned from it and related the joy and the pain
in vivid detail. Imagine talking to your own mother about an affair that turned sour.

Scott must be as clear in your mind as the photograph he may have given you. Perhaps as an artist you painted him. This is a woman who paints pictures with words.

Paint the building where you lived, the room, the liquor store, hear the street sounds, imagine the smells, the horror at finding your lover "shooting up," see the "sky's the limit" potential burned out.

Think about the nausea and the gradual realization, the moment of truth, and the sense of triumph that you were strong enough to "close the door."

This is not a character plagued by remorse or full of despair. She is strong, rebellious, crusading, vulnerable, and filled with pride. Find her humor.

CHAPTER 20

THE SOAP OPERA AUDITION

I walked in and I was confident. I was in control of the material and it gave me room to play.
—LAURA BONARRIGO, *Cassie,* One Life to Live

In this chapter we are fortunate to have three examples of authentic audition material.

If you have watched *General Hospital* and *All My Children*, you will have seen the actors who won the auditions — performers who studied these pages just as you are doing and connected so forcefully with the material that the producers, directors, writers, and network executives agreed that they were the ones who must be chosen for the roles.

SCENE ANALYSIS

Here we list some general directions for you to follow in exploring the audition scene. Each guideline will help you to see the action or your character from a different angle.

- Read the scene over at least five times. Find the rhythm, structure, character relationships, and mood changes.

- Read both parts. Understand where the other character in the scene is coming from. Not only is this awareness essential to the give-and-take nature of acting, but you may be asked to switch roles at the audition, and you want to be prepared.

- Decide where the character has been the moment before the scene starts and where the character is going the moment after the scene is ended.

- In most scenes, there is a central conflict which creates the tension that is essential to the situation, whether it is dramatic or comic. Discover the cause: sexual frustration; opposing value systems; mixed signals; greed; a double standard; mistaken identity; role-reversal; cowardice, and so on.

- Look for emotional "buttons" or beats in the scene. Mark each of these, breaking it down into moments. Clues exist in stage directions, pauses, and interrupted lines. Find the attack, the build, and the resolution. Your understanding of the structure of the scene will tell you how to play it with truthfulness and integrity. In the excitement of the audition, these moments can be rushed, or forgotten. Forced emotion is shallow and jeopardizes the truth of the situation.

- Who is the "third person"? The third person is a presence, not physically in the scene. Someone who is talked about, or who has influenced the character's behavior and philosophy, such as a parent, teacher, spouse, or mentor. This third person can be living or dead, historical or fictional.

- What is the secret each character is keeping from the other?

- Always find the "child" within the character.

- Always find the sense of humor, even if it isn't obvious.

- Whether you'll be performing in an office or on a bare stage, gain a sense of place by sketching a simple set design. For example, if your scene takes place in a living room, choose the furniture, the wall colors, carpets, floral arrangements, and so forth. By putting the design on paper, it will then be etched in your mind.

THE CHARACTER'S BACKGROUND
Write a mini-biography to flesh out the character. So often, you will be provided with only a limited description and "back story." Focus on the following:

- Roots: ancestry, ethnicity, family tree. For example, if there is aristocracy in the character's background, he or she may be influenced by this knowledge.

- Parents: who raised the character is key to that person's development, behavior, and physicality.

- Childhood memories: happy and sad events in the early years through grade school may impact on decisions made in later life.

- Environment: where the character was raised will affect the way he or she fits in socially, intellectually, and emotionally, and influence goals and the ability to succeed.

- Education: analyzing the language of the scene will tell you about the character's schooling and how the character communicates and articulates thoughts and feelings. Notice grammar, use of metaphor, imagery, slang, idioms, puns, and regional expressions.

- Religion: what is the character's spiritual connection? An organized religion or Eastern religion? Scientology? The information comes from examining heritage, parental beliefs, and occupation.

- Health: what's your character's medical history? Childhood diseases, accidents, addictions, disabilities, skin disorders, inherited conditions?

- Goals: depend upon your knowledge of education, parents, and environment.

- Love story: an active romantic agenda will determine if the character is interested in long-term commitment, and how active she or he is sexually.

- Marital status: number of marriages, divorces, determination not to marry. Belief in the institution of marriage can be found in your analysis of the relationship.

- Spouse: if not married in the scene, focus on the ideal spouse. Define the match made in heaven.

- Children: some characters will have at least one, some won't. Some may be unable to have any. Either way, children can be a source of great tension in the relationship.

- Work history: what is the character's occupation? Prepare a resumé the character might give to a personnel director.

- Fame: celebrity, notoriety, and how the character feels about power.

- Fortune: character's finances will depend upon ancestry, parents, present occupation, education, marital partner, and career goals.

- Favorite actors: who the character connects with indicates cultural background and role-model selection. A young man who idolizes James Dean might copy the way he dresses, talks, and moves. Some characters may only come alive when they are at the movies or seeing a play. For Bella, in *Lost in Yonkers*, a love relationship at the movies makes her real life with a tyrannical mother bearable.

- Fantasies: investigate the character's fantasy life. Who would he or she wish to be stranded on a desert island with? Everyone daydreams about a better place, job, social position, life on the big screen.

- Favorite books: your choices will affect the character's imagination, thoughts, feelings. What's in the character's library? Bill Moyers or D.H. Lawrence? Edith Wharton or Danielle Steel? Comic books? Biographies, how-to, self-help, cookbooks, and so on?

- Favorite foods: spaghetti, pheasant under glass, or hamburger and fries? Rich pastries, low-fat yogurt?

- Restaurants: Where would the character choose to eat, and is this the same as where the character *does* eat?

- Sounds: find the character's favorite music. You might bring it to the audition in a Walkman and use it to put yourself in the character's place and present.

- Colors: choose the character's favorite color by analyzing personality, emotional state, temperament, and humor.

- Wardrobe: depends on background, social status, occupation, and financial means—even rural or urban location. A sense of style will help in selecting what to wear for the part. The right colors will make the choice memorable.

- Favorite games: does the character play chess, checkers, Monopoly, charades, billiards, backgammon, poker, gin rummy, Trivial Pursuit?

• Sports: is the character athletic? At outdoor or indoor sports? In water, with a racket, on horseback, on ice, on roller blades?

• Hobbies: Stamp collecting, saxophone playing, wine tasting . . . or?

Furnishing the character's closet is another good background exercise, for the closet is a metaphor for the mind—there are myriad possibilities within that boundless space. The closet needn't contain just clothing. It may be filled with sporting gear, safe deposit boxes, old chests, cars, foreign countries, animals, love letters, collectibles—everything that can make up the life of the individual and give that life its shape and uniqueness. List ten items in the closet.

In the closet, discover one prop: something personal, such as a clothing accessory, or something practical, such as a clipboard, a book, or a letter — whatever you think is appropriate for the character in the scene. Do not choose a cigarette, cigar, or pipe, and avoid chewing on a toothpick, match stick, or gum.

Transport yourself into the rhythm of the character. Realize that the character's vocal quality, physical gestures, and habits should not be identical to yours. From your analysis of the scene, find an activity that is appropriate to the character, which helps you with the character's physical behavior, such as combing hair, applying makeup, examining self in the mirror, dressing, exercising, walking, running, sitting, and so on. Experiment with the sound of the character by changing your rhythm, accent, tone, pitch, and projection.

Enjoy the process of creation and discovery!

AUDITION SCENE 1

Mary Mae and Laura, *General Hospital*

MARY MAE

So you like my house? I say "my house." It's yours, of course. But it was part of me, and me of it, for a long, long time. My children grew there, and my husband died, and those things tie you to a place.

LAURA

(A smile:) We can share.

MARY MAE

You're a nice young woman.

LAURA

You're still part of it. I felt it when we walked through the door ... that people in that house had loved one another.

MARY MAE

It was a home. We had porch geraniums, and supper every night at six.

LAURA

We're rebuilding the porch.

MARY MAE

Well, that's good news.

LAURA

And there was sadness, too.

MARY MAE

No life was ever lived without it. No life worth living.

LAURA

May I ask how your husband died, Mrs. Ward?

MARY MAE

First of all, my name is Mary Mae. My friends call me
MaeMae. 'Course, most of my friends nowadays average
about two and a half years in age, y'know what I'm
saying?

LAURA

I like MaeMae.

MARY MAE

I like it, too. And yes, you can surely ask me anything.
Almost anything. My husband? I had two husbands. The first
one drowned in the guts of a destroyer on the floor of the
Pacific Ocean in nineteen hundred and forty two. In that
war, the Navy didn't officially segregate black men; they
just put them to work in the engine rooms. Understand me,
I didn't begrudge life or the lifeboats to the white boys
who made it to the rail and over the side. God knows,
they had wives and mothers, too. But I was mad. And I
took it out on myself....

LAURA

How?

MARY MAE

In the ways that women do. Or used to do. I think young
women have a little more sense in these days.... Papa
said I was going too fast. Mama lay face down in the
chenille bedspread and cried for me. She was right to
cry... I was lost. I was singing in a club outside
Norfolk, and I was eighteen years old, and my young
husband was dead. A tall, handsome Navy lieutenant came
in one night and sat at a table by himself and just
listened to the music. That set him apart right there

.... He came back again, and the next four nights
running, and he stayed through both my sets .... I used to
do a fine arrangement of "Ev'ry Time We Say Goodbye," and
after the second night, he asked for it in every set ....
I didn't fall in love with him; I was in love with
appreciation.

                    LAURA
Did you marry him?

                    MARY MAE
Honey, he was white ... though black and white didn't have
anything to do with what happened between us. It was the
music, and it was my frame of mind .... In the course of
time, he shipped out, and I had a baby. Which brought me
back to reality, let me tell you. (A smile) Babies have a
way of doing that. As I suspect you know.

                    LAURA
Yes, I do.

                    MARY MAE
Anyway, the next year I married the best man I ever knew,
and he was the father to my son, and another one after
that, and my daughter. And we came here.

                    LAURA
And bought the house?

                    MARY MAE
And bought the house, which was home to us, and then to
my first son and his wife and babies ... until I had to let
it go.

                    LAURA
Did you ever see the Navy lieutenant again?

                    MARY MAE
Yes. Oh, yes ... I did, indeed. (A moment) Come on with me,
now. I want to show you our play-yard.

ANALYSIS OF MARY MAE AND LAURA

After reading this scene several times you conclude that Mary Mae is an African-American woman in her sixties who has lived deeply: She has raised four children, one of whom is the illegitimate offspring from an affair with a white Navy lieutenant. There is a great deal of exposition as she shows her new friend Laura the house and tells of her past career as a chanteuse in a club near the big naval base at Norfolk, Virginia. Imagine how the scandal that her affair would have caused at that time may have scarred her.

As the facts of Mary Mae's past emerge we find a rather complicated tapestry of life experience: a dead husband by the time she was eighteen, a job in a nightclub, exposure to a tawdrier kind of life, a handsome white man, to whom she was attracted because she was "in love with appreciation." Having his baby, she openly admits, gave her a solid dose of reality. She then found the "best man she ever knew," whom she married, and they came to this house that Luke and Laura are now buying. A lot of history has occurred in a place that was also a home to her first son, his wife, and their children. An important element in the scene is that Laura, who has insight and sensitivity, feels the waves of love shared in this house. When Laura remarks that the porch is being rebuilt, Mary Mae is suddenly reminded of all the experiences, the comings and goings, lemonade drinks, and intimacies that happened on the old one. This sense of her past dominates the scene.

Laura is intrigued with this intensely aware, loving survivor, and Mary Mae encourages Laura to call her what all the toddlers do. Mary Mae has had her share of discrimination, intimidation, and pain, but in Port Charles has enjoyed a good, balanced life tending to her geraniums and watching her babies grow like the flowers.

Laura actively pursues a rapport between the women in the scene. What fascinates her most is the mystery of the lieutenant who fathered one of the children. Yes, Mary Mae admits, she did see him again, then quickly changes the subject. This is her strongest action in the scene. Could it be that the character will re-emerge? That is the cliffhanger that soap operas depend upon to keep audiences glued.

In this scene the focus is clearly on Mary Mae. (Laura has been an established character on the show for many years). The scene is unevenly balanced, giving the bulk of the interest to the older actress.

As an exercise to flesh out Mary Mae, make the list of closet items recommended earlier. Remember that the closet, as a metaphor for the mind/imagination, has no spatial boundaries. You could put an airplane in your closet and have room for an infinite number of objects, even people. Let's start out with ten items that could give texture to the character. Be as specific as possible:

1. The chenille bedspread that belonged to her mother.

2. A faded photograph of her first husband, who died during World War II.

3. The wedding dress she wore when she married her second husband is white taffeta, with a white veil and a coronet of silk flowers.

4. Records, including some old 78s, of Ella Fitzgerald, Billie Holliday, and Duke Ellington.

5. A charm bracelet that her children designed for her sixtieth birthday, of the milestones of her life.

6. A photo album containing baby pictures and snaps of her late husband, her parents, graduation pictures of her grandchildren.

7. Gardening tools, packets of zinnia seeds, marigolds, carrots, okra, and tomatoes.

8. A coat, from the late 1940s, with a fur collar, that she can't bear to part with.

It was a gift from her late husband. He did without things because he wanted to buy it for her.

9. Assorted eyeglass cases and bifocal frames, watch-fob chains, cuff links, old buttons.

10. A red cocktail dress that has never been worn — still waiting for the right occasion.

Starting to compose lists will start a chain reaction. Before you know it, you will have created a character with a past, present, and definite future. An old movie stub might spark a whole scenario. You'll have hints of a definite future, too. The writer of this scene has given enough autobiographical information about Mary Mae to write diary entries, letters, or even songs. Your responsibility is to use your imagination, trust your instincts, and find enjoyment in the discovery.

AUDITION SCENE 2
Decker and Felicia, *General Hospital*

THE AREA OUTSIDE THE TV STUDIO. LATE AFTERNOON.

DECKER MOVES IN ALONE, BRANDISHING A HYMNAL, ANGRY AND FRUSTRATED AFTER JUST HUMILIATING COLTON IN A LIVE BROADCAST.

> DECKER
> Step right up, sinners! Repent! Save yourselves from Satan's clutches. Let Brother Colton show you the way. And bless you, brothers, bless you. Bull!

HE FLINGS THE BOOK ACROSS THE ROOM AS FELICIA ENTERS, UPSET.

> FELICIA
> How could you do that?

> DECKER
> Easy. Lift your arm and let it go.

> FELICIA
> To Colt! How could you humiliate him like that in front of all those people?

> DECKER
> All I did was give him an argument. It livened up the show. That's what we have out there, isn't it? A circus? A sideshow? A carny barker selling salvation? (Picking up the hymnal) Let us open the book to Hymn 34 and lift our voices in praise. "The Judgment Day Comes." Sing, sister.

FELICIA

You're enjoying this, aren't you?

DECKER

Tents, TV studios. When you come right down to it, there's not much difference. One's got sawdust on the floor, the other has wires and cables. If you don't watch your step, you can trip yourself up in both places.

FELICIA

Colt helps people. He makes them feel good about themselves.

DECKER

Clowns do that, too. And acrobats. And elephant trainers. And freaks. Freaks make people feel best of all. Thank Heaven, they say, we're not like that.

FELICIA

It is all a show to you, isn't it?

DECKER

It's a ring-toss. We keep throwing them out hoping we'll catch onto something big. Most of us miss.

FELICIA

Why'd you come here?

DECKER

To join the circus!

FELICIA

You grew up in one.

DECKER

I was never in the ring with Colton.

FELICIA

You make it sound more like a fight than a circus.

DECKER

Again, there's not much difference. Only Colt never loses. No sirreebob. Not Brother Colt. Step right up, ladies and gentlemen! See a real live genuine good person! All my life I heard that about him. When Charlene came to my Dad, I'd hear her talk. He was somebody, so I could be

somebody. But never as good as him. I got that
message loud and clear, too. Not from Colt. He
only met me once. I was a kid. He didn't give two
hot damns about me. But to me, he was center
ring. I was sideshow.

> FELICIA

You resent that, don't you?

> DECKER

No, not him. Now that I've been around long
enough to watch his act, I resent the way he
fools people. And himself. There's only one real
thing in his life. That's you.
A long look between them, eyes locked.

> FELICIA

When we first met, why didn't you tell me you were
Colt's brother?

> DECKER (MOVING CLOSER)

You were real to me, too. The first real thing in
my life. I wanted to reach out and take hold of
you. Preacher-man wouldn't like that. He'd have a
name for it. He'd call it "sin."

> FELICIA (IN HIS HOLD)

The show's almost over.

> DECKER

It's just begun.

HE KISSES HER. SHE RESPONDS.

FADE OUT.

Analysis of Decker and Felicia

This scene is an audition piece for Decker. The actor auditioning for this character
has to have a certain kind of danger, body language, physical look, and charm. We
have to believe that Felicia would get on his Harley-Davidson and leave everything
behind if he asked her, for as the conclusion of this scene makes clear, the two principals are physically drawn to each other. There is a rage and a passion that drives
Decker to unmask his brother Colton, the evangelist.

Before the scene starts, Decker has already humiliated Colton by starting an
argument in front of an audience. He is determined to get even for being forced to
live in his older brother's shadow all his life. He unsettles Felicia, who is caught up
in his frenzy and his drive.

Is all this explosive energy for Felicia's benefit? It is apparent that he is drawn to
her goodness, her reality, her lack of pretense.

Two brothers interested in the same woman, at odds with each other, is a common theme in the Bible and in novels, and soap operas love to use this kind of triangle to heat up the screen.

This is a scene that demands a greater output of energy right at the top than most scenes. Before you go in to the audition, you have to visualize the sequence of events that led up to that opening moment.

Think *red* for Decker. He is aggressive, physical, ambitious, passionate, capable of self-sacrifice, and equally capable of violence and verbal abuse. You might think about wearing a red turtleneck, sweater, kerchief, or work shirt.

As an exercise, here is an example of a diary entry which Decker might make after the confrontation with Colton and the final moment with Felicia when his physical desire for her takes over.

> I finally found Colt. It's taken me long enough. I thought he'd be charming folks with his silver tongue in New York City, and he's here in Hicksville! But I ain't about to leave till I get my revenge for all the time I've had to live in his shadow. And there's this girl, an angel named Felicia. She is going to be the answer to my prayers. Colt is stuck on her, but I know she is attracted to me. And I will use everything I've got to take her away from him. I will prove to the people here that Colt is a phony, and when I'm through doing that I can start making it big time, with Miss Felicia at my side.

You would probably find items like the following in Decker's closet:

1. Denim jacket with Harley-Davidson patch

2. Publicity pictures of Colton

3. Father's hunting knife

4. Khaki pants

5. Camouflage wear

6. Clown hat, fake nose and wig

7. Bible, with pages missing

8. Dark blue work shirt

9. Leather jacket with zippers

10. Sunglasses

11. Pendleton shirt

12. Belt with native American buckle

13. Picture of mother who died when he was two

14. U.S. road atlas

15. Brother's block letter sweater that he stole from him

AUDITION SCENE 3

This audition scene is for the role of Katie Kennicott, on *All My Children*. When you receive an audition script, very often you will find included with it the "back story," a detailed history of what has occured before the scene begins. The material below is provided to fully acquaint you with the character, and it is worth your attention.

Katie and Charlie, *All My Children*

Katie Kennicott, the youngest of the large Kennicott brood who grew up on a farm in New Hampshire, has the honesty and goodness of one who has a devoted family and a deep-rooted sense of fair play.

At present, Katie is in her last year of nurse's training. Into her life comes Charlie Brent, who has come east from California, where he dropped out of Stanford Medical School. Charlie has recently become engaged to Katie's friend Melanie and then done an about-face, deciding that he was precipitous in leaving medical school. Most people credit this change to his engagement to Melanie and a desire to make their future secure. Katie has been helping Melanie plan her wedding.

On this night, Katie and Charlie have been working together in a hospital emergency room on an accident case that came in past midnight. The life of the patient was saved. They need a break, and Charlie has suggested they walk outdoors.

> KATIE
> (Takes a deep breath) Mm. It feels good to be out in the fresh air.

> CHARLIE
> I'll say .... You were terrific tonight, Katie.

> KATIE
> Well, thank you. You weren't too bad yourself, Dr. Brent.

> CHARLIE
> I'm not really a doctor yet.

> KATIE
> You will be soon. I'm so glad you went back to medicine, Charlie.

> CHARLIE
> You are?

KATIE

Well — yes. Because you — you were meant to be a doctor and I know how happy Melanie is about it.

CHARLIE

Melanie ... right.

KATIE

She'll be the perfect doctor's wife, too.

CHARLIE

Katie ....

KATIE

Yes?

CHARLIE

I didn't go back to medicine because of Melanie.

KATIE

Well, naturally you went back because you realized that it's what you want to do with your life. But she will make an ideal doctor's wife —

CHARLIE

(Interrupting) You're the one who made me realize I wanted to go back to medicine.

KATIE

Me?! Oh, come on.

CHARLIE

I'm serious ... When I saw how into nursing you were, I began to realize I still felt that way about medicine.

KATIE

Melanie helped you with that decision more than I did.

CHARLIE

Melanie had nothing to do with it. It was you, Katie. You must know that.

KATIE

Well, I don't want to get into an argument about it.

CHARLIE

I don't either, but I'd like to talk ... about Melanie, I mean. And me.

                    KATIE
I don't think we should.

                    CHARLIE
We have to. Or maybe more to the point, talk
about you and me.

                    KATIE
Charlie, I've got to get back to the hospital.

                    CHARLIE
(He stops her) We've still got ten minutes. Sit
down, Katie. (They sit) Don't you know how much
I've come to care about you?

                    KATIE
What I know is that Melanie is one of my best
friends and you are going to marry her.

                    CHARLIE
I'm engaged to her. Being engaged doesn't mean
being married.

                    KATIE
It certainly means you'll be married soon.

                    CHARLIE
I think that would be a big mistake. Don't you?

                    KATIE
No! I certainly do not, and I resent your asking
me such a thing.

                    CHARLIE
Please don't get angry.

                    KATIE
How do you expect me to react? I've been helping
Melanie plan her wedding and trousseau. I'm
addressing invitations for her. I'm going to be
in your wedding. You are being very disloyal to
Melanie, and that's bound to make me angry.

                    CHARLIE
I don't think you're angry so much as guilty.

                    KATIE
Guilty!?

                    CHARLIE
Because Melanie is your friend and you're such a

loyal person, you feel guilty about what's
happening between us.

KATIE

Nothing is happening between us! (She jumps up)
Just get that through your thick head, Charlie. I
like you as a friend and that's all. That's all
it will ever be. And I don't appreciate your
trying to flirt with me behind Melanie's back.

CHARLIE

(He rises) You know that's not what I'm doing....
The last thing I expected was to fall in love
with you.

KATIE

Don't say that!

CHARLIE

But it's true, Katie.

KATIE

I'm going inside and the subject is closed.
Permanently.

(CHARLIE GRABS HER ARM AND PULLS HER BACK)

CHARLIE

 Okay if that's the way you want it, but I won't
marry Melanie in any case.

KATIE

You — !

CHARLIE

Because I know I don't love her. And before you
go just look me in the eye and tell me you don't
care anything about me. That you don't feel a
little bit of what I feel for you.

KATIE

Of course I don't. I don't feel anything.

CHARLIE

Katie....

(HE TAKES HER IN HIS ARMS. SHE STARTS TO PULL AWAY, AND
THEN HE KISSES HER.)
You still don't feel anything? Tell the truth.

```
                         KATIE
        Oh, Charlie .... (They embrace.) Charlie, what are
        we going to do?
```

ANALYSIS OF KATIE AND CHARLIE

Destiny plays an important role in all lives, but in soap opera it is a deciding factor! Katie, despite her loyalty to Melanie, is too much a contemporary young woman not to be aware of the attraction she feels for Charlie. But also she is such a "straight arrow" that she represses her feelings as being an inconsequential crush and tells herself that she has only a sincere friendship with Charlie. A clear example of her inner conflict!

The setting is outdoors, on a pathway with a bench. Think about the atmosphere — the night air, chirping of crickets — so that when Katie takes that first breath we appreciate the sensation she is experiencing. We have to believe that Charlie is looking at her with love in his eyes. It is tonight or never. The wedding date is getting closer, and he knows he can't go through with it — which demonstrates his inner conflict.

Katie's sweetness is reflected in her initial action: she admires Charlie. Her emotional openness makes Charlie more anxious to get the "moment of truth" over with. Then Katie protests, but this doesn't weaken Charlie's position. Finally, she yields to his persistence and purpose, and she admits her deep affection for him.

Here is an example of a letter that Katie might write to her mother about her dilemma:

Pine Valley, PA

Dear Mom,

I miss you and Dad, the farm and my bedroom with your homemade quilt, the smells of your pies and Dad's pipe — and of course, the best Labrador God ever created. Kiss Polly for me.

But Mom, I miss talking to you in the late-night hours, getting your advice about life's upsets. Well, you've heard me talk about Charlie Brent. He and I have been seeing a lot of each other at the hospital, and he happens to be engaged to one of my best friends, Melanie Cortlandt (you remember Melanie — she stayed with us one Thanksgiving). I started to notice him looking at me with more than friendly appreciation. I have been playing it down, but then last night, Charlie admitted to me that he has a deep attraction to me and now he wants to break off his engagement.

Oh, Mom, I am so confused! I tried to get him to rethink his abrupt decision, and he took me in his arms and kissed me. I know you of all people will understand how I felt after that kiss. I was all warm and dizzy and I felt safe for the first time since I left home.

I need your help Mom to get through this. I am so torn. You are and always will be my best friend. I am coming back to the farm for a few days to clear my head. I love you. See you soon.

Katie

Again, let's list the possible items to be found in Katie's closet.

1. Two pairs white work shoes

2. Two standard nurse's uniforms

3. Senior prom dress — pink ballet-length skirt, fitted bodice, spaghetti straps

4. Dyed pink shoes

5. Framed photo of family on Fourth of July picnic

6. Riding outfit

7. A pair of worn Levis

8. Antique cameo pin left to her by maternal grandmother

9. Pine Valley U. sweatshirt

10. A pea coat

11. A pair of Reeboks

12. A biography of Clara Barton

13. A copy of *Brides* magazine

14. Navy blue blazer and pleated skirt

We recommend that you practice the diary, letter, and closet exercises for all future soap opera auditions. Another element we haven't emphasized, but one worth remembering, is the music that each character connects with. Helen Hayes was having trouble finding the character of the Duchess in the Broadway play, *Time Remembered*. One morning, she heard 18th-century harpsichord music on the radio and later told a prominent critic that she had "found the Duchess."

Each character connects to a certain type of music. For example, a small town rural girl like Katie might gravitate to a singer like Bonnie Raitt. Mary Mae would love Billie Holiday. Decker would go for heavy metal and the Rolling Stones. Find the music of the character, put it in your Walkman, and let it create the moment before the audition.

CHAPTER 21

THE PRIME-TIME SERIES AUDITION

*If I have to do TV I prefer sitcom. It's like a one-act play,
you have a live audience and you have to learn your lines
each week.*

—KEENE CURTIS

While a soap opera affords the actor a significant amount of time to develop the life of the character, a prime-time series demands that the characters establish an immediate love affair with the audience on the first or second episode.

We have witnessed the cancellation of prime-time series early in a season, to see them replaced by mid-season backups, which in turn last for only a few episodes. Therefore it is crucial that the actor bring to the audition enough personality, charisma, uniqueness, physicality, vulnerability, and talent to convince the producer, writers, directors, and network executives to take the very costly chance on using him or her.

ONE-SHOT ON A SITCOM

After thirteen years as a working actor in New York, Bruce Nozick had done a spate of films, had a terrific tape, and, along with his wife, decided that the time was right to try Los Angeles. He also happened to look very much like another actor, Jay Thomas, one of the stars of *Love and War*. So when the writers of that show had an idea for an episode in which one of the leading ladies dates a Jay Thomas look-alike, one would expect that Bruce Nozick would immediately get the call. Here's what happened:

> Nobody at that production office knew me. Luckily, I had auditioned for Julie Hutchinson, director of comedy casting at CBS, and she alerted me. Then my agent was able to get me an audition. That was a funny scene. There were about fifteen other guys there, and none of them looked like Thomas! They all just stared at me! They knew I fit the description. When the show's casting director came out of her office, they said, "Look, why don't we all go home? He's the guy!"
>
> But still, I had to audition, and then I had to come back again, to be

> seen by the producer. I was one of three actors at the callback. Then
> they told me I had the job. Only, there was no script. It was just an idea.
> I guess they wouldn't write the script without knowing there was some-
> one to play the part. The audition I won didn't turn into a job until two
> and a half months later.

The series is taped in front of a live audience. The show normally works a five-day
schedule, with a read-through and blocking on Monday, rehearsals the next three
days, with dress rehearsal and taping on Friday.

> They called me early on Monday to say the script wasn't ready. They
> finally faxed it to me late Monday evening. So, Tuesday was my first day
> of rehearsal.
>
>   The director, Michael Lembeck, couldn't have been nicer. And every-
> one in that cast was supportive; the atmosphere is so nice, relaxed,
> happy, and comfortable. I was the only one who was nervous. Of course,
> they all knew what they were supposed to be doing. We read through
> the script and did the blocking. Everyone was so comfortable that we
> only had a half-day rehearsal on Wednesday. We worked the whole day
> on Thursday, and then Friday was it. I was terrified I'd forget my lines. I
> didn't; some of the others did. And when that happened, they just
> stopped, and started the scene over again. No sweat. Everyone says it
> was one of the best episodes they did. And the company has another
> show going into pilot, so maybe I'll get a chance to work on that.
>
>   —BRUCE NOZICK

The two audition pieces that follow are two especially well-written scenes from *The
Wonder Years*, an award-winning prime-time series. The scripts provided to the auditioning actors state who the characters are, give pertinent information about where
the scenes take place, and tell what happened before they start. An important fact for
the actors to remember that the time is 1968. Researching this period — in magazines, movies, TV programs, and books — is recommended.

     There should be no difficulty in finding the humor in these characters. They have
wit, intelligence, and a flair for sarcasm. You like them and want to know more about
them. They have the ability to reach us through their vulnerability, their imperfec-
tions, and their truth.

     The general directions for script analysis in Chapter 20 apply here.

AUDITION SCENE 1

Jack: a typical father — hard-working, tense, moody. He loves his family, but has a
great deal of trouble expressing it.

Kevin: a twelve-and-a-half-year-old boy.

Jack's father, Kevin's grandfather, has had a heart attack and is in the hospital. Jack
has just been in to see his father, who is in critical condition. Jack and his father were
never close.

INTERIOR: HOSPITAL WAITING ROOM

JACK STANDS ALONE, STARING OUT THE WINDOW. KEVIN ENTERS UNNOTICED, LOOKS AT HIS FATHER FROM BEHIND FOR A WHILE.

> KEVIN
>
> Hi, Dad.

(JACK DOESN'T SEEM TO HEAR HIM. KEVIN TAKES A TENTATIVE STEP CLOSER.)

> KEVIN
>
> (A little louder) Hi, Dad.

(JACK TURNS, SEES KEVIN, COVERS HIS PREOCCUPATION.)

> JACK
>
> (Too casual) Oh. Hi, Sport.

> KEVIN
>
> Mom and Karen are in there, now.

> JACK
>
> Oh, uh-huh, good. Good.

> JACK
>
> (A long beat) Come on over here. We can, you know, sit here and catch up.

> KEVIN
>
> Yeah. (Beat.) Catch up on what?

> JACK
>
> Oh, you know — you, school, all that stuff.

> KEVIN
>
> Well ... I've been married twice.

> JACK
>
> (Oblivious) Good.

> KEVIN
>
> I have four sons.

> JACK
>
> Good. Great. (A beat.) What did you say?

> KEVIN
>
> (Shrugs) Nothing. School's okay.

> JACK
>
> Good. Your schooling's very important, you know. You get out of it what you put in.

                         KEVIN

Yeah. (A beat.) How come we never go visit Granny
and Grandpa??? I mean, before this?

                         JACK

(Immediately) Because they live too far away.

(KEVIN LOOKS SCEPTICAL. JACK SENSES IT.)

                         KEVIN

Do you think Grandpa's going to die?

                         JACK

What? Are you kidding me? It's gonna take a hell
of a lot more that one little heart attack to
kill my father.

                         KEVIN

The doctor said it was a major heart attack.

                         JACK

Yeah...well...that's because he's a doctor and
they get paid according to the size of the heart
attack.

                         KEVIN

Rich Vogel's father died from a minor —

                         JACK

Dammit, Kevin! I said he's gonna be fine, he's
gonna be fine!

(KEVIN LOOKS DOWN. JACK LOOKS SORRY, BUT HE CAN'T SAY
IT.)

                         JACK

(Finally) So, what, uh...what did you learn this
week in school?

                         KEVIN

(Shrugging) I learned that if you cut a frog open
the wrong way his liver explodes.

                         JACK

(Sorry he asked) No kidding.

                         KEVIN

Karen says the reason we never go visit Granny
and Grandpa is because you hate your father
because he never had time for you. (JACK's eyes
flash angrily.)

JACK
(Flat, furious) Karen is a smartass teenage girl
who thinks she knows everything. (Beat, still
furious) Do you want to stop at Howard Johnson's
on the way home?

ANALYSIS OF SCENE 1

This scene is about the relationship between a father and son who have difficulty communicating. The crisis of Grandpa's physical condition has brought them together. The problem isn't resolved but at least an attempt has been made to bridge the gap. The actor playing the son must let the father have the moment at the beginning to remember his father and the ambivalent feelings he has for him. The son's repetition of "Hi, Dad," snaps him out of it. The overall feeling of the scene is highlighted by the number of *beats*, or pauses. The reactive moments are heightened, as when Jack gets defensive about the visits to the grandparents and his father's state of health in answer to his son's questions.

Look for levels in the scene, as the characters say one thing and cover something else. In his attempt to reach his father, Kevin shows a perception, a maturity, and a humor beyond his years. The father at times becomes more like the child.

Take the scene apart, moment by moment. There is a definite rhythm and a slow build to the father's outburst at the end. Don't rush these moments (but don't prolong them — find a balance). The tension is broken when Dad invites son to Howard Johnson's. This indirect apology is another key to understanding the father's character. While the son's reaction is not written, a positive response should be indicated by the actor. The "moment after" can be imagined.

As previously recommended, make a list of ten items in each character's closet. Make this list as specific as possible, describing articles of clothing, old toys, souvenirs, jewelry, shoes, accessories, and any other object that your character might keep there.

AUDITION SCENE 2

Karen: A sixteen-year-old girl in 1968. Bright, rebellious, absolutely convinced of the enlightenment of the principles of "the movement" — peace, free love, very little underwear — and the nefariousness of the principles of her parents' generation.

Norma: A typical mother — stable, wise, anxious, loving.

INTERIOR: ARNOLD KITCHEN, MORNING.

NORMA WORKS AT THE STOVE. KAREN COMES IN WEARING JEANS, A
TIE-DYED T-SHIRT AND NO BRA. NORMA STARTS OVER WITH SOME
EGGS. NOTICES KAREN IS BRA-LESS.

NORMA
(Shaking her head) No.

                    KAREN
Thank you for that warm and positive greeting.

                    NORMA
You're not going to school like that.

                    KAREN
Like what?

                    NORMA
You know like what. You know exactly like what.

                    KAREN
If you're referring to the fact that I'm not
wearing the traditional western undergarment that
binds the female torso into one rigid piece of
flesh, yes I am.

                    NORMA
Put on a bra.

                    KAREN
How can you live with yourself knowing that you
let a male-dominated design culture dictate your
tastes, your values, your very morality?

                    NORMA
I can't. You don't know how many times I've tried
to take my own life. But until I succeed, I want
you to wear a bra.

                    KAREN
The answer is no, Mom. I'm not ashamed of my body
and I don't think you should be either.

                    NORMA
(Sighing deeply) Oh, Karen. Honey, I'm not
ashamed of your body. (A beat) I'd just as soon
you didn't go out for the next five years, but —

                    KAREN
Exactly. You're afraid of the world and you want
me to be afraid of the world, too. But I'm not. I
happen to love the world if that's okay with you.

                    NORMA
Can't you love the world and put a piece of
fabric over your — (Gestures vaguely at her
chest)

KAREN

Nipples? See, you can't even say it. A beautiful, natural part of your own body and you can't even say it. That's really sad. (She starts to head out)

NORMA

I think your father may have something to say about this.

KAREN

I don't think my breasts are any of my father's business. (She exits)

NORMA

(Shouting after her) You may not think so, but I happen to know that your breasts are very close to your father's heart!

ANALYSIS OF SCENE 2

This scene not only presents a slice-of-life confrontation between mother and daughter but underscores the year 1968, an important year in the evolution of the women's liberation movement. The opening line is motivated by the daughter's choice to go bra-less. This is a universal situation and one which actors should connect to effortlessly. It doesn't have to be about to bra or not to bra. It could deal with dating, using the car, wearing a skirt instead of jeans, and returning the hair to its natural shade, or clearing the dishes before going to school.

In the previous scene there was a communication problem between father and son. That does not exist in this scene. These women tell it like it is. Again, the language of the daughter implies a sophistication which is slightly intimidating to the mother. However, the daughter can only mouth phrases she has read in Betty Freidan and Gloria Steinem. Emotionally, she is not as mature as she thinks she is. Mom doesn't have the intellectual advantage, but she demonstrates natural, protective concerns for her teenager. Despite the central argument in the scene, these two love each other — and that comes through.

There is more fluidity in this scene due to fewer beats between lines. Each character takes a position and sticks to it. Look for the humor in the daughter's description of a bra. The moment when Mom can't say "nipples" and the clever final exchange about the father's involvement will amuse the audience, but the actor must stay in the reality of the moment, not play for laughs.

To help flesh out these characters, each actress should write a letter to a close friend. The daughter could write about why she connects to the feminist movement, the mother could write about her daughter's behavior and why she is so concerned.

CHAPTER 22

THE FILM AUDITION

I'm ready for my closeup, Mr. DeMille.

—NORMA DESMOND

For these scenes from his teleplay for a Movie of the Week, *The Stranger Within,* we are indebted to John Pielmeier, who was particularly eager for newcomers to have the opportunity to work with authentic, current material. It is published with the understanding that it may not be reprinted or broadcast.

AUDITION SCENE 1

The story's setting is a small town in New England. The year at the beginning is 1974. Mare Blackburn's life was turned upside down when she received the news that her husband Luke had been gunned down in Vietnam, leaving her to raise their son. She is once more thrown into upheaval when she takes the three-year-old to the local grocery store and, while she is looking for cereal in the back of the store, an unseen person lifts the boy out of the cart and disappears with him.

Characters: Emma and Mare

INT. KITCHEN — AFTERNOON

MARE SITS AT THE KITCHEN TABLE — A ROUND, RUSTIC ONE IN THE CENTER OF THIS FARMHOUSE KITCHEN — WITH A CUP OF COFFEE AND THE PHONE BEFORE HER. THE BLACK PUPPY LIES DESPONDENT AT HER FEET. EMMA ENTERS AND STANDS BEHIND HER DAUGHTER. SHE PLACES HER HANDS ON MARE'S SHOULDERS.

                    EMMA
    It's not gonna ring any sooner with you sitting
    there.

MARE RISES AND PULLS AWAY —

                    MARE
    It's been three days, Mother. It's not gonna ring
    at all.

— TO EMPTY HER COLD COFFEE INTO THE SINK.

EMMA'S FACE HARDENS

> EMMA
>
> Stop that kind of thinking. That's not how we get
> through life in this family. You're feeling sorry
> for yourself. That's not the kind of daughter I
> raised you to be.

EMMA TURNS TO THE STOVE TO PUT ON SOME MILK FOR HOT
CHOCOLATE.

> EMMA
>
> I know what you're thinking, it's not easy, but
> you've gotta fight those thoughts, Mare, you've
> gotta remember what the officer said, he'll turn
> up. This happens all the time. They find these
> children.

> MARE
>
> What if they don't find him? What if he's dead,
> Mother? What if they ....

> EMMA
>
> (OVERLAPPING) That's enough. I'm making hot
> chocolate, you want some hot chocolate?

MARE LEAVES THE ROOM. EMMA, MILK CARTON IN HAND, WATCHES
HER DAUGHTER —

INT. DINING ROOM — AFTERNOON

— AS SHE WALKS PAST THE STAIRS THROUGH THE DINING ROOM

INT. LIVING ROOM — AFTERNOON

— TO THE DOOR OF THE LIVING ROOM. SHE STOPS, WATCHING THE
TV. OVER HER SHOULDER WE SEE EMMA, IN THE KITCHEN
DOORWAY, HOLDING THE CARTON OF MILK AND A SAUCEPAN.

> EMMA
>
> I swear, Mare, you're just like your father.

EMMA HAS TURNED BACK TO THE STOVE.

> EMMA
>
> You're too soft, you always were soft, and
> life'll get you if you don't watch out, kid.

MARE IN THE FOREGROUND, FINALLY BEGINS TO CRY.

> EMMA
>
> (OBLIVIOUS) It'll turn out just fine in the end.

You gotta believe that.

EMMA TURNS AND SEES HER DAUGHTER'S TEARS. SHE COMES TO
HER, MILK CARTON IN HAND, AND TAKES HER IN HER ARMS.

>   EMMA
> Listen to me. I'm just a tough old bossy bird.

>   MARE
> It's my fault, mother, it's all my fault.

>   EMMA
> No, it's not.

MARE IS BECOMING HYSTERICAL, LOSING ALL LOGIC, SPEAKING
WHEN SHE CAN BETWEEN TEARS.

>   MARE
> You always told me not to leave him alone. I'm a
> terrible mother. I was a terrible wife! Luke
> would be ashamed of me for what I've done with
> our son!

>   EMMA
> Sssssh. Luke loved you, honey.

>   MARE
> I left my baby alone! It's all my fault!!

>   EMMA
> Mare, no ...

>   MARE
> I don't deserve to be a mother!!!

SHE TEARS AWAY FROM HER MOTHER AND TURNS UP THE STAIRS.
EMMA FOLLOWS.

INT. CHILD'S BEDROOM — AFTERNOON

MARE TEARS INTO THE ROOM, IN HYSTERICS. SHE GRABS BUZZY
FROM OFF THE BED AND HUGS HIM — TOO TIGHT. SHE SOBS. EMMA
ARRIVES AT THE DOOR.

>   MARE
> Luke said I was too careless with the baby. He
> said I had to take better care ....

SHE HITS HERSELF, STRIKING HER FIST AGAINST HER CHEST,
PUNISHING THIS BAD MOTHER.

>   EMMA
> Mare, no!

AS EMMA MOVES IN TO STOP HER, SHE PULLS AWAY.

                    MARE
He fell down the stairs last month! I wasn't
watching!

                    EMMA
Honey, you can't watch them...(all the time).

                    MARE
(OVERLAPPING) It was my fault! I'm a terrible
mother!

                    EMMA
You're only human, Mare....

MARE'S EYES FALL ON THE OPEN SAFETY PINS ON THE DRESSER.

                    MARE (O.C.)
Look at this!

                    EMMA
(CONTINUING OVER) ...we're all...(only human).

                    MARE
(OVERLAPPING) He could have hurt himself.

SHE SWEEPS UP THE OPEN PINS IN ONE HAND.

                    EMMA
Mare....

                    MARE
It would have been my fault!

                    EMMA
Nonsense, dear....

                    MARE
Why did God make me a mother?! I don't deserve to
be a mother!!!

SHE IS SQUEEZING HER HAND, FILLED WITH OPEN SAFETY PINS,
TIGHT...

                    EMMA
My God, Mare....

                    MARE
He's dead! He's gone! I killed him!!!

...AND NOW STRIKES HER CHEST AS HARD AS SHE CAN.

CUT.

ANALYSIS OF SCENE 1

In this scene between Mare and her mother, Emma, Mare is a nervous wreck and clearly blames herself for what happened. Emma's objective in the scene is to try to calm her down, give her hope that the police will arrive at any moment with the child. As the scene progresses there is a feeling of sweeping momentum. Mare's restlessness, not being able to stay put; her mother's stance and strength. Emma warns her that life will get her for being as soft as her father was. This criticism is too much for Mare, and the dam bursts.

Hysteria builds until she tears away from her mother and goes upstairs to the child's bedroom. She hugs his teddy bear, for it is linked to her son. Echoes of her dead husband's criticism — that she was too careless with the baby — lead her to strike herself in an act of self-punishment. Then she recalls incidents that happened prior to the kidnapping — he fell downstairs because she wasn't paying attention, she left safety pins lying around which could hurt him. Finally, her hysteria leads to the irrational conclusion that she killed him.

These two women are very different. It is very difficult to play this kind of build on one take, much less in seven or eight takes. The actress playing Mare doesn't have much time in the sequence of events before she is thrown into an hysteria. This is where emotional recall has to save the day, that technique that José Ferrer described as the key to inspiration.

AUDITION SCENE 2

The preceding scene is the only time we get to see Mare at this age. This scene takes place fifteen years later. Mare never stops blaming herself. But while she has never remarried or had any more children, she is having a relationship with a handsome, healthy, and very confident divorced man, Max Vance. One evening there is a knock at the door. An eighteen-year-old youngster named Mark claims to be her long-lost son. He says he was raised by elderly people on a farm in Iowa. After their death, he found clippings regarding his true identity.

From then on, life changes drastically for Mare. Mark seems sure about his childhood before he was kidnapped. He even has a scar where hot chocolate scalded him prior to the tragedy. But he is also full of contradictions. However, suppressing her doubts, Mare takes him in. As the story unfolds, however, we discover that Mark is a sociopath.

She discovers she is pregnant with Max's baby, and the action accelerates. Mark is jealous of Max, and in the scene that follows, it is apparent that Max is suspicious of Mark.

Characters: Mark and Max

EXT. WOODED LAKE — MORNING

SNOW IS FALLING, COVERING THE GROUND. MAX JOGS AROUND THE
EDGE OF THIS NEAR-FROZEN LAKE, NOT FAR FROM THE HOUSE.
HIS BREATH PUFFS FROM HIS MOUTH AS HE TRAVELS. AT ONE END
OF THE LAKE IS A SMALL DAM, WITH WATER SPILLING OVER THE

TOP TO FORM A STREAM BELOW, AND IT IS HERE THAT HE STOPS, CATCHING HIS BREATH. ACROSS THE DAM, MARK STEPS FROM THE WOODS ONTO THE PATH. THEY FACE EACH OTHER IN SILENCE FOR A MOMENT — A STAND-OFF. THEN MARK BREAKS THE ICE.

MARK

Hi.

MAX

Hi.

MAX MOVES ACROSS THE DAM TO MARK.

MAX

Sleep O.K.?

MARK

Yeah. Sure. Just thought I'd get some morning air.

HE REACHES MARK AND CONTINUES WALKING, THE BOY SHOULDERING ON BESIDE HIM.

MARK

You do this every day?

MAX

When I can. Getting old. Sometimes it's easier to sleep that extra hour.

MARK

Max, why don't you believe me?

MAX STOPS; MARK TOO. MAX LOOKS HIM OVER, WEIGHING THOUGHTS.

MARK

Why would I want to do this if she's not my Mom? I mean she's not rich, I'm not gonna get any money off her.

MAX MAKES NO REPLY.

MARK

I need love, Max. So does she. I don't pretend it's always gonna be as nice and easy as it is now, but come on, what parent—child relationship is perfect? (Throwing a tiny dart) I mean, you ought know that.

MAX IS STUNG.

                              MAX
What do you mean?

                              MARK
    (Innocent) She told me you have a kid somewhere,
    that's all.

SILENCE.

                              MARK
    You do, don't you?

MAX DOES NOT ANSWER, LOOKS AWAY.

                              MARK
    I mean, I'm not saying I'm not her son, Max, I'm
    saying that if she can give me the kind of love I
    never had ... (then ...)

                              MAX
    (On the attack) I thought you said you had that
    love?

MARK LOOKS AT HIM: WHAT DO YOU MEAN?

                              MAX
    Gram and Gramps. You said you had a perfect
    childhood ....

                              MARK
    I did.

                              MAX
    (continuing over) ... you said they were saints,
    too good to be true.

                              MARK
    They are.

A BEAT OF SILENCE.

                              MARK
    They are.

MAX PUZZLES OUT THIS PRESENT-TENSE ANSWER.

CUT.

ANALYSIS OF SCENE 2
This example is useful for seeing how "stage directions" can give you the sense of place and the physicality of the action. As you read this scene, think of the eyes of each character. Mark, we have seen, is a sociopath who constantly invents stories —

dangerous, clever, manipulative. How do Mark's eyes look? Does he establish eye-contact with Max? Or does he avoid Max's penetrating stare?

Max suspects foul play in Mark — he could be a danger to Mare — so there is a silent moment before the dialogue begins.

Think of the characters' objectives. There is a key plot point (not in this scene), in which Mare has revealed to Mark that Max's teenaged son, a drug addict, had jumped to his death. Even though Mare has asked him not to bring it up, Mark reveals to Max that he knows about his son. Mark's line, "What parent–child relationship is perfect?" is, as the stage direction says, like a dart being thrown. Max's tension mounts as Mark persists in mentioning the dead son to gain the advantage over Max. But then the contradictions begin. Mark says, "if she can give the kind of love I never had." And Max says, "I thought you said you had that love?" This rejoinder is Max's dart thrown back to Mark. "You said you had a perfect childhood." The actor playing Max must end the scene with another silence that shows his strong distrust of Mark.

AUDITION SCENE 3

Mark sees to it that while ice-fishing, Max falls into the water and drowns. There are no witnesses. Now the man whose baby Mare is carrying is dead. In shock, she returns to her home with Mark and her dog, Thornton.

Characters: Mare and Mark

INT. LIVING ROOM — DUSK

A FIRE ROARS IN THE FIREPLACE. MARE AND MARK SIT IN FRONT
OF IT. HE DRINKS FROM A BOTTLE OF BOURBON; SHE HOLDS A
HALF-EMPTY GLASS. THORNTON RESTS BESIDE THEM. HER EYES
ARE RED FROM WEEPING.

> MARK
>
> He didn't feel anything, Mom. Soon as he hit the
> water, he was numb.

> MARE
>
> How did it happen?

> MARK
>
> (He takes a swallow from the bottle.) He was
> upset about your fight last night. He was drinking
> a lot. He took a sip of your coffee. Burned his
> mouth, spilled it on his hands. Lost his balance.
> Fell in.

SILENCE.

> MARK
>
> What were you fighting about?

SILENCE.

> MARK
>
> Whatever it was, whatever you said to him, that set him off. You should have talked to him this morning, Mom.

> MARE
>
> You're saying this was my fault?

> MARK
>
> No. Don't be paranoid, Mom. It was an accident. All I'm saying is that, maybe, if you had smoothed things over, talked things out, made the coffee a little less hot, any one of a dozen little things, events might be different. But you can't control these things, Mom. So just don't think about it.

MARE IS STARING AT HIM, AS IF BEGINNING TO SEE HIM FOR THE FIRST TIME. HE IS BECOMING PROGRESSIVELY MORE DRUNK.

> MARK
>
> It's like Gram and Gramps. There were a lot of things that I might have done to save them, but it was still an accident.

> MARE
>
> You said they died ... years apart.

> MARK
>
> Did I? No, I just didn't want to tell you. You wanna hear? Everything?

MARE WATCHES HIM, ANSWERING NEITHER YES NOR NO.

> MARK
>
> See, I wasn't the only kid there. There were three. John, he was the oldest. He came to them when he was about four, so he kinda remembered his past. Then came Joey. Then me. We were only two or three when they got us, so we thought we'd always been there. (He smiles, remembering.)

> MARK
>
> Gram loved babies. That's why they took us, I guess. She was always happy with a baby around. The problem with babies is, they grow up.

TEARS SPRING TO HIS EYES. HE TAKES ANOTHER DRINK.

>   MARK
> Gram would have these ... bad times, see? When
> she'd ... do things to us you don't wanna know
> about. We didn't have any friends. Missed a lot
> of school. But, John. He remembered. A better
> home, a different life. It's the memories, Mom,
> that really screwed it up. (He wipes his tears;
> others follow. Painful memories.) I mean, you
> don't know how bad things really are, until you
> remember that things were better once.

HE GETS CONTROL — ANOTHER DRINK AND HE CALMS.

>   MARK
> They'd always told everyone we were adopted, see,
> so John started trying to find out who his real
> parents were. He was digging around in the attic
> one day, and he came across these clippings. They
> always subscribed to lots of newspapers, and they
> musta saved everything they could find about each
> of us. Like maybe they thought if they clipped
> the articles no one would ever know, or maybe
> they were proud of what they had done, I don't
> know, but John found them and told them he was
> going to the police. Next day he was gone. Wasn't
> until about aweek later that Joey and I found ...
> where they'd buried him in the basement.

THE TEARS COME AGAIN. HE TAKES ANOTHER DRINK TO KEEP
THEM BACK.

>   MARK
> Joey tried to run. Gramps caught him. It was
> awful. He made me watch. Made me swear I'd be a
> good boy. He rubs the burn on his finger.

>   MARK
> That night there was a fire. By the time help
> came, everyone was dead. Gramps, Gram, Joey,
> John. Everyone but me. (He sighs, stares into the
> fire.)

>   MARK
> The hardest part was after ... when they took me
> away ... when I saw ... what other kids had ... the
> love ... something I never missed until then.

HE WIPES HIS TEAR, AND TURNS TO MARE, SMILING.

```
                          MARK
    But now, I have you.

MARE IS IN SHOCK, FRIGHTENED, UNCERTAIN HOW TO RESPOND.
THERE IS A KNOCK AT THE DOOR. THORNTON BARKS.

CUT.
```

ANALYSIS OF SCENE 3

In this scene Mark is making an attempt to comfort Mare following Max's death. She is in a state of shock. Think of how the atmosphere contributes to the emotions of the scene: It is growing dark, and the characters' faces are lit by firelight.

Mark is getting drunk. As he lies about Max's death, he places blame on Mare for the fight that led to the "accident." It is a "mind game" that causes the light of discovery to dawn in Mare's mind. She gazes at him and wonders: "Why have there been so many 'accidents' since his arrival? Who is this young man?"

Mark loosens up under the influence of the liquor and recounts the "truth" of his background. This further inventing of stories by the character (this time to make himself seem innocent) suggests that in actuality he was responsible for all the deaths he describes, including the elderly couple's. However, the actor playing this part must tell everything with absolute conviction. And he has lived so many fantasies that the ultimate lie has become his only reality: This strange woman is his mother.

As the writer states, Mare is uncertain how to respond. There is a knock at the door. Here the actress might seem to freeze up to portray her fear, or jump at the sound. (Yes, it is a police investigator. In the story's chilling finale, Mark dies as the police rescue Mare from him. She is wounded, but delivers a healthy baby.)

In the best situations, when you have an audition for a made-for-TV movie or feature film, you will be given the entire script to read. We hope so, but there are times when you will be handed only scenes, or pages of dialogue. You have to look at the nature of the relationship and make quick decisions based upon what the characters' objectives are. Making a strong choice based on your understanding of the emotional nature of the scene and how it changes, will put you in control.

CHAPTER 23

THE COMMERCIAL AUDITION

When an actor takes control of the copy, doing it his way,
that is when an actor stands out. The copy makes sense.
—ARISTA BALTRONIS, *casting director, Grey Advertising*

The filmed or taped commercial is normally a sales message, from ten to sixty seconds long, about a product or service. There are several types: A spokesperson delivering the sales pitch directly to the audience; a dramatization, involving husband and wife, sister and brother, mother and child, or a group of people who might gather at a resort, a party, a bank, and so forth; an off-camera announcer may deliver the message as we watch the action.

Some commercials are funny; some are low-key or *soft sell*; some use a forceful *hard sell*.

The actor's approach to commercial copy will utilize training in sense memory, improvisation, mime, characterization, voice production, concentration, and timing.

There is a facility that comes with constant auditioning which affects the reading so that it may sound too glib. We hope that understanding the overall purpose of each commercial message presented in these samples — through the exploration of the dynamic, language, punctuation, emphasis, copy points, structure, and rhythm — will provide you with guidelines for all future auditions and will help keep you from becoming too slick.

A recommended exercise is to write your own commercial about a product you enjoy using. Practice telling a friend about the product; attempt to persuade the person to buy it. All of us do commercials every day — whenever we tell a friend about a book we enjoyed, the cologne we just purchased, last night's terrific restaurant, or the new camera we simply have to buy. Notice your own enthusiasm and concentration at those moments. Bring that enthusiasm to the audition with you.

To feel at home with any piece of copy, you may want to put it in your own words. Just remember: at the audition, you still keep it natural, but you read the *copywriter's* words.

Always read over the copy at least five times. Make this your general rule for all auditions.

COMMERCIAL 1

WIND DRIFT® AFTER-SHAVE AND COLOGNE   (30 SECONDS)
    You're tired.
    You've had a rough week in a grimy city.
    But now you're at the shore.
    The sea is pounding and the air is fresh.
    You fill your lungs and
        breathe deeply of the clean, fresh air with
        a tang of salt and the sound of waves.
    You're not tired anymore.
    WIND DRIFT does that to you.
    because WIND DRIFT is about the sea.
    WIND DRIFT After-Shave and Cologne.

ANALYSIS OF COMMERCIAL 1

• Voice-over: action on camera

• Motivation: To help a tired friend feel revitalized by using the correct and most refreshing after-shave and cologne.

• Objective: Compare the soothing influence of the shore to the product using sense memory.

Personalize the copy. Talk to someone you know. You are using yourself to reach your friend. Be specific. It will be far more effective than trying to sound like the stereotypical announcer.

Visualize the grimy city, the shore, the color of the sea. In your mind you can see that tired, sweaty, pale, bedraggled nine-to-fiver. Think about August in New York or Dallas or wherever you have been uncomfortable from the heat. Bus fumes pollute the air. Soot and litter are pervasive, and the smell of it all is inescapable. When you have this picture clearly drawn from your own experience you'll be prepared to tackle the first line.

You'll use a certain tone in the second line elaborating on the "tired" state. Underscore the words "rough" and "grimy." They describe the unpleasantness you are trying to express.

Then there is a major transition on "But now . . ."; this takes you and your tired friend to the shore. There should be an implied feeling of Ahhhh! Hear the sound of the waves, taste the salt that is connected to the waves. Sense the filling of the lungs with clean, fresh air. Hear the pounding of the sea on the beach. You are praising the clean, fresh seashore environment. "Tired" no longer exists. The metaphor is complete for the product pitch: Wind Drift takes you to the seashore. It makes you feel just as clean and fresh as the sea air.

By appealing to your senses, the qualities of the after-shave and cologne are enhanced. The sponsor doesn't have to tell you to buy the product. The message speaks for itself. This is a soft-sell commercial. A mood piece.

COMMERCIAL 2

EASY-OFF® OVEN CLEANER   (30 SECONDS)

ANNCR (EXCITED BUT CONFIDENTIAL): America, here's a
wonderful new way to clean your oven:
EASY-OFF® Oven Cleaner. We cut the fumes, kept the power.
Let's discover the difference.
WOMAN: It'll take EASY-OFF® to get grease this bad.
ANNCR: How's this smell?
WOMAN (SNIFFS): Nice and fresh. Bet it won't work like
EASY-OFF®!
ANNCR (VO, STILL CONFIDENTIAL): The EASY-OFF® power
cleaners cut through grease *fast*.
ANNCR (LIVE): Okay, wipe.
WOMAN: Sparkling clean! EASY-OFF® Oven Cleaner! Smells
great, works great.
ANNCR (VO): Get *improved* EASY-OFF®. We cut the fumes,
kept the power.

Analysis of Commercial 2

• Announcer (male) and housewife (female)

• Product demonstration commercial

Note the stage directions in the announcer's copy: "Excited but confidential." This is the tone used by sports announcers at the eighteenth hole as they describe the final strokes that will determine the winner of the PGA trophy.

The announcer must be dynamic and intent on informing us that this product is improved because the maker has cut its fumes but kept its power. He establishes contact with a housewife who doesn't know about the new improved brand. (In the filming, there is a cover label hiding the product's real label.)

As a woman auditioning for this commercial, you have to imagine a grease-caked oven. The homemaker knows about Easy-Off, as is evident from her first line. Common sense dictates that the product name is emphasized in this line.

The announcer sprays some oven cleaner and asks the woman what she thinks of the odor. Now she must sniff. (Note: clients and producers pay critical attention to actors' sensory reactions. Actors have lost coffee commercials, for instance, because their coffee-tasting responses weren't convincing.) We know he has fooled her. She thinks the smell is nice and fresh, so it can't work like the Easy-Off she knows, an industrial-strength product with a strong aroma.

The announcer still uses a one-to-one confidential tone to address America. He reiterates that Easy-Off has the *power* to cut through grease *fast*. These words are italicized in the script for emphasis. "Fast" is the operative word and when she wipes the oven, she reacts with surprise. Now he removes the cover label and reveals the hero of the day — Easy-Off. She is convinced of the product's claims.

The *voice-over tag* (VO) is heard over a product shot with a reprise of the opening claim: "We cut the fumes, kept the power."

This is not an easy commercial because its dynamic is intense and at a higher pitch than a "real-people" commercial. It challenges the announcer to use low-voice excitement to address the nation with important news about oven cleaners. He is figuratively winking at us and playfully leading on the housewife with a seeming Brand X he knows is the preferred cleaner. He is doing this so she will discover that the product does work, minus the fumes. The word "improved" must get a headline emphasis. It is a major selling point.

The actress playing the consumer, in the age range twenty-five to thirty-five, should know about cleaning an oven. When the sparkling clean oven emerges from the grime, your vocal contrast is important in the interpretation. The reactions must sound real, not forced. To anticipate the outcome is a common trap. You must play each moment — from doubt to skepticism to the thrill of discovery.

COMMERCIAL 3

JERGENS DIRECT-AID® (30 SECONDS)

VIDEO	AUDIO	
SFX Alarm Clock	SHE:	Good morning
2 hands touch	HE:	G'morning. Hey — your hands.
	SHE:	Mmmmm?
His hand caresses hers.	HE:	They're so soft.
She reaches out of frame, bring in product	SHE:	I've discovered Jergens Direct-Aid
	HE:	You put it on before bed?
She takes out a tiny dab, rubs it on finger	SHE:	Uh, huh. And wake up to softer hands.
	HE:	Hmm ... smoother, too.
	SHE:	Jergens starts working instantly to soothe and soften. S'nongreasy.
	HE:	Can you use it during the day?
	SHE:	Sure. Honey ...?
	HE:	Mmmm?
	SHE:	How about you making breakfast?

ANALYSIS OF COMMERCIAL 3

• Voice-over

• Husband and wife

• Hand demonstration: "Talking hands"

Imagine the place — the bed, night table, alarm clock, morning light. Imagine how the product feels to the woman and how her hands feel to her husband. Visualization will help the interpretation of the copy. In the beginning, the voices should sound a little sleepy. We see hands groping for the alarm clock. The contact prompts the dialogue. He says, "Hey—your hands." She has a throwaway reaction, "Mmmm?" He then says, "They're so soft." A major selling point. No mention yet of the product. This is her discovery. She describes the method. Before bed she applies the lotion, and then she wakes up to smoother hands. He concurs that her hands are indeed smoother. She enlightens him: "Jergens starts working instantly to soothe and soften" — important selling words, along with "nongreasy." Another transition follows: "Honey," she purrs, "How about *you* making breakfast?" We must sense that she has him in the palm of her hands.

This dialogue is written in a conversational rhythm. The product message is important, but it is not sledge-hammered home. Read both parts so you can get a sense of how to listen and react. Notice the contractions used in the dialogue: "G'morning" and "S'nongreasy." Relaxed people do not punch every word in a dialogue, especially in bed, so the writer intended an ease in the conversation. Practice saying: soft, soften, smooth, smoother, and soothe. The video direction has his hand caressing hers. The voices should sound just as caressing as they relate to the product. That is your objective.

When auditioning with a partner, see if you can find out in advance who that person will be; get together and rehearse. You won't have much time, so make each moment meaningful.

COMMERCIAL 4

WHITE CLOUD® TISSUE   (60 SECONDS)

SFX: BREAKFAST SOUNDS
MAN: Ann ....
WOMAN: Yes, dear.
MAN: Why is bathroom tissue on our table?
WOMAN: You noticed!
MAN: (VOICE-OVER) I noticed.
WOMAN: Harold, I am such a terrific shopper ... listen ... I
        found White Cloud ... One touch, and I knew it was
        for us. C'mon, I want you to touch it ... just once!
MAN: Can I have my coffee?

```
WOMAN: After one touch. C'mon.
MAN:   Aw, what can one touch prove?
WOMAN: You'll see. Feel ours.
MAN:   Feels soft.
WOMAN: Now the White Cloud — one touch, mind you.
MAN:   Feels different! Softer!
WOMAN: The softest.
MAN:   Smooth — like velvet. Feels velvety, like...your
       robe. Y'know, Ann, you are a terrific shopper.
WOMAN: And you're a terrific husband. Here's your coffee,
       Harold.
MAN:   One touch did prove it!
WOMAN: One touch.
ANNCR: White Cloud. One touch tells you it's softest. One
       touch tells someone you care.
```

ANALYSIS OF COMMERCIAL 4

The commercial is made up of the following elements:

• Slice-of-life dramatization

• Husband/wife relationship

• Sound effects (SFX): Breakfast sounds

In this sixty-second commercial, Ann and Harold discuss bathroom tissue. The White Cloud is on the breakfast table. Key words in this copy are: *touch, soft, velvet, caring*. Ann convinces her husband of the special qualities of the product. As with the oven cleaner, this is a comparison test — our tissue versus theirs. Let's check the difference. Harold is more interested in his morning coffee than in complying with her touch test. He gives in.

Both characters have interesting personalities. She is outgoing and vivacious from the start. He is more tongue-in-cheek and skeptical. His major transition occurs naturally after he feels the tissue. He becomes sensually involved to the point of touching her velvet robe. Then the praise pours forth and he is a convert. Coffee is his reward.

The theme is restated by the voice over announcer: "One touch tells you it's softest."

Do an improvisation using different products that would not normally be on the kitchen table at mealtime — shaving cream, perfume, hand lotion, bath powder. Have one person explain why one shaving cream is better than another.

In this commercial the wife is wearing a velvet robe. What is the man wearing? How long have they been married? He works for a living. What does he do? Does she work outside the home or is she a full-time housekeeper and mother? They are a happily married couple and appear to be very comfortable with each other. Be specific about their relationship.

PROGRAM-LENGTH COMMERCIALS

The latest selling tool is the thirty-minute commercial, or "infomercial." These are actually enlargements of the soft-sell, slice-of-life commercial. Whether the players are a group of friends, a roomful of recognizable celebrities, or a discussion leader with a cluster of disciples, it's still an assortment of people talking enthusiastically about the exceptional virtues of a specific product. And, at some point in the copy, the viewer, rather than being told to go out and buy some, is given the convenient opportunity to order directly. There's an element of secret treasure, of something so wondrous that it's not available to the general public, or at least not the general public who shop in stores — only to the general public who happen to watch television and are willing to shop over the telephone.

For the actor, the assignment remains the same: read the copy over at least five times. Analyze the language, improvise the situation, be specific, make the situation real to yourself, in the writer's words.

AUDITION INTELLIGENCE

These and the other audition selections presented in this book illustrate the range of material you will encounter. They represent the kinds of scenes being done on stage, on television, and in film today. The material has been chosen also to illustrate the various formats employed in The Business — there are many ways to set down dramatic material on the printed page. Each medium has its own conventions. A scene from a play will not look like an excerpt from a television show. Commercial copy does not resemble a page from a film script.

Yet, for all their differences in appearance, these selections — and any others that you will work on — make the same demands upon the actor: careful investigation of the circumstances, exploration of the possibilities, consideration of the character's objectives, realization of the moments before the scene begins and after it ends. Most important, they require a soaring imagination.

In all cases, what we hope to see is truth, illuminated by your singular talent!

EPILOGUE

*I never, ever thought of giving up. People told me the best
thing I could do would be to get out of this business, but I
never. . . . Even if Alfie hadn't come along, and I was still in
England, doing repertory for £100 a week, I'd be doing it.*

—MICHAEL CAINE

We have come to the end of our guided journey. What happens now is up to you.

You must ask yourself if it is absolutely necessary to journey to New York or Los
Angeles. Have you explored every possibility in your own neighborhood? Are you
the outstanding talent in your group? Have you measured yourself against the best
of what you see and hear?

Is it necessary to be in Los Angeles or New York to accomplish what you want to
do? We have shown you how The Business works for performers in regional markets, and how enthusiastic they are about remaining near their home base. We have
told you about excellent, respected theater companies flourishing outside the major
production centers. Many of today's young playwrights prefer to have their works
performed in these regional theaters. Actors like John Malkovich, Gary Sinise, Ann
Pitoniak, and Robert Prosky come quickly to mind as examples of performers who
were "discovered" in productions that originated thousands of miles from Broadway
or Century City.

If the theater is what lures you, how strong is your foundation? Are you expecting your boundless enthusiasm to carry you farther than it can?

Examine your motives and determination. Can you envision a life in The Business
without becoming a star? Because that is what we are talking about. A life of work.

The words of the late Mervyn Nelson, who worked in every branch of The Business as a teacher, performer, producer, and filmmaker and was responsible for many
great careers, are very moving:

> If someone is going to be a star, in spite of the masochistic nature of The
> Business, I've never seen, in all my years, *talent* go unrecognized, pro-
> vided the talent is dedicated, because talent itself is an addiction. You
> don't need anything else but talent. That's your addiction. One day Roy
> Scheider came to me when I was teaching him and said, "I don't fit any-
> where. I'm not a leading man, I'm not really a character. There is no
> cliché for me to be." I told him that has nothing to do with it. "You have

talent. Hold on. Hold on." I have never known really wonderful talent to
be ignored. Somehow they found their way, if they held on.

If the talent and desire are so strong within you, perhaps the next question is which
city: Los Angeles or New York? These are two dissimilar cultures.
Mervyn Nelson again:

> I believe people are not born *in* New York, they are born *for* it. And I
> think people out in L.A. are lost because they went out there. Then I sit
> with people in New York and say, "Go West!" There are people who can
> be put into a niche. Hollywood is a place of niches. You must be able to
> be given a title by them. If you can do that, if you have that kind of charis-
> ma, New York is wrong for you. If you are an actor or actress with a lot
> of stretch and don't seem to fit into a particular category, you shouldn't
> go to the Coast, but to New York. If Hollywood finds you in New York,
> then they'll take you, no matter what.
>
> The competition in the most important cultural city in the world is
> such that if you come here too soon, you're going to be a waiter the rest
> of your life. The competition is too strong. You must be able to compete
> with the best. What is considered off-Broadway in Hollywood and lasts
> for a year would last in New York off-off-Broadway one night.

The working actor who continues to grow and keeps his soul intact and stays sane
is the one who will last. Such actors are ready when the wonderful accident happens
— the sudden, unpredictable marriage of *preparation* and *opportunity* that is the true
meaning of luck.

And luck may find you anywhere in our rapidly changing, expanding universe.
Before the millennium, we expect that you will be able to audition for a job in Turkey
or Tahiti without leaving your living room. The script will be delivered via your fax.
The casting director's face will appear on your monitor, to give you hints about what
the client wants. You will record your own performance — beefing up or softening
your tone, possibly changing the color of your hair, the shape of your nose — on your
own equipment. Editing your audition, you'll perhaps combine bits and pieces of several takes in order to achieve the desired performance. And then you'll zap it along
the fiber-optic highway to the casting director, the client, or, perchance, to another
machine. Of course, you'll still have to wait to find out whether the job is yours. . . .

Wherever you are working, in whatever capacity — whether in Chicago or
Miami, Dallas or Minneapolis, Philadelphia or Seattle, Los Angeles or New York —
what is essential is to be your professional best. And that is an ongoing process.

But suppose, as you inch along this pathway, that you discover, or decide, that the
journey is too hard and not sufficiently rewarding. There may be more to life than,
say, the next audition, another rehearsal, or one more cross-country tour. The time
you will have spent in The Business will then have been the best, the most valuable
experience you could hope for, in learning how to communicate with others, appreciate yourself and strive enthusiastically for excellence. Everything in this book is
geared to your professionalism — as well as to your ultimate and continuing success.

RECOMMENDED READING

Acker, Iris Y. *The Secret of How to Audition for Commercials*, 1980.

Adler, Stella. *The Technique of Acting*, New York: Bantam Books, 1988.

Allen, John. *Summer Theatre Guide*, Theatre Guide Update, Box 2129, New York, 10185. Includes detailed information on non-Equity theaters, from an actor's viewpoint.

Anderson, Virgil. *Training the Speaking Voice*, New York: Oxford University Press, 1977.

Ball, William. *A Sense of Direction*, New York: Drama Book Publishers, 1984.

Caine, Michael. *What's It All About?* New York: Random House, 1992.

Callow, Simon. *Being an Actor*, New York: Grove Press, 1988.

Carson, Nancy, and Fawcett, Alan. *Kidbiz: How to Help Your Child Succeed in Show Business*, New York: Warner Books, 1986.

Charles, Jill, ed. *Directory of Professional Theatre Training Programs*, Annual Publication, Dorset Theatre Festival and Colony House, Box 519, Dorset, VT 05251. Also available are the same editor's annual *Summer Theatre Directory* and *The Regional Theatre Directory*.

Chekhov, Michael. *To the Actor*, New York: Harper and Brothers, 1953.

Clurman, Harold. *The Fervent Years*, New York: Knopf, 1945.

Eaker, Sherry. *The Back Stage Handbook for Performing Artists*, New York: Back Stage Books, 1989.

Funke, Lewis, and Booth, John E. *Actors Talk About Acting*, New York: Random House, 1961.

Gam, Rita. *Actress to Actress*, New York: Nick Lyons Books, 1986.

Gielgud, John. *An Actor and His Time*, New York: Clarkson Potter, 1980.

Goldman, William. *Adventures in the Screen Trade*, New York: Warner Books, 1983.

Guinness, Alec. *Blessings in Disguise*, New York: Knopf, 1986.

Hagen, Uta. *A Challenge for the Actor*, New York: Scribner's, 1991.

———. *Respect for Acting.* New York: Macmillan, 1973.

Hart, John. *Lighting for Action*, New York: Amphoto, 1992.

———. *Professional Headshots*, New York: Amphoto, 1994.

Hartman, Tori, and Strauss, Carolyn. *Specialty Modeling*, New York: Dutton, 1988.

Herman, Lewis, and Herman, Marguerite Shalett. *A Manual of American Dialects*, New York: Theatre Arts Books, 1943.

———. A Manual of Foreign Dialects, New York: Theatre Arts Books, 1943.

Hunt, Gordon. *How to Audition*, New York: Harper and Row, 1979.

Kilhret, Peg. *Encore: More Winning Monologs for Young Actors*, Colorado Springs: Meriwether Publishing, 1987.

Lessac, Arthur. *The Use and Training of the Human Voice*, Mountain View, Calif.: Mayfield Publishers, 1967.

Lewis, M.K., and Lewis, Rosemary. *Your Film Acting Career*, Los Angeles: Samuel French, 1993.

Lewis, Robert. *Advice to the Players*, New York: Stein and Day, 1980.

———. *Method or Madness?* New York: Samuel French, 1958

———. *Slings and Arrows*, New York: Stein and Day, 1984

Linklater, Kristin. *Freeing the Natural Voice*, New York: Drama Books, 1976.

Meisner, Sanford, and Longwell, Dennis. *On Acting*, New York: Random House, 1987.

Mekler, Eve. *The New Generation of Acting Teachers*, New York: Penguin Books, 1988.

Monos, Jim. *Professional Actor Training in New York City*, New York: Broadway Press, 1989.

Olivier, Laurence. *Confessions of an Actor*, New York: Simon & Schuster, 1982.

Padol, Brian A., and Simon, Alan. *The Young Performer's Guide*, New York: Betterway Publications, 1990.

Pielmeier, John. *Impassioned Embraces: Pieces of Love and Theatre*, New York: Dramatists Play Service. 1989.

Richardson, Ralph. *An Actor's Life*, New York: Limelight Editions, 1982.

Schickel, Richard. *Intimate Strangers*, New York: Doubleday, 1985.

Schulman, Michael, and Mekler, Eve, eds. *The Actor's Scenebook*, New York: Bantam Books, 1984.

Searle, Judith. *Getting the Part*, New York: Fireside, 1991.

Seldes, Marian. *The Bright Lights*, Boston: Houghton Mifflin, 1978.

Shurtleff, Michael. *Audition!* New York: Walker and Company, 1978.

Silver, Fred. *How to Audition for the Musical Theatre*, New York: Newmarket Press, 1985.

Skinner, Edith, and Monich, Timothy. *Good Speech for the American Actor*, New York: Drama Book Publishers, 1980

Small, Edgar. *From Agent to Actor*, Hollywood: Samuel French, 1991

Weist, Dwight. *On Camera!*, New York: Walker and Company, 1982.

BOOKS ON IMAGE AND WARDROBE

Begoun, Paula. *Blue Eyeshadow Should Be Illegal*, second edition, Seattle: Beginning Press, 1986.

———. *Don't Go to The Cosmetics Counter Without Me*, Seattle: Beginning Press, 1994.

Bixler, Susan. *The Professional Image*, New York: Putnam's, 1985.

Cho, Emily, and Fisher, Neila. *It's You: Looking Terrific Whatever Your Type*, New York: Random House, 1986.

Cho, Emily, and Glover, Linda. *Looking Terrific: Express Yourself Through the Language of Clothing*, New York: Putnam's, 1978.

Flusser, Alan. *Clothes and the Man*, New York: Villard Books, 1985.

Head, Edith. *How to Dress for Success*, New York: Random House, 1967.

Karpinski, Kenneth J. *The Winner's Style: The Modern Male's Passport to Good Grooming*, New York: Acropolis, 1987.

Lucas, Jacqui, and Lundell, Coralyn. *You and Your Image*, Los Gatos, Calif.: Appearance Designers, 1991.

Mathis, Carla, and Connor, Helen Villa. *The Triumph of Individual Style*, Timeless Editions, 1993.

McGill, Leonard. *Stylewise: A Man's Guide to Looking Good for Less*, New York: Putnam's, 1983.

Michelle, Colette. *Look Like a Million*, San Diego: Fashion Promotions, 1986.

Parente, Diane and Parsons, Alyce. *Universal Style*, Ross, Calif.: Parente and Parsons, 1991.

Parente, Diane, and Parsons, Alyce, and Henricks, Joan. *Universal Style for Men*, Ross, Calif.: Parente and Parsons, 1992.

Pooser, Doris. *Always in Style*, Los Altos, Calif.: Crisp Publications, 1989.

Rasband, Judith. *Fabulous Fit*, New York: Fairchild Publications, 1994.

Singer Sewing Reference Library. *The Perfect Fit*, Minnetonka, Minn.: Cy De Cosse, 1987.

Thompson, Jacqueline, ed. *Image Impact: The Complete Makeover Guide*, New York: Bristol Books, 1990.

Villarosa, Riccardo, and Angeli, Giuliano. *The Elegant Man*, New York: Random House, 1990.

BOOKS ON COLOR

Birren, Faber. *Color and Human Response*, New York: Van Nostrand Reinhold, 1978

Color Psychology and Color Therapy, New York: Citadel Press, 1978.

Color: A Survey in Pictures and Words, New York: Citadel Press, 1961.

Caygill, Suzanne. *Color: The Essence of You* , Celestial Press, 1980.

Don, Frank. *Color Your World*, New York: Destiny Books, 1983.

Eiseman, Leatrice. *Alive with Color*, New York: Acropolis, 1983.

Fujii, Donna. *Color with Style*, New York: Graphic-Sha Publishing, 1991.

Jackson, Carol. *Color Me Beautiful*, New York: Ballantine Books, 1981.

———. *Color for Men*, New York: Ballantine Books, 1984.

Munsell, Albert H. *Nature of Light and Color in the Open Air*, New York: Dover, 1954.

Patton, Jean E. *Color to Color: The Black Woman's Guide to a Rainbow of Fashion and Beauty*, New York: Fireside, 1991.

Walker, Dr. Morton. *The Power of Color*, New York: Avery Publishing Group, 1991.

INDEX

HOEBERMANN STUDIO

Mari Lyn Henry has been developing talent for the stage and screen for over twenty years. After thirteen years as the director of casting for ABC, she now runs her own consulting firm, Persona Image Enhancement.

Lynne Rogers has appeared in scores of soap operas and commercials over the past several decades. She is the author of *The Love of Their Lives*, a behind-the-scenes look at the soap opera industry.

Senior editor: Paul Lukas
Associate editor: Dale Ramsey
Designer: Jay Anning
Production manager: Ellen Greene